CONTENTS

I have always believed that education provides a means for accomplishing a person's dreams. I guess I learned that idea from my parents and teachers in high school. When I started college at the University of New Mexico, it was the beginning of a great adventure which was to last my lifetime. I can still recall being a college freshman. I had attended a small school in northern New Mexico, Pojoaque High School. I was a good student in high school and was motivated to succeed in college. As a freshman, I had career goals that were pretty unrealistic and changed from week to week. I thought about becoming the first woman president or maybe a diplomat. Since Nancy Drew was my heroine, I thought about being a spy or detective like Nancy Drew. Deciding on a major and career was a monumental task.

When I started at the University of New Mexico, I was soon overwhelmed. I did not know how to take notes, remember what I read, or manage my time. I remember that I was anxious and stressed out about taking tests. I worked and went to school during the day and tried to study at night. Sometimes I studied all night and then the next day forgot what I had studied. College was not fun, and I wished that someone had written a book on how to survive in college. I decided that I would figure out how to be successful and maybe someday write a book about it so that other people would not have to struggle as much as I did.

I learned how to survive and was very successful in college, completing my bachelor's, master's, and doctorate degrees. I enjoyed the college environment so much that I ended up being a college counselor and teacher. That was pretty far from being Nancy Drew, but it has been a career that I have found very satisfying. In 1978, the vice-president of newly opened Cuyamaca College in El Cajon, California, asked if I would design a college success course for the new college. I was excited to design a course that would help students to be successful in college. I was motivated because I believed in the value of education and remembered what it was like to be a new college student. It is now 36 years later and I am still designing and teaching college success courses. Every semester that I teach, I learn more from students and continue to develop ideas for a college success course that makes a positive difference in students' lives. My experiences as a student and faculty member have helped me design a class with proven success. I have also done research on student success and designed this textbook based on my research findings.

What do students need to be successful? First of all, they need to know how to study. This includes being able to apply memory techniques, read effectively, listen to lectures, take notes, and prepare for exams. Without these skills, students may wrongly decide that they are not capable of doing college work. If students know these techniques and apply them, they can be confident in their abilities and reach their true potential. With confidence, they can begin to relax and meet the challenges of tests and term papers. They might even learn to like education.

Being able to study is not enough. Students need to know what to study, so having a career goal is important. I have observed that students choose their career goals for a variety of reasons. Just like I wanted to be Nancy Drew, some students choose their occupations based on some person that they admire. Some choose their career based on familiarity. They choose occupations that they have observed in their families or communities. Others choose a career by accident; they obtain whatever job is available. We now have a great deal of information on how to choose a satisfying career goal. The first step is personal assessment. What are the students' personality types, interests, aptitudes, and values? Once these are determined, what careers match these personal characteristics? What careers will be a good choice for the future? These are all questions that need to be answered in order to continue to study in college.

Managing time and money and setting goals are important. Like many other students, I had always worked while attending college. While getting my master's and doctorate degrees, I worked and had a family. I have felt the pressures of these many roles and learned how to manage them. Students can learn these important life skills to make the journey easier.

Learning how to speak and write well has been a great asset to me in college and in my career. These skills did not come easily. I remember getting papers back with so many red corrections that they looked like decorated Christmas trees. I learned from the mistakes and kept practicing. These are skills that all college students need to master early in their college careers.

One of the goals of a college education is to learn to think critically and creatively. The world is full of complex issues with no easy answers. We find solutions by working with others, questioning the status quo, looking at different alternatives, respecting the opinions of others, and constructing our own personal views. Through creative thinking, we can come up with ideas to solve problems in our careers and personal lives.

I had the advantage of growing up with two cultures and speaking two languages. This has given me an appreciation for different groups of people. Appreciating others and working with diverse groups of people are skills needed by everyone today because the world is becoming more diverse. If we have hope for being able to live peacefully in the world, we will need to understand and appreciate this diversity.

Probably the most important skill for success is that of positive thinking. I truly believe that we accomplish what we think we can do. We need to become aware of our thoughts, and when they are negative, we need to change them. I often ask students to notice their negative thoughts and then, as if rewinding a tape, change their negative thoughts to positive thoughts. Positive thoughts are powerful influences on attitude and behavior.

What good does it do to attend college if students do not enjoy good health? I have resolved to emphasize achieving wellness and maintaining good health in all my college classes. In the new millennium, we are all supposed to live to be 100 years old. I collect stories about seniors who climb mountains, orbit the earth, write bestselling novels, and become famous artists. We can learn from them about how to live long, healthy, and productive lives.

Through the study of psychology, we have discovered many ways to help people to be successful. I have briefly introduced these theories and the names of the psychologists who have done research in this area. It is not enough to know the theory or idea; it is necessary to know how to apply it. This book contains many exercises designed to assist students apply the material learned.

The sections titled "Keys to Success," located near the end of each chapter, are my personal philosophies of life developed from being in education for over 45 years. Although I still remember being a college freshman, that was a long time ago, and I have learned a lot since then. If I could survive in college, you can too. I wrote that book that I thought about many years ago. I hope that it makes your journey through college, your career, and your life a little easier.

- Topics include both college and career success.

- Students learn to take responsibility for their success by applying tools for motivation, positive thinking, and learning positive behavior.

- Positive psychology is used to help students understand their personal strengths and multiple intelligences and how they are related to choosing a major.

- Throughout the text, students are encouraged to build on their strengths and think positively about the future.

- New material on emotional intelligence enhances personal as well as career success.

- The **Do What You Are (DWYA)** personality assessment and the **Productivity Environmental Preference Survey (PEPS)** are included.

- An online portfolio summarizes the results of the DWYA and PEPS and provides links to career information.

- Personality type, learning style and multiple intelligences are key themes throughout the text.

- The textbook help students become lifelong learners by understanding their learning preferences and improving reading, memory, note taking, writing, speaking, and test taking.

- Interactive activities within the text help students to practice the material learned.

- Frequent quizzes and answer keys within the chapters help students with reading comprehension and check understanding of key concepts.

- Journal entries help students think critically and apply what they have learned to their personal lives.

- Individual and group exercises are included at the end of each chapter.

- The **College Success Website** at http://www.collegesuccess1.com has resources for students and faculty. Student resources include key ideas and Internet links related to each chapter and Word documents for the journal entries. Resources for faculty include the **Instructor Manual** and **Faculty Resources** for teaching college success courses.

I would like to give my sincere thanks to:

- My parents, Betty and Clarence Finley, who taught me the value of education,

- My seven brothers and sisters, who taught me to laugh at life,

- My children, Mark and Sara Fralick, who assisted with editing and shared their New Millennial perspective,

- Paul Delys, who provided love and encouragement and shared many of his ideas and materials for this book,

- The instructors of College and Career Success at Cuyamaca Community College who tried out my material, gave valuable feedback, and shared their ideas,

- The many students who have taken my course over the years and shared their insights and experiences with me.

About the Author

Marsha Fralick has been employed in the field of education for over 45 years, including 35 years of teaching college success courses. She has brought together theories from counseling, psychology, career development, and health to provide students with strategies for college, career, and lifelong success. Her College and Career Success Program at Cuyamaca College in El Cajon, California, is recognized as an exemplary program by students and statewide organizations. Her college success materials are now used by community colleges and universities nationwide. She has a doctorate from the University of Southern California in higher education with an emphasis in career counseling, a master's degree in counseling from the University of Redlands, and a bachelor's degree in Spanish and English from Arizona State University.

CHAPTER 1

Getting Started

Learning Objectives

Read to answer these key questions:

- What do I want from college?

- What is the value of a college education?

- How do I choose my major and career?

- How can I motivate myself to be successful?

- How can I begin habits that lead to success?

- How can I be persistent in achieving my goal of a college education?

- How does health affect learning?

Most students attend college with dreams of making their lives better. Some students are there to explore interests and possibilities, and others have more defined career goals. Being successful in college and attaining your dreams begin with motivation. It provides the energy or drive to find your direction and to reach your goals. Without motivation, it is difficult to accomplish anything.

Not everyone is successful in college. Unfortunately, about one-third of college students drop out in the first year. Forty percent of students who start college do not finish their degrees. Having a good understanding of your gifts and talents, reasons for attending college, career goals, and how to motivate yourself will help you to reach your dreams.

What Do I Want from College?

Succeeding in college requires time and effort. You will have to give up some of your time spent on leisure activities and working. You will give up some time spent with your friends and families. Making sacrifices and working hard are easier if you know what you want to achieve through your efforts. One of the first steps in motivating yourself to be successful in college is to have a clear and specific understanding of your reasons for attending college. Are you attending college as a way to obtain a satisfying career? Is financial security one of your goals? Will you feel more satisfied if you are living up to your potential? What are your hopes and dreams, and how will college help you to achieve your goals?

When you are having difficulties or doubts about your ability to finish your college education, remember your hopes and dreams and your plans for the future. It is a good idea to write these ideas down, think about them, and revise them from time to time.

What Is the Value of a College Education?

Many college students say that getting a satisfying job that pays well and achieving financial security are important reasons for attending college. By going to college you can get a job that pays more per hour. You can work fewer hours to earn a living and have more time for leisure activities. You can spend your time at work doing something that you like to do. A report issued by the Census Bureau in 2012 listed the following education and income statistics for all races and both genders throughout the United States.[1] Lifetime income assumes that a person works thirty years before retirement.

Average Earnings Based on Education Level

Education	Yearly Income	Lifetime Income
High school graduate	$33,904	$1,017,120
Some college, no degree	$37,804	$1,134,120
Associate degree	$40,820	$1,224,600
Bachelor's degree	$55,432	$1,662,960
Master's degree	$67,600	$2,028,000
Professional degree	$90,220	$2,706,600

Notice that income rises with educational level. Over a lifetime, a person with a bachelor's degree earns 66% more than a high school graduate. Of course these are average figures across the nation and some individuals earn higher or lower salaries. People fantasize about winning the lottery. The reality is that the probability of winning the lottery is very low. In the long run, you have a better chance of improving your financial status by going to college.

Let's do some further comparisons. A high school graduate earns an average of $1,017,120 over a lifetime. A college graduate with a bachelor's degree earns $1,662,960 over a lifetime. A college graduate earns $645,840 more than a high school graduate does over a lifetime. So how much is a college degree worth? It is worth $645,840 over a lifetime. Would you go to college if someone offered to pay you $645,840? Here are some more interesting figures we can derive from the above table:

Completing one college course is worth $16,146.
($645,840 divided by 40 courses in a bachelor's degree)

Going to class for one hour is worth $336.
($16,146 divided by 48 hours in a semester class)

Would you take a college class if someone offered to pay you $16,146? Would you go to class today for one hour if someone offered to pay you $336? Of course, if this sounds too good to be true, remember that you will receive these "payments" over a working lifetime of thirty years.

Education beyond high school will become increasingly important. It will take place in a variety of forms: community college courses, training on the job, private training sessions, and learning on your own. Those who do not keep up with the new technology will find that their skills quickly become obsolete. Those who do keep up will find their skills in demand.

According to the Bureau of Labor Statistics, occupations that require a postsecondary degree will account for nearly half of all new jobs from 2008 to 2018, with the fastest growth in jobs requiring an associate's degree or higher. In addition, higher education will result in higher earnings and lower unemployment.[2] While college graduation does not guarantee employment, it increases your chances of finding a job. In 2012, high school graduates had an unemployment rate of 12.4% as compared to college graduates who had an unemployment rate of 4.5%.[2] Increase your chances of employment by continuing your education.

Young people who do not continue their education are likely to be stuck in lower-paying jobs, while those who continue their education will have higher-paying jobs. Author Joyce Lain Kennedy believes that the middle class is becoming an endangered species.[3] She states that many jobs traditionally held by the middle class have been "dumbed down," making them so simple that anyone can do them. These jobs pay very little and offer no benefits, no employment stability, and little opportunity for advancement. Young people often hold these jobs in their teens and twenties. At the other end of the job continuum are jobs requiring a college education or training beyond high school. These high-end jobs often require technical or computer skills. These are the jobs that pay better and offer benefits. It seems that we are becoming a nation of haves and have-nots who are separated by their education and technical skills.

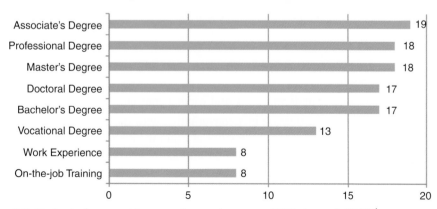

Figure 1.1 Projected percent increase in employment, 2008 through 2018.[4]

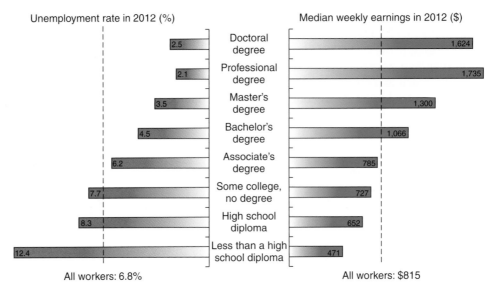

Figure 1.2 Education pays, unemployment rate and median weekly earnings, 2009.

Money is only one of the values of going to college. Can you think of other reasons to attend college? Here are some less tangible reasons.

- College helps you to develop your potential.
- College opens the door to many satisfying careers.

© 2014, sergign. Used under license with Shutterstock, Inc.

- College prepares you to be an informed citizen and fully participate in the democratic process.
- College increases your understanding and widens your view of the world.
- College allows you to participate in a conversation with the great minds of all times and places. For example, reading the work of Plato is like having a conversation with that famous philosopher. You can continue great conversations with your faculty and fellow students.
- College helps to increase your confidence, self-esteem, and self-respect.

Choosing a Major and Career

Having a definite major and career choice is a good motivation for completing your college education. It is difficult to put in the work necessary to be successful if you do not have a clear picture of your future career; however, three out of four college students are undecided about their major. For students who have chosen a major, 30 to 75 percent of a graduating class will change that major two or more times.[5] Unclear or indefinite career goals are some of the most significant factors that identify students at risk of dropping out of college.[6] Students often drop out or extend their stay in college because they are uncertain about their major or want to change their major. Choosing an appropriate college major is one of the most difficult and important decisions that college students can make.

© 2014, iQoncept. Used under license with Shutterstock, Inc.

How can you choose the major that is best for you? The best way is to first understand yourself: become aware of your personality traits, learning style, interests, preferred lifestyle, values, gifts, and talents. The next step is to do career research to determine the career that best matches your personal characteristics. Then, plan your education to prepare for your career. Here are some questions to answer to help you understand yourself and what career and major would be best for you.

To learn about yourself, explore these areas:

- **What is my personality type?** Assessing your personality type will help you to become more aware of your individual gifts and talents and some careers that will give you satisfaction.
- **What is my learning style?** Being aware of your learning style will help you identify learning strategies that work best for you and increase your productivity in college, on the job, and in your personal life.
- **What are my aptitudes?** Focus on your strengths by identifying your multiple intelligences.
- **What are my interests?** Knowing about your interests is important in choosing a satisfying career.
- **What kind of lifestyle do I prefer?** Think about how you want to balance work, leisure, and family.
- **What are my values?** Knowing what you value (what is most important to you) will help you make good decisions about your life.

To learn about career possibilities, research the following:

- **What careers match my personality, learning style, aptitudes, interests, lifestyle, and values?** Learn how to do career research to find the best career for you. Find a career that has a good outlook for the future.

- **How can I plan my education to get the career I want?** Once you have identified a career that matches your personal strengths and interests, consult your college catalog or advisor to make an educational plan that matches your career goals.

By following the above steps, you can find the major that is best for you and minimize the time you spend in college.

Journal Entry #2

Write a paragraph about deciding on your ideal major and career. Use any of these questions to guide your thinking: If you have chosen a major, why is it the best major for you? How does it match your interests, aptitudes, and values (what is most important to you)? Does this major help you to live your preferred lifestyle? If you have not chosen a major, what are some steps in choosing the right major and career? What qualities would you look for in an ideal career? Can you describe some of your interests, aptitudes, and values? What is your preferred lifestyle?

"The purpose of our lives is to give birth to the best which is within us."
Marianne Williamson

How to Be Motivated

There are many ways to be motivated.

- You can **think positively about the future** and take the steps necessary to accomplish your goals.
- You can begin your studies by **looking for what is interesting** to you.
- You can **improve your concentration** and motivation for studying by managing your external and internal distractions.
- You can be motivated by internal or external factors called **intrinsic or extrinsic motivation.**
- You can become aware of your **locus of control,** or where you place the responsibility for control over your life. If you are in control, you are more likely to be motivated to succeed.
- You can join a club, organization, or athletic team. **Affiliation motivation** involves taking part in school activities that increase your motivation to stay in college.
- **Achievement** and competition are motivating to some students.
- You can **use rewards** as a motivation to establish desirable behaviors.

Let's examine each type of motivation in more detail and see if some of these ideas can be useful to you.

Thinking Positively about the Future

You can motivate yourself to complete your education by thinking positively about the future. If you believe that your chances of graduating from college are good, you can be motivated to take the steps necessary to achieve your goals. Conversely, if you think that your chances of graduating are poor, it is difficult to motivate yourself to continue. The degree of optimism that you possess is greatly influenced by past experiences. For example, if you were a good student in the past, you are likely to be optimistic about the future. If you struggled with your education, you may have some negative experiences that you will need to overcome. Negative thoughts can often become a self-fulfilling prophecy: what we think becomes true.

How can you train yourself to think more optimistically? First, become aware of your thought patterns. Are they mostly negative or positive? If they are negative, rewind the tape and make them more positive. Here is an example.

Pessimism

I failed the test. I guess I am just not college material. I feel really stupid. I just can't do this. College is too hard for me. My (teacher, father, mother, friend, boss) told me I would never make it. Maybe I should just drop out of college and do something else.

Optimism

I failed the test. Let's take a look at what went wrong, so I can do better next time. Did I study enough? Did I study the right material? Maybe I should take this a little slower. How can I get help so that I can understand? I plan to do better next time.

Can a person be too optimistic? In some circumstances, this is true. There is a difference between optimism and wishful thinking, for example. Wishful thinking does not include plans for accomplishing goals and can be a distraction from achieving them. Working toward unattainable goals can be exhausting and demoralizing, especially when the resources for attaining them are lacking. Goals must be realistic and achievable. Psychologists recommend that "people should be optimistic when the future can be changed by positive thinking, but not otherwise."[7] Using optimism requires some judgment about possible outcomes in the future.

There are some good reasons to think more positively. Psychologists have done long-term studies showing that people who use positive thinking have many benefits over a lifetime, including good health, longevity, happiness, perseverance, improved problem

solving, and enhanced ability to learn. Optimism is also related to goal achievement. If you are optimistic and believe a goal is achievable, you are more likely to take the steps necessary to accomplish the goal. If you do not believe that a goal is achievable, you are likely to give up trying to achieve it. Being optimistic is closely related to being hopeful about the future. If you are hopeful about the future, you are likely to be more determined to reach your goals and to make plans for reaching them. Be optimistic about graduating from college, find the resources necessary to accomplish your goal, and start taking the steps to create your success.

ACTIVITY

Are you generally an optimist or pessimist about the future? Read the following items and rate your level of agreement or disagreement:

Rate the following items using this scale:

5   I definitely agree
4   I agree
3   I neither agree or disagree (neutral)
2   I disagree
1   I strongly disagree

_____   My chances of graduating from college are good.

_____   I am confident that I can overcome any obstacles to my success.

_____   Things generally turn out well for me.

_____   I believe that positive results will eventually come from most problem situations.

_____   If I work hard enough, I will eventually achieve my goals.

_____   Although I have faced some problems in the past, the future will be better.

_____   I expect that most things will go as planned.

_____   Good things will happen to me in the future.

_____   I am generally persistent in reaching my goals.

_____   I am good at finding solutions to the problems I face in life.

Add up your total points and multiply by two. My total points (× 2) are _____.

90–100	You are an excellent positive thinker.
80–89	You are a good positive thinker.
70–79	Sometimes you think positively, and sometimes not. Can you re-evaluate your thinking?
60 and below	Work on positive thinking.

Journal Entry #3

Write five positive statements about your college education and your future.

Find Something Interesting in Your Studies

If you can think positively about what you are studying, it makes the job easier and more satisfying. Begin your studies by finding something interesting in the course and your textbook. Contrast these two ideas:

I have to take economics. It is going to be difficult and boring. What do I need economics for anyway? I'll just need to get through it so I can get my degree.

I have to take economics. I wonder about the course content. I often hear about it on the news. How can I use this information in my future? What can I find that is interesting?

Make sure to attend the first class meeting. Remember that the professor is very knowledgeable about the subject and finds the content interesting and exciting. At the first class meeting, the professor will give you an overview of the course and should provide some motivation for studying the material in the course. Look at the course syllabus to find what the course is about and to begin to look for something that could be interesting or useful to you.

Skimming a textbook before you begin a course is a good way to find something interesting and to prepare for learning. Skimming will give you an organized preview of what's ahead. Here are the steps to skimming a new text:

1. **Quickly read the preface or introduction.** Read as if you were having a conversation with the author of the text. In the preface or introduction, you will find out how the author has organized the material, the key ideas, and his or her purpose in writing the text.

2. **Look at the major topics in the table of contents.** You can use the table of contents as a window into the book. It gives a quick outline of every topic in the text. As you read the table of contents, look for topics of special interest to you.

3. **Spend five to 15 minutes quickly looking over the book.** Turn the pages quickly, noticing boldfaced topics, pictures, and anything else that catches your attention. Again, look for important or interesting topics. Do not spend too much time on this step. If your textbook is online, skim through the website.

4. **What resources are included?** Is there an index, glossary of terms, answers to quiz questions, or solutions to math problems? These sections will be of use to you as you read. If your book is online, explore the website to find useful features and content.

Skimming a text or website before you begin to read has several important benefits. The first benefit is that it gets you started in the learning process. It is an easy and quick step that can help you avoid procrastination. It increases motivation by helping you notice items that have appeal to you. Previewing the content will help you to relax as you study and remember the information. Early in the course, this step will help you verify that you have chosen the correct course and that you have the prerequisites to be successful in the class.

Improving Your Concentration

Have you ever watched lion tamers concentrate? If their attention wanders, they are likely to become the lion's dinner. Skilled athletes, musicians, and artists don't have any trouble concentrating. They are motivated to concentrate. Think about a time when you were totally focused on what you were doing. You were motivated to continue. You can improve your concentration and motivation for studying by managing your external and internal distractions.

Manage your external environment. Your environment will either help you to study or distract you from studying. We are all creatures of habit. If you try to study in

> "No pessimist ever discovered the secrets of the stars, or sailed to an uncharted land, or opened a new doorway for the human spirit."
> Helen Keller

> "A pessimist sees the difficulty in every opportunity; an optimist sees the opportunity in every difficulty."
> Winston Churchill

© 2014, Karramba Production. Used under license with Shutterstock, Inc.

front of the TV, you will watch TV because that is what you are accustomed to doing in front of the TV. If you study in bed, you will fall asleep because your body associates the bed with sleeping. If you study in the kitchen, you will eat. Find an environment that minimizes distractions. One idea is to study in the library. In the library, there are many cues that tell you to study. There are books and learning resources and other people studying. It will be easier to concentrate in that environment. You may be able to set up a learning environment in your home. Find a place where you can place a desk or table, your computer, and your materials for learning. When you are in this place, use it for learning and studying only.

Increase your concentration and motivation as well as your retention by varying the places where you study and the content of what you are studying. Study at home, in the library, outside, in a coffee shop or any place where you can focus your attention on your studies. You can also increase learning effectiveness by varying the content and subjects that you are studying. Athletes maintain concentration and motivation by including strength, speed and skill practice in each workout. Musicians practice scales, different musical pieces and rhythm exercises in one practice session. In your studies you can do the same. For example, when studying a foreign language, spend some time on reading, some time on learning vocabulary and some practice in speaking the language. Then do some problems for your math class.

Manage your internal distractions. Many of our distractions come from within. Here are some techniques for managing these internal distractions:

1. **Be here now.** Choose where you will place your attention. As I'm sure you have experienced, your body can be attending a lecture or at the desk reading, but your mind can be in lots of different and exciting places. You can tell yourself, "Be here now." You cannot force yourself to pay attention. When your mind wanders, notice that you have drifted off and gently return your attention to your lecture or reading. This will take some practice, since attention tends to wander often.

2. **The spider technique.** If you hold a tuning fork to a spider web, the web vibrates and the spider senses that it has caught a tasty morsel and goes seeking the food. After a while, the spider discovers that there is no food and learns to ignore the vibrations caused by the tuning fork. When you are sitting in the library studying and someone walks in talking and laughing, you can choose to pay attention either to the distraction or to studying. Decide to continue to pay attention to studying.

3. **Set up a worry time.** Many times worries interfere with concentration. Some people have been successful in setting up a worry time. Here's how it works:

   a. Set a specific time each day for worrying.

   b. When worries distract you from your studies, remind yourself that you have set aside time for worrying.

   c. Tell yourself, "Be here now."

   d. Keep your worry appointment.

   e. During your worry time, try to find some solutions or take some steps to resolve the things that cause you to worry.

4. **Take steps to solve personal problems.** If you are bothered by personal problems, take steps to solve them. See your college counselor for assistance. Another strategy is to make a plan to deal with the problem later so that you can study now.

5. **Use the checkmark technique.** When you find yourself distracted from a lecture or from studying, place a checkmark on a piece of paper and refocus your attention on the task at hand. You will find that your checkmarks decrease over time.

6. **Increase your activity.** Take a break. Stretch and move. Read and listen actively by asking questions about the material and answering them as you read or listen.

7. **Find an incentive or reward.** Tell yourself that when you finish, you will do something enjoyable.

8. **Change topics.** Changing study topics may help you to concentrate and avoid fatigue.

Intrinsic or Extrinsic Motivation

Intrinsic motivation comes from within. It means that you do an activity because you enjoy it or find personal meaning in it. With intrinsic motivation, the nature of the activity itself or the consequences of the activity motivate you. For example, let's say that I am interested in learning to play the piano. I am motivated to practice playing the piano because I like the sound of the piano and feel very satisfied when I can play music that I enjoy. I practice because I like to practice, not because I have to practice. When I get tired or frustrated, I work through it or put it aside and come back to it because I want to learn to play the piano well.

© 2014, fotoscool. Used under license with Shutterstock, Inc.

You can be intrinsically motivated to continue in college because you enjoy learning and find the college experience satisfying. Look for ways to enjoy college and to find some personal satisfaction in it. If you enjoy college, it becomes easier to do the work required to be successful. Think about what you say to yourself about college. If you are saying negative things such as "I don't want to be here," it will be difficult to continue.

Extrinsic motivation comes as a result of an external reward from someone else. Examples of extrinsic rewards are certificates, bonuses, money, praise, and recognition. Taking the piano example again, let's say that I want my child to play the piano. The child does not know if he or she would like to play the piano. I give the child a reward for practicing the piano. I could pay the child for practicing or give praise for doing a good job. There are two possible outcomes of the extrinsic reward. After a while, the child may gain skills and confidence and come to enjoy playing the piano. The extrinsic reward is no longer necessary because the child is now intrinsically motivated. Or the child may decide that he or she does not like to play the piano. The extrinsic reward is no longer effective in motivating the child to play the piano.

You can use extrinsic rewards to motivate yourself to be successful in college. Remind yourself of the payoff for getting a college degree: earning more money, having a satisfying career, being able to purchase a car and a house. Extrinsic rewards can be a first step in motivating yourself to attend college. With experience and achievement, you may come to like going to college and may become intrinsically motivated to continue your college education.

If you use intrinsic motivation to achieve your goal, you will be happier and more successful. If you do something like playing the piano because you enjoy it, you are more likely to spend the time necessary to practice to achieve your goal. If you view college as something that you enjoy and as valuable to you, it is easier to spend the time to do the required studying. When you get tired or frustrated, tell yourself that you are doing a good job (praise yourself) and think of the positive reasons that you want to get a college education.

Locus of Control

Being aware of the concept of locus of control is another way of understanding motivation. The word **locus** means place. The locus of control is where you place the responsibility for control over your life. In other words, who is in charge? If you place the responsibility on yourself and believe that you have control over your life, you have an internal locus of control. If you place the responsibility on others and think that luck or fate determines your future, you have an external locus of control. Some people use the internal and external locus of control in combination or favor one type in certain situations. If you favor an internal locus of control, you believe that to a great extent your actions determine your future. Studies have shown that students who use an internal locus of control are likely to have higher achievement in college.[8] The characteristics of students with internal and external loci of control are listed below.

"Ability is what you're capable of doing. Motivation determines what you do. Attitude determines how well you do it."
Lou Holtz

Students with an internal locus of control:

- Believe that they are in control of their lives.
- Understand that grades are directly related to the amount of study invested.
- Are self-motivated.
- Learn from their mistakes by figuring out what went wrong and how to fix the problem.
- Think positively and try to make the best of each situation.
- Rely on themselves to find something interesting in the class and learn the material.

Students with an external locus of control:

- Believe that their lives are largely a result of luck, fate, or chance.
- Think that teachers give grades rather than students earning grades.
- Rely on external motivation from teachers or others.
- Look for someone to blame when they make a mistake.
- Think negatively and believe they are victims of circumstance.
- Rely on the teacher to make the class interesting and to teach the material.

ACTIVITY

Internal or External Locus of Control

Decide whether the statement represents an internal or external locus of control and put a checkmark in the appropriate column.

Internal	External	
_____	_____	1. Much of what happens to us is due to fate, chance, or luck.
_____	_____	2. Grades depend on how much work you put into it.
_____	_____	3. If I do badly on the test, it is usually because the teacher is unfair.
_____	_____	4. If I do badly on the test, it is because I didn't study or didn't understand the material.
_____	_____	5. I often get blamed for things that are not my fault.
_____	_____	6. I try to make the best of the situation.
_____	_____	7. It is impossible to get a good grade if you have a bad instructor.
_____	_____	8. I can be successful through hard work.
_____	_____	9. If the teacher is not there telling me what to do, I have a hard time doing my work.
_____	_____	10. I can motivate myself to study.
_____	_____	11. If the teacher is boring, I probably won't do well in class.
_____	_____	12. I can find something interesting about each class.
_____	_____	13. When bad things are going to happen, there is not much you can do about it.
_____	_____	14. I create my own destiny.
_____	_____	15. Teachers should motivate the students to study.
_____	_____	16. I have a lot of choice about what happens in my life.

As you probably noticed, the even-numbered statements represent internal locus of control. The odd-numbered statements represent external locus of control. Remember that students with an internal locus of control have a greater chance of success in college. It is important to see yourself as responsible for your own success and achievement and to believe that with effort you can achieve your goals.

Affiliation

Human beings are social creatures who generally feel the need to be part of a group. This tendency is called affiliation motivation. People like to be part of a community, family, organization, or culture. You can apply this motivation technique in college by participating in student activities on campus. Join an athletic team, participate in a club, or join the student government. In this way, you will feel like you are part of a group and will have a sense of belonging. College is more than going to class: it is participating in social activities, making new friends, and sharing new ideas. Twenty years after you graduate from college, you are more likely to remember the conversations held with college friends than the detailed content of classes. College provides the opportunity to become part of a new group and to start lifelong friendships.

Achievement

Some students are motivated by achievement. Individuals who are achievement-motivated have a need for success in school, sports, careers, and other competitive situations. These individuals enjoy getting recognition for their success. They are often known as the best student, the outstanding athlete, or the employee of the year. These people are attracted to careers that provide rewards for individual achievement, such as sales, law, architecture, engineering, and business. They work hard in order to enjoy the rewards of their efforts. In college, some students work very hard to achieve high grades and then take pride in their accomplishments. One disadvantage of using this type of motivation is that it can lead to excess stress. These students often need to remember to balance their time between work, school, family, and leisure so that they do not become too stressed by the need to achieve.

Using a Reward

You can use rewards to manage your own behavior. If you want to increase your studying behavior, follow it by a positive consequence or a reward. Think about what is rewarding to you (watching TV, playing sports, enjoying your favorite music). You could study (your behavior) and then watch a TV program (the reward). The timing of your reward is important. To be effective, it must immediately follow the behavior. If you watch TV and then study, you may not get around to studying. If you watch the TV program tomorrow or next week, it is not a strong reinforcement because it is not an immediate reward.

Be careful about the kinds of rewards you use so that you do not get into habits that are detrimental to your health. If you use food as a reward for studying, you may increase

© 2014, Andy Dean Photography. Used under license with Shutterstock, Inc.

your studying behavior, but you may also gain a few pounds. Using alcohol or drugs as a reward can start an addiction. Buying yourself a reward can ruin your budget. Good rewards do not involve too many calories, cost too much money, or involve alcohol or drugs.

You can also use a negative consequence to decrease a behavior. If you touch a hot stove and get burned, you quickly learn not to do it again. You could decide to miss your favorite television program if you do not complete your studying. However, this is not fun and you may feel deprived. You might even rebel and watch your favorite TV show anyway. See if you can find a way to use positive reinforcement (a reward) for increasing a behavior that is beneficial to you rather than using a negative consequence.

When we are young, our attitudes toward education are largely shaped by positive or negative rewards. If you were praised for being a good reader as a child, it is likely that you enjoyed reading and developed good reading skills. Maybe a teacher embarrassed you because of your math skills and you learned to be anxious about math. Think about areas of your education in which you excel, and see if you can recall someone praising or otherwise reinforcing that behavior. If you are a good athlete, did someone praise your athletic ability when you were younger? How was it rewarded? If you are not good at math, what were some early messages about your math performance? These early messages have a powerful influence on later behavior. You may need to put in some effort to learn new and more beneficial behaviors.

As a college student, you can use a reward as a powerful motivator. Praise yourself and think positively about your achievements in college even if the achievements come in small steps.

QUIZ

Motivation

Test what you have learned by selecting the correct answers to the following questions:

1. If the behavior is followed by a reward
   a. it is likely to be increased.
   b. it is likely to be decreased.
   c. there will probably be no effect.

2. For rewards to be effective, they must occur
   a. before the behavior.
   b. immediately after the behavior.
   c. either before or after the behavior.

3. Manage your internal distractions by
   a. forcing yourself to concentrate.
   b. telling yourself not to worry about your problems.
   c. noticing when your attention has wandered and choosing where you want to focus your attention.

4. To be successful in college, it is best to use
   a. intrinsic motivation.
   b. extrinsic motivation.
   c. an external locus of control.

5. An example of internal locus of control is:
   a. It is impossible to get a good grade if you have a bad professor.
   b. If the teacher is boring, I probably won't do well in class.
   c. Grades depend on how much work you put into it.

How did you do on the quiz? Check your answers: 1. a, 2. b, 3. c, 4. a, 5. c

Get Started, Get Healthy!

Being in good health is important for your success in learning as well as your quality of life. You can learn better if you get enough sleep, exercise, eat well and learn to relax. Getting a college education is also an investment in the quality of your life in the future. Enjoying this increased quality of life depends on maintaining your good health. Get started on your education by adopting some healthy patterns of living.

Get the Right Amount of Sleep

Getting the proper amount of sleep helps you to pay attention in class and remember what you have studied. College students often miss out on sleep while cramming for exams, enjoying an active social life, and trying to balance work and school. If you are sleep-deprived, it is more difficult to read, perform arithmetic tasks, study, store information in long-term memory and reason logically. Drinking caffeinated beverages will make you feel less sleepy, but your ability to pay attention and remember what you have studied is still reduced with lack of sleep.

© 2014, Andrey_Kuzmin. Used under license with Shutterstock, Inc.

Getting enough sleep is important for optimal brain function. Nobel Laureate Francis Crick, who studies the brain at the Salk Institute in California, has proposed that the purpose of sleep is to allow the brain to "take out the trash."[9] Sleep gives the brain time to process the day's events, store what is needed, and delete irrelevant material. Sleep is necessary to properly store the experiences of each day in the brain. Without sleep, your ability to remember what you have studied is decreased. It is believed that sleeping helps the brain store needed information and to replenish its energy supplies.[10]

Not getting enough sleep results in a decline in mental performance. Colonel Gregory Belenky of the Walter Reed Army Institute of Research studied the effects of sleeplessness on military personnel.[11] He found that mental performance declined by 25 percent in every 24-hour sleepless period. Another researcher found that being awake for 24 hours causes the same mental impairment as being drunk.[12] After 24 hours of continuous simulated combat, artillery teams lost track of where they were and what they were firing at. During the Persian Gulf War, sleep-deprived soldiers lost a sense of where they were and began firing on their own tanks, destroying two of them. Lack of sleep impairs higher cognitive functions such as critical thinking. It becomes more difficult to make decisions, pay attention to detail, and react to new information. College students who stay up all night studying for exams suffer from the same declines in mental performance.

Depriving yourself of sleep also has negative impacts on your health.[13] Lack of sleep can harm brain cells, weaken the immune system, and decrease muscle-building growth hormones.

It can lead to diabetes, hypertension and obesity. Blood levels of the stress hormone cortisol are increased. Sleep deprivation can cause increased stress and risk of illness as well as the growth of fat instead of muscle. Researchers are now finding evidence that lack of sleep hastens the aging process.[14] Lack of sleep can make you less energetic, increase your irritability, cause depression, and make you accident-prone. It is estimated that sleepy drivers cause about 100,000 car accidents each year.

So, how much sleep do you need? Everyone has different needs for sleep. One way to determine your personal need for sleep is to think about how much sleep you get at the end of a long vacation when you do not have to get up at a certain time. At first you may sleep longer to make up for any sleep deficits. Toward the end of the vacation, you will probably be getting the amount of sleep your body needs for optimum performance. Gregory Belenky recommends, "If you simply want to put one foot in front of the other, five hours will do. But if you want to be doing things where you're required to think, plan, or anticipate, then you probably need eight or eight and a half hours of sleep."[15] It is interesting to note that current research shows that it is not healthy to sleep more than eight hours because too much sleep can alter sleep patterns and lead to sluggishness, fatigue, and other health problems.[16]

Get Some Exercise

Getting enough exercise has many benefits related to education and general health. It can help you to pay attention and improve memory. Improving your cardiovascular fitness increases the supply of oxygen and energy to the brain and keeps it healthy. Aerobic exercise even reduces your chances of getting Alzheimer's disease by 60%.[17] There are many additional benefits to regular physical activity:

- Increases your fitness, endurance, and strength
- Maintains healthy bones, muscles, and joints
- Helps in managing weight
- Lowers risk of cardiovascular disease, colon cancer, and Type 2 diabetes
- Promotes psychological well-being
- Reduces depression and anxiety

Two kinds of physical activity are recommended. Aerobic activity speeds up your heart rate and breathing and increases cardiovascular fitness. Strength and flexibility exercises such as lifting weights and stretching help to maintain strong bones. Choose activities that you enjoy and include them in your daily routine. It is important to remain active throughout your life. New federal guidelines suggest the need for 30 to 60 minutes of moderately intense physical activity each day. These activities could include an hour of walking, slow

"Walking is the best possible exercise. Habituate yourself to walk very far."

Thomas Jefferson

swimming, leisurely bicycle riding, or golfing without a cart. More intense exercise such as jogging can provide needed exercise in a shorter time.[18] Regular exercise is one of the most important factors in living a long and healthy life.

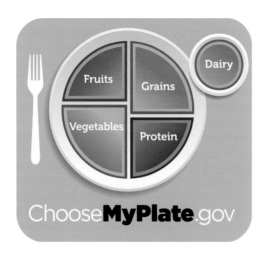

Eating Healthy

A good diet helps you to enjoy life and feel your best. Use the government dietary guidelines at http://www.choosemyplate.gov/ to make good nutritional choices. At this site you can enter your personal information for a customized recommendation of the types and amounts of food to eat for optimal health. The plate icon below provides a visual of the five different food groups with half of the plate filled with fruits and vegetables and the other half filled with whole grains and proteins.[19]

Here are some suggestions for making healthy food choices:

- In establishing a pattern of healthy eating, it is recommended that plant foods form the foundation of a good diet. Two-thirds of the dinner plate should be covered with fruits, vegetables, whole grains, and beans. Use meats and dairy products in moderation and use fats and sweets sparingly. This type of diet is helpful in controlling weight as well as reducing your risk of cancer.[20]

- Eat a variety of grains daily, especially whole grains. Whole grains include brown rice, cracked wheat, graham flour, whole-grain corn, oatmeal, popcorn, barley, whole rye, and whole wheat. Whole grains provide vitamins, minerals, and fiber, which helps you to feel full with fewer calories.

- Eat a variety of fruits and vegetables daily. Eating many kinds and colors of fruits and vegetables provides important vitamins and minerals. Enjoy five servings of fruits and vegetables each day with at least two servings of fruit and three servings of vegetables.

- Limit the use of solid fats such as butter, lard, margarines, and partially hydrogenated shortenings. Solid fats raise blood cholesterol and increase your chances of coronary heart disease. Use vegetable oils instead. Aim for a fat intake of no more that 30 percent of your calories.

- Moderate your intake of sugar. Foods containing added sugars have added calories and little nutritional value. The number one source of added sugar is soft drinks. Drink water instead of or in addition to soft drinks. Sweets, candies, pies, cakes, cookies, and fruit drinks are also major sources of added sugars. Eating too many foods with added sugar contributes to weight gain or eating less of the nutritious foods. Added sugar also contributes to tooth decay.

- Choose and prepare foods with less salt. Eating too much salt can increase your chances of having high blood pressure. High salt intake causes thecauses the body to secrete calcium, which is necessary for healthy bones. Only small amounts of salt occur naturally in foods. Most salt is added during food processing. Eat fresh fruits and vegetables to avoid eating too much salt.

Maintaining a healthy weight is one of the keys to a long and healthy life. Being overweight increases the risk of high blood pressure, high blood cholesterol, heart disease, stroke, diabetes, cancer, arthritis, and breathing problems. The problem of overweight children and adults is a major health concern today. The best way to lose weight is by establishing patterns of healthy eating and exercise.

ACTIVITY

Body Mass Index

The Body Mass Index (BMI) is a commonly used method of evaluating a person's weight. It is based on the ratio of weight to height. To calculate your BMI, first answer these two questions:

1. What is your height in inches? _____

2. What is your weight in pounds?_____

Calculate your BMI using the following formula:

$$BMI = (705 \times body\ weight) \div (height \times height)$$

Example: A person who is 66 inches tall and weighs 155 pounds:

$$BMI = (705 \times 155) \div (66 \times 66) = 25$$

Calculate your BMI here. To evaluate your weight, locate your BMI in the chart below.

My BMI = (705 × my weight ____) ÷ (my height in inches____ × my height in inches _____) = _____

Body Mass Index Categories

BMI	Weight
Less than 18.5	Underweight
18.5–24.9	Normal weight
25–29.9	Overweight
30 and above	Obese

There are some exceptions to consider when using BMI to evaluate weight:

- Bodybuilders and other athletes may have a higher BMI because muscle weighs more than fat.
- For the elderly, a BMI between 25 and 27 may be healthier and protect against osteoporosis.
- The BMI is not designed to be used with children.

Another way to evaluate your weight is to simply measure around your waist. A measurement of over 35 inches for women or 40 inches for men places a person at greater risk of health problems. If your BMI is over 25 or your waist measurement increases, reduce calories and increase activity.

If you need to lose weight, you are not alone! Increasing numbers of adults in the United States are struggling with being overweight or obese. The Centers for Disease Control report that approximately 33 percent of adults are overweight and another 33 percent are obese.[21] Being overweight is defined as having a BMI between 25 and 29.9. Obesity is defined as having a BMI of 30 or above. For example, a woman who is five feet four inches tall and weighs 180 pounds is considered obese. Maintaining your ideal weight is a matter of balancing calories in from food and beverages with calories expended through physical activity.

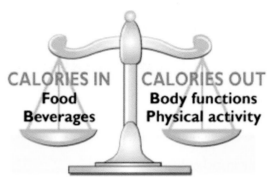

Source: From the U.S. Center for Disease Control, 2010.

Here are some practical suggestions for losing weight if your BMI is over 25 and you are not an athlete:

- Stop drinking sodas. One out of every five calories consumed in the United States is from sodas, and they are the biggest contributors to obesity.[22] Instead of drinking sodas, substitute water or unsweetened tea. Flavor your water with lemons, oranges, limes, strawberries, or mint. Be careful not to substitute sugary fruit juice, coffee, or tea for the sodas, since these drinks are often higher in calories.
- Exercise at least an hour to an hour and a half daily. Exercise is needed to burn the excess calories.
- Use the information at choosemyplate.gov to determine the number of calories needed to maintain your ideal weight. For example, the average 18-year-old female needs 2,000 calories a day. To lose weight, subtract 300 to 500 calories a day from this total.
- Eat five servings of fruits and vegetables a day. Use these fruits and vegetables as snacks.
- To control hunger, eat several small meals of 300 to 400 calories each.
- Make sure to eat breakfast. Eating breakfast helps to provide energy and avoid hunger, which leads to overeating.
- Eat smaller portions. Use a salad plate instead of a dinner plate. When you eat out, save half of your food for another meal.
- Minimize eating out at fast-food restaurants, since it is difficult to make good food choices there.
- If you are sad or anxious, try exercise instead of eating to relieve these symptoms. Practice stress reduction techniques.

Learn to Relax

Too much stress interferes with learning and memory. Practice some physical and mental relaxation techniques to deal with stress. Here are a few suggestions:

- Listen to soothing music. Choose music that has a beat that is slower than your heart rate. Classical or New Age music can be very relaxing.
- Take a few deep breaths.
- Focus on your breathing. If you are thinking about breathing, it is difficult to think about your worries.
- Lie down in a comfortable place and tense and relax your muscles. Start with the muscles in your head and work your way down to your toes. Tense each muscle for five to 10 seconds and then release the tension completely.

© 2014, Tatiana Popova. Used under license with Shutterstock, Inc.

- Imagine yourself in a pleasant place. When you are actually in a beautiful place, take the time to make a mental photograph. Memorize each detail and then close your eyes to see if you can still recall the scene. Return to this place in your mind when you feel stressed. Some people visualize the mountains, the beach, the ocean, a mountain stream, waterfalls, a tropical garden, or a desert scene. Choose a scene that works for you.
- Use positive thinking. Look for the good things in life and take the time to appreciate them.
- Maintain a healthy diet and get enough exercise.
- Practice yoga or tai chi.
- Keep things in perspective. Ask yourself, "Will it be important in 10 years?" If so, do something about it. If not, just relax.
- Focus on the positives. What have you learned from dealing with this problem? Has the problem provided an opportunity for personal growth?
- Discuss your feelings with a friend who is a good listener or get professional counseling.
- Keep your sense of humor. Laughter actually reduces the stress hormones.
- Maintain a support network of friends and loved ones.
- Practice meditation. It is a way of calming the mind.
- Get a massage or give one to someone else.
- Visit Health Services at your college for more help in dealing with excessive stress.

Success Is a Habit

We establish habits by taking small actions each day. Through repetition, these individual actions become habits. I once visited the Golden Gate Bridge in San Francisco and saw a cross section of the cable used to support the bridge. It was made of small metal strands twisted with other strands; then those cables were twisted together to make a stronger cable. Habits are a lot like cables. We start with one small action, and each successive action makes the habit stronger. Have you ever stopped to think that success can be a habit? We all have learned patterns of behavior that either help us to be successful or interfere with our success. With some effort and some basic understanding of behavior modification, you can choose to establish some new behaviors that lead to success or to get rid of behaviors that interfere with it.

"Habits are first cobwebs, then cables."
Spanish Proverb

"We are what we repeatedly do. Excellence, then, is not an act but a habit."
Aristotle

Health

Test what you have learned by selecting the correct answers to the following questions.

1. If you do not sleep for 24 hours, your mental performance decreases by:

    a. 50%
    b. 25%
    c. 10%

2. Exercise is important because:

    a. It increases the supply of oxygen and energy to the brain
    b. It helps you to relax
    c. All of the above

3. If you are not an athlete and your BMI is over 25, it is probably a good idea to:

    a. Severely limit caloric intake.
    b. Go on a diet that limits food choices.
    c. Reduce calories and increase activities.

4. It is suggested that two-thirds of the dinner plate be covered with:

    a. Potatoes
    b. Plant foods such as fruits, vegetables, whole grains, and beans
    c. Meats, fish, or poultry

5. Learn to relax by:

    a. Focusing on the negatives so you can improve
    b. Imagining the worst
    c. Asking yourself, "Will it be important in 10 years?"

How did you do on the quiz? Check your answers: 1. b, 2. c, 3. c, 4. b, 5. c

Journal Entry #4

Write a paragraph with at least three ideas about how you can motivate yourself to be successful in college. Use any of the following questions to think about your answer: How can you use positive thinking to be successful? How can you find something interesting in your studies? How can you improve your concentration? What are your intrinsic motivators for attending college? Remember that intrinsic motivators are those activities that you do because you enjoy them or they are personally meaningful to you. What are some extrinsic motivators? Are you motivated by money or achievement? How can you use the concept of locus of control to improve your chances of success in college? Do you believe that you create your own success? What are some rewards you can use to increase your positive behavior? How can being healthy improve attention and memory?

Seven Steps to Change a Habit

You can establish new habits that lead to your success. Once a habit is established, it can become a pattern of behavior that you do not need to think about very much. For example, new students often need to get into the habit of studying. Following is an outline of steps that can be helpful to establish new behaviors.

1. **State the problem.** What new habit would you like to start? What are your roadblocks or obstacles? What bad habit would you like to change? Be truthful about it. This is sometimes the most difficult step. Here are two different examples:

   - I need to study to be successful in college. I am not in the habit of studying. I easily get distracted by work, family, friends, and other things I need to do. At the end of the day, I am too tired to study.

   - I need to improve my diet. I am overweight. I eat too much fast food and am not careful about what I eat. I have no time for exercise.

2. **Change one small behavior at a time.** If you think about climbing a mountain, the task can seem overwhelming. However, you can take the first step. If you can change one small behavior, you can gain the confidence to change another. For example:

   - I plan to study at least one hour each day on Mondays through Fridays.

   - I plan to eat more fruits and vegetables each day.

State the behavior you would like to change. Make it small.

3. **State in a positive way the behavior you wish to establish.** For example, instead of the negative statements "I will not waste my time" or "I will not eat junk food," say, "I plan to study each day" or "I plan to eat fruits and vegetables each day."

4. **Count the behavior.** How often do you do this behavior? If you are trying to establish a pattern of studying, write down how much time you spend studying each day. If you are trying to improve your diet, write down everything that you eat each day. Sometimes just getting an awareness of your habit is enough to begin to make some changes.

5. **Picture in your mind the actions you might take.** For example:

   - I picture myself finding time to study in the library. I see myself walking to the library. I can see myself in the library studying.

   - I see myself in the grocery store buying fruits and vegetables. I see myself packing these fruits and vegetables in my lunch. I see myself putting these foods in a place where I will notice them.

6. **Practice the behavior for 10 days.** In 10 days, you can get started on a new pattern of behavior. Once you have started, keep practicing the behavior for about a month to firmly establish your new pattern of behavior. The first three days are the most difficult. If you fail, don't give up. Just realize that you are human and keep trying for 10 days. Think positively that you can be successful. Write a journal entry or note on your calendar about what you have accomplished each day.

7. **Find a reward for your behavior.** Remember that we tend to repeat behaviors that are rewarded. Find rewards that do not involve too many calories, don't cost too much money, and don't involve alcohol or drugs. Also, rewards are most effective if they directly follow the behavior you wish to reinforce.

Seven Steps to Change a Habit

1. State the problem
2. Change one small behavior at a time
3. Be positive
4. Count the behavior
5. Picture the change
6. Practice the behavior
7. Reward yourself

"The difference in winning and losing is most often . . . not quitting."
Walt Disney

"It's not that I'm so smart; it's just that I stay with problems longer."
Albert Einstein

Ten Habits of Successful College Students

Starting your college education will require you to establish some new habits to be successful.

1. Attend class.

College lectures supplement the material in the text, so it is important to attend class. Many college instructors will drop you if you miss three hours of class. After three absences, most students do not return to class. If your class is online, log in frequently.

2. Read the textbook.

Start early and read a little at a time. If you have a text with 400 pages, read 25 pages a week rather than trying to read it all at once.

3. Have an educational plan.

Counselors or advisors can assist you in making an educational plan so that you take the right classes and accomplish your educational goal as soon as possible.

4. Use college services.

Colleges offer valuable free services that help you to be successful. Take advantage of tutoring, counseling, health services, financial aid, the learning resources center (library) and many other services.

5. Get to know the faculty.

You can get to know the faculty by asking questions in class or meeting with your instructors during office hours. Your instructors can provide extra assistance and write letters of recommendation for scholarships, future employment, or graduate school.

6. Don't work too much.

Research has shown that full-time students should have no more than 20 hours of outside employment a week to be successful in college. If you have to work more than 20 hours a week, reduce your college load. If you are working 40 hours a week or more, take only one or two classes.

7. Take one step at a time.

If you are anxious about going to college, remember that each class you attend takes you another step toward your goal. If you take too many classes, especially in the beginning, you may become overwhelmed.

8. Have a goal for the future.

Know why you are in college and what you hope to accomplish. What career will you have in the future? Imagine your future lifestyle.

9. Visualize your success.

See yourself walking across the stage and receiving your college diploma. See yourself working at a job you enjoy.

10. Ask questions if you don't understand.

Asking questions not only helps you to find the answers, but it shows you are motivated to be successful. Starting your college education will require you to establish some new habits to be successful.

Persistence

There is an old saying that persistence will get you almost anything eventually. This saying applies to your success in life as well as in college. The first two to six weeks of college are a critical time in which many students drop out. Realize that college is a new experience and that you will face new challenges and growth experiences. Make plans to persist, especially in the first few weeks. Get to know a college counselor or advisor. These professionals can help you to get started in the right classes and answer any questions you might have. It is important to make a connection with a counselor or faculty member so that you feel comfortable in college and have the resources to obtain needed help. Plan to enroll on time so that you do not have to register late. It is crucial to attend the first class. In the first class, the professor explains the class requirements and expectations and sets the tone for the class. You may even get dropped from the class if you are not there on the first day. Get into the habit of studying right away. Make studying a habit that you start immediately at the beginning of the semester or quarter. If you can make it through the first six weeks, it is likely that you can finish the semester and complete your college education.

It has been said that 90 percent of success is just showing up. Any faculty member will tell you that the number one reason for students dropping out of college is lack of attendance. They know that when students miss three classes in a row, they are not likely to return. Even very capable students who miss class may find that they are lost when they come back. Many students are simply afraid to return. Classes such as math and foreign languages are sequential, and it is very difficult to make up work after an absence. One of the most important ways you can be successful is to make a habit of consistently showing up for class.

You will also need commitment to be successful. Commitment is a promise to yourself to follow through with something. In athletics, it is not necessarily the one with the best physical skills who makes the best athlete. Commitment and practice make a great athlete. Commitment means doing whatever is necessary to succeed. Like the good athlete, make a commitment to accomplishing your goals. Spend the time necessary to be successful in your studies.

When you face difficulties, persistence and commitment are especially important. History is full of famous people who contributed to society through persistence and commitment. Consider the following facts about Abraham Lincoln, for example.

- Failed in business at age 21.
- Was defeated in a legislative race at age 22.
- Failed again in business at age 24.
- Overcame the death of his sweetheart at age 26.
- Had a nervous breakdown at age 27.
- Lost a congressional race at age 34.
- Lost a congressional race at age 36.
- Lost a senatorial race at age 45.
- Failed in an effort to become vice president at age 47.
- Lost a senatorial race at age 49.
- Was elected president of the United States at age 52.[23]

You will face difficulties along the way in any worthwhile venture. The successful person keeps on trying. There are some precautions about persistence, however. Make sure that the goal you are trying to reach is attainable and valuable to you. As you learn more about yourself, you may want to change your goals. Also, persistence can be misguided if it involves other people. For example, if you decide that you want to marry someone and this someone does not want to marry you, it is better to focus your energy and attention on a different goal.

One of the best ways to be persistent is to accomplish your goals one step at a time. If you look at a mountain, it may seem too high to climb, but you can do it one step at a time. Araceli Segarra became the first Spanish woman to climb Mount Everest. At 29,028 feet, Mount Everest is the highest mountain in the world. It is so high that you need an oxygen tank to breathe at the top. So how did Araceli climb the mountain? She says that it took strength and concentration. She put one foot

(continued)

in front of the other. When she was near the top of the mountain, she was more tired than she had ever been in her life. She told herself that she would take 10 more steps. When she had taken 10 steps, she said, "I'm OK. I made it." Then she took 10 more steps until she reached the top of the mountain.

The goal of getting a college education may seem like a mountain that is difficult to climb.

Break it into smaller steps that you can accomplish. See your college counselor or advisor, register for classes, attend the first class, read the first chapter, do the first assignment, and you will be on the road to your success. Then continue to break tasks into small, achievable steps and continue from one step to the next. And remember, persistence will get you almost anything eventually.

Journal Entry #5

What will you do if you are tempted to drop out of college? What steps can you take to be persistent in achieving your college goals? Are there times when it is best to change goals rather than to be persistent if your efforts are not working? Write a paragraph about how you will be persistent in reaching your college goals.

JOURNAL ENTRIES
Understanding Motivation

Go to http://www.collegesuccess1.com/JournalEntries.htm for Word files of the Journal Entries

Success over the Internet

Visit the *College Success Website* at http://www.collegesuccess1.com/

The *College Success Website* is continually updated with new topics and links to the material presented in this chapter. Topics include:

- How to improve concentration
- Motivation
- Positive attitude
- Balancing work, school, and social life
- Success factors for new college students
- How to change a habit
- Dealing with cravings and urges

Contact your instructor if you have any problems accessing the *College Success Website*.

Notes

1. U.S. Census Bureau, "Earnings and Unemployment by Educational Attainment 2012," retrieved from http://www.bls.gov/emp/ep_chart_001.htm

2. U.S. Bureau of Labor Statistics, Occupational Handbook, 2010–11 Edition, "Overview of the 2008–18 Projections," accessed from http:data.bis.gov

3. Joyce Lain Kennedy, *Joyce Lain Kennedy's Career Book* (Chicago, IL: VGM Career Horizons, 1993),32.

4. U.S. Census Bureau, "Earnings and Unemployment by Educational Attainment 2012" retrieved from http://www.bls.gov/emp/ep_chart_001.htm

5. W. Lewallen, "The Impact of Being Undecided on College Persistence," *Journal of College Student Development* 34 (1993): 103–12.

6. Marsha Fralick, "College Success: A Study of Positive and Negative Attrition," *Community College Review* 20 (1993): 29–36.

7. Christopher Peterson, *A Primer in Positive Psychology* (New York: Oxford University Press, 2006), 127.

8. M. J. Findlay and H. M. Cooper, "Locus of Control and Academic Achievement: A Literature Review," *Journal of Personality and Social Psychology* 44 (1983): 419–27.

9. Scott LaFee, "A Chronic Lack of Sleep Can Lead to the Big Sleep," *San Diego Union Tribune,* October 8, 1997.

10. Ronald Kotulak, "Skimping on Sleep May Make You Fat, Clumsy and Haggard," *San Diego Union Tribune,* June 14, 1998.

11. Gregory Belenky, Walter Reed Army Institute of Research, *Sleep, Sleep Deprivation, and Human Performance in Continuous Operations,* 1997.

12. Lindsey Tanner, "AMA Backs 80-hour Workweek Limit for Doctors-in-Training," *San Diego Union Tribune,* June 21, 2002.

13. Ronald Kotulak, "Skimping on Sleep."

14. Nicole Ziegler Dizon, "Aging Men's Flab Tied to a Lack of Deep Sleep," *San Diego Union Tribune,* August 16, 2000.

15. From http://www.thirdage.com/cgi-bin/NewsPrint.cgi, 2002.

16. Francesco Cappuccio, Warwick Medical School, "Researchers Say Lack of Sleep Doubles Risk of Death . . . But So Can Too Much Sleep," http://www2warwick.ac.uk, 2008.

17. John Medina, *Brain Rules* (Seattle: Pear Press, 2008), p. 16.

18. U.S. Department of Agriculture, http://www.mypyramid.gov.

19. Ibid.

20. Associated Press, "Proper Diet Urged to Fight Cancer, Not Supplements," *San Diego Union Tribune,* September 5, 2000.

21. U.S. Centers for Disease Control and Prevention, "Overweight and Obesity," accessed August 3, 2010, http://www.cdc.gov/obesity/causes/index.html.

22. Marilyn Marchione, "Soda Causes Obesity, Researchers Report," *San Diego Union Tribune,* March 5, 2006.

23. Anthony Robbins, *Unlimited Power* (New York: Ballantine Books, 1986), 73.

Name _____   Date _____

A good way to begin your success in college is to assess your present skills to determine your strengths and areas that need improvement. Complete the following assessment to get an overview of the topics presented in the textbook and to measure your present skills.

Measure Your Success

The following statements represent major topics included in the textbook. Read the following statements and rate how true they are for you at the present time. At the end of the course, you will have the opportunity to complete this assessment again to measure your progress.

5 Definitely true
4 Mostly true
3 Somewhat true
2 Seldom true
1 Never true

© 2014, Kenishirotie. Used under license with Shutterstock, Inc.

_____ I am motivated to be successful in college.

_____ I know the value of a college education.

_____ I know how to establish successful patterns of behavior.

_____ I understand how my health impacts attention and learning.

_____ I am attending college to accomplish my own personal goals.

_____ I believe to a great extent that my actions determine my future.

_____ I am persistent in achieving my goals.

_____ **Total points for Getting Started**

_____ I can describe my personality type.

_____ I can list careers that match my personality type.

_____ I can describe my personal strengths and talents based on my personality type.

_____ I understand how my personality type affects how I manage my time and money.

_____ I know what college majors are most in demand.

_____ I am confident that I have chosen the best major for myself.

_____ Courses related to my major are interesting and exciting to me.

_____ **Total points for Personality and Major**

_____ I can describe my learning style.

_____ I can list study techniques that match my learning style.

_____ I understand how my personality affects my learning style.

_____ I understand the concept of emotional intelligence and how it affects personal and career success.

_____ I understand the concept of multiple intelligences.

_____ I can list my multiple intelligences and matching careers.

_____ I create my own success.

_____ **Total points for Learning Style and Intelligence**

_____ I have a list or mental picture of my lifetime goals.

_____ I know what I would like to accomplish in the next four years.

_____ I spend my time on activities that help me accomplish my lifetime goals.

_____ I effectively use priorities in managing my time.

_____ I can balance study, work, and recreation time.

_____ I generally avoid procrastination on important tasks.

_____ I am good at managing my money.

_____ **Total points for Managing Time and Money**

_____ I know memory techniques and can apply them to my college studies.

_____ I can read a college textbook and remember the important points.

_____ I know how to effectively mark a college textbook.

_____ I can quickly survey a college text and select the main ideas.

_____ I generally have good reading comprehension.

_____ I can concentrate on the material I am reading.

_____ I am confident in my ability to read and remember college-level material.

_____ **Total points for Memory and Reading**

_____ I know how to listen for the main points in a college lecture.

_____ I am familiar with note-taking systems for college lectures.

_____ I know how to review my lecture notes.

_____ I feel comfortable with writing.

_____ I know the steps in writing a college term paper.

_____ I know how to prepare a speech.

_____ I am comfortable with public speaking.

_____ **Total points for Taking Notes, Writing, and Speaking**

_____ I know how to adequately prepare for a test.

_____ I can predict the questions that are likely to be on the test.

_____ I know how to deal with test anxiety.

_____ I am successful on math exams.

_____ I know how to make a reasonable guess if I am uncertain about the answer.

_____ I am confident of my ability to take objective tests.

_____ I can write a good essay answer.

_____ **Total points for Test Taking**

_____ I have self-confidence.

_____ I use positive self-talk and affirmations.

_____ I have a visual picture of my future success.

_____ I have a clear idea of what happiness means to me.

_____ I usually practice positive thinking.

_____ I am confident of my ability to succeed in college.

_____ I am confident that my choice of a major is the best one for me.

_____ **Total points for Future**

Total your points:

_____ Getting Started

_____ Personality and Major

_____ Learning Style and Intelligence

_____ Managing Time and Money

_____ Memory and Reading

_____ Taking Notes, Writing, and Speaking

_____ Test Taking

_____ **Grand total points**

If you scored

253–280   You are very confident of your skills for success in college. Maybe you do not need this class?

225–252   You have good skills for success in college. You can always improve.

197–224   You have average skills for success in college. You will definitely benefit from taking this course.

Below 196   You need some help to survive in college. You are in the right place to begin.

Use these scores to complete the Success Wheel that follows this assessment.

Success Wheel

Name _____ Date _____

Use your scores from the Measure Your Success assessment to complete the following Success Wheel. Use different colored markers to shade in each section of the wheel.

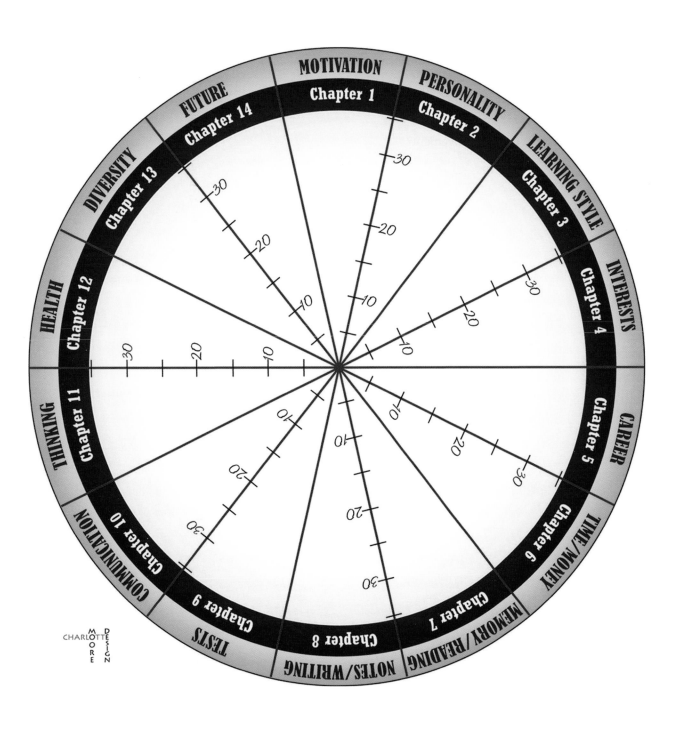

CHARLOTTE MOORE DESIGN

1. What are your best areas?

2. What are areas that need improvement?

Name _____   Date _____

Justin

It is the first day of class in the college success course. Justin is feeling excited and a little apprehensive as he walks into the class on the first day. He wonders if this is the right course for him. He managed to be successful in high school without much effort and thinks that college should be the same. His college advisor has recommended the course for all new students. He thinks that this course should be at least an easy A grade and it is not too important to attend every class. Justin has just graduated from high school and is looking forward to more freedom and independence. Justin has just been employed at a local sporting goods store. He is enjoying the job and the extra spending money. He started out working on Saturday only, but has now agreed to work 30 hours a week so that he can buy a new truck. School is not one of his top priorities, but his parents are insisting that he attend college so that he can get a better job in the future. How can Justin motivate himself to be successful in this course?

Anna

Anna walks into the classroom on the first day with a great deal of anxiety. She is returning to school 15 years after her high school graduation. Her children are getting a little older and she has decided to return to school to finish that degree that she has always wanted. Although having a college degree has been a lifelong dream of hers, she is uncertain about which major would be best. She is hoping to choose a major that leads to a well-paying job so that she can help her children with college expenses in the near future. She has a busy family life and is not sure how to add all the college activities to her schedule. The college success course seems like a good place to start. She looks around the classroom, notices that she is one of the older students in class, and hopes she can keep up with the younger students who have just graduated from high school. What steps can Anna take to be successful in this course?

What Do I Want from College?

Name _____ Date _____

Read the following list and place checkmarks next to your reasons for attending college. Think about why you are attending college and add your own personal reasons to the list.

_____ **1.** To have financial security

_____ **2.** To find a satisfying career

_____ **3.** To explore possibilities provided by college

_____ **4.** To expand my options

_____ **5.** To become an educated person

_____ **6.** To figure out what I want to do with my life

_____ **7.** To develop my potential

_____ **8.** To become a role model for my children

_____ **9.** To make my parents happy

_____ **10.** To respect myself

_____ **11.** To feel good about myself

_____ **12.** To see if I can do it

_____ **13.** To meet interesting people

_____ **14.** To have something to do and prevent boredom

_____ **15.** To become the best I can be

_____ **16.** To have better job opportunities

_____ **17.** To have no regrets later on

_____ **18.** To prepare for a good job or profession

_____ **19.** To have job security

_____ **20.** To gain confidence in myself

_____ **21.** To get a degree

_____ **22.** To gain a greater understanding of the world

_____ **23.** To have fun

_____ **24.** To understand myself

_____ **25.** To learn how to think

_____ **26.** To enjoy what I do for a living

_____ **27.** To reach my potential

_____ **28.** Because my parents want me to get a degree

_____ **29.** For my own personal satisfaction

_____ **30.** To make a difference in other people's lives

_____ **31.** To have a position of power

_____ **32.** To have respect

_____ **33.** To have prestige

_____ **34.** To have time and money for travel

_____ **35.** To acquire knowledge

_____ **36.** _____

_____ **37.** _____

What are your top six reasons for attending college? You may include reasons not listed above. If you are tempted to give up on your college education, read this list and think about the reasons you have listed below.

1. _____   **4.** _____

2. _____   **5.** _____

3. _____   **6.** _____

Name _____ Date _____

© 2014, iQoncept. Used under license with Shutterstock, Inc.

Students come to college with a dream of making a better future for themselves. What is your dream? Your instructor may have you share your ideas with other students in the course.

Place a checkmark next to any item that could be a roadblock to your success in college.

_____ Too much work	_____ Family obligations	_____ Lack of study skills
_____ Financial difficulties	_____ Social life	_____ Using time wisely
_____ Lack of confidence	_____ Computer games	_____ Speaking in class
_____ Difficulty with reading	_____ Social media	_____ Negative thinking
_____ Difficulty with writing	_____ Phone use and texting	_____ Lack of motivation
_____ Difficulty with math	_____ Lack of career goals	_____ Learning disabilities
_____ Difficulty with tests	_____ Dislike of homework	_____ Lack of persistence
_____ Difficulty with memory	_____ Dislike of school	_____ Health problems

List any other roadblocks in addition to the items checked above:

What are your top three roadblocks?

1. _____

2. _____

3. _____

Spend 5 minutes skimming through the table of contents in your textbook and looking quickly through the chapters to find ideas that will help you overcome any roadblocks to your success. List 5 topics from the textbook that can help you to be successful in college.

1. _____

2. _____

3. _____

4. _____

5. _____

What are other resources that can help you to overcome your roadblocks? (tutoring, financial aid, advising, family support, self-motivation)

Your instructor will help the class brainstorm ideas for overcoming roadblocks. What is your plan for overcoming the roadblocks to achieve your hopes and dreams for the future?

How Healthy Is Your Diet?

Name _____ Date _____

Use the following worksheet to analyze your diet. This plan is based on 2,000 calories. Go to www.choosemyplate.gov/ to find your individualized recommendations.

Food Groups	Recommended	List Actual Food Choices
Grains	6 ounce equivalents (1 ounce equivalent is about 1 slice of bread, I cup dry cereal, or ½ cup rice or pasta)	How many ounces?
Vegetables	2½ cups (Includes dark green, orange, starchy, dry beans and peas, and other veggies)	How many cups?
Fruits	2 cups	How many cups?
Oils	6 teaspoons	How many teaspoons?
Milk	3 cups (1½ ounces of cheese = 1 cup milk, a large pizza contains 16 ounces of cheese)	How many cups?
Meat and Beans	5.5 ounces (1 ounce equivalent is 1 ounce of meat, poultry or fish, 1 tablespoon peanut butter, ½ ounce nuts, ¼ ounce dry beans or peas)	How many ounces?
Discretionary Calories	100–300 calories	List foods high in fat or sugar.

1. How much do you exercise daily outside of your daily routine?

2. Compare your results to the recommended dietary guidelines. What did you discover?

3. What changes will you make as a result of this exercise?

What Is Your Stress Index?*

Name _____ Date _____

Do you frequently: Yes   No

1. Neglect your diet?   _____   _____

2. Try to do everything yourself?   _____   _____

3. Blow up easily?   _____   _____

4. Seek unrealistic goals?   _____   _____

5. Fail to see the humor in situations others find funny?   _____   _____

6. Act rude?   _____   _____

7. Make a big deal out of everything?   _____   _____

8. Look to other people to make things happen?   _____   _____

9. Have difficulty making decisions?   _____   _____

10. Complain you are disorganized?   _____   _____

11. Avoid people whose ideas are different from your own?   _____   _____

12. Keep everything inside?   _____   _____

13. Neglect exercise?   _____   _____

14. Have only a few supportive relationships?   _____   _____

15. Use psychoactive drugs, such as sleeping pills and tranquilizers, without   _____   _____
    physician approval?

16. Get too little rest?   _____   _____

17. Get angry when you are kept waiting?   _____   _____

18. Ignore stress symptoms?   _____   _____

19. Procrastinate?   _____   _____

20. Think there is only one right way to do something?   _____   _____

21. Fail to build in relaxation time?   _____   _____

22. Gossip?   _____   _____

23. Race through the day?   _____   _____

24. Spend a lot of time lamenting the past?   _____   _____

25. Fail to get a break from noise and crowds?   _____   _____

*From Andrew Slaby, *Sixty Ways to Make Stress Work for You*.

Score 1 for each yes answer and 0 for each no. Total score: _____

1–6   There are a few hassles in your life. Make sure, though, that you aren't trying so hard to avoid problems that you shy away from challenges.

7–13   You've got your life in pretty good control. Work on the choices and habits that could still be causing some unnecessary stress in your life.

14–20   You're approaching the danger zone. You may well be suffering stress-related symptoms and your relationships could be strained. Think carefully about choices you've made and take relaxation breaks each day.

Above 20   Emergency! You must stop now, rethink how you are living, change your attitudes, and pay scrupulous attention to your diet, exercise, and relaxation programs.

How to Change a Habit

Name _____ Date _____

The following exercise will help you to practice the process of beginning successful new habits. Choose *one* of these simple 10-day projects:

- Monitor how many minutes you study each day.
- Monitor how many minutes you exercise each day.
- Monitor how you spend your money each day. Write down all your expenditures.
- Make a goal of eating breakfast. Write down what you eat for breakfast each day.
- Keep a list of the fruits and vegetables you eat each day.
- Count how many sodas you drink each day.
- Keep a log of time you sleep each night and make a note of how rested you feel the next day.
- Make a goal of making your bed or picking up your clothes. Record your progress each day.
- You can choose another behavior as long as it is realistic and achievable. You must be able to count it or describe the outcome. Consult with your instructor if you choose this option.

1. First, state the problem. Describe the behavior you want to change. What are your roadblocks or obstacles?

   For example: I get stressed when I run out of money before my next paycheck. I would like to manage my money better. One obstacle is my attitude that if I have money, I can spend it.

2. Choose one small behavior at a time. If you can change one small behavior, you can gain the confidence to change another.

   For example: A goal like improving money management is broad and vague. A good way to begin is to choose a small first step. A good first step is to keep track of expenditures so that you can begin to understand how you spend your money. The projects listed earlier are examples of small behaviors. If you are working on a different project, is it a small behavior that can be counted and one that can realistically be accomplished? List the small behavior that you will use for this project.

3. State in a positive way the behavior you wish to establish.

   For example: Instead of saying, "I will not spend all of my money before payday," say, "I will keep a money monitor for 10 days." Of course, the next step would be to work on a budget. If necessary, rewrite your goal in a positive way.

4. Count the behavior. Sometimes just becoming aware of your habit is enough to begin making some changes.

   For example: For the next 10 days, I will write down all my expenditures.

5. Picture in your mind the actions you might take to accomplish your goal and write them down in the following space.

   For example: I see myself writing down all my expenses on a sheet of paper. I will do this each day so that I can find out where I spend my money and begin to manage my money better. I see myself less stressed because I will have money for the things I need.

6. What reward will you use to reinforce the behavior? Rewards are most effective if they directly follow the behavior you wish to reinforce. Remember that good rewards do not have too many calories, cost too much money, or involve alcohol or drugs. List your rewards.

7. Practice the behavior for *10 days*. The first three days are the most difficult. If you fail, don't give up. Just realize that you are human and keep trying for 10 days. Think positively that you can be successful. Use the space below or a separate sheet of paper to count how many times you did the behavior each day and what happened. Remember, you can get started on a new habit in 10 days, but you will need to continue for about a month to firmly establish your new pattern of behavior.

Day 1: _____

_____

_____

Day 2: _____

_____

_____

Day 3: _____

_____

_____

Day 4: _____

_____

_____

Day 5: _____

_____

_____

Day 6: _____

_____

_____

Day 7: _____

_____

_____

Day 8: _____

_____

_____

Day 9: _____

_____

_____

Day 10: _____

_____

_____

How did this project work for you?

Textbook Skimming

Name _____ Date _____

Use this text or any new text to answer the following questions. Challenge yourself to do this exercise quickly. Remember that a textbook survey should take no longer than five to 15 minutes. Try to complete this exercise in 15 minutes to allow time for writing. Notice the time when you start and finish.

1. Write two key ideas found in the introduction or preface to the book.

2. Looking at the table of contents, list the first five main ideas covered in the text.

3. Write down five interesting topics that you found in the book.

4. What did you find at the back of the book (e.g., index, glossary, appendixes)?

5. How long did it take you to do this exercise? _____

6. Briefly, what did you think of this textbook skimming exercise?

CHAPTER 2

Exploring Your Personality and Major

Learning Objectives

Read to answer these key questions:

- What are the different personality types?

- What is my personality type?

- What are my personal strengths?

- How is personality type related to choice of a major and career?

- What are the characteristics of my ideal career?

- How does personality type affect decision-making, communication, time management, and money management?

- What careers and majors should I consider based on my personality type?

- What are some other factors in choosing a major?

To assure your success in college, it is important to choose the major that is best for you. If you choose a major and career that match your personality, interests, aptitudes, and values, you will enjoy your studies and excel in your work. It was Picasso who said that you know you enjoy your work when you do not notice the time passing by. If you can become interested in your work and studies, you are on your way to developing passion and joy in your life. If you can get up each morning and enjoy the work that you do (at least on most days), you will surely have one of the keys to happiness.

Choose a Major That Matches Your Gifts and Talents

The first step in choosing the major that is right for you is to understand your personality type. Psychologists have developed useful theories of personality that can help you understand how personality type relates to the choice of major and career. The personality theory used in this textbook is derived from the work of Swiss psychologist Carl Jung (1875–1961). Jung believed that we are born with a predisposition for certain personality preferences and that healthy development is based on the lifelong nurturing of inborn preferences rather than trying to change a person to become something different. Each personality type has gifts and talents that can be nurtured over a lifetime.

While assessments are not exact predictors of your future major and career, they provide useful information that will get you started on the path of career exploration and finding the college major that is best suited to you. Knowledge of your personality and the personalities of others is not only valuable in understanding yourself, but also in appreciating how others are different. This understanding of self and others will empower you to communicate and work effectively with others. Complete the Do What You Are personality assessment that is included with this textbook before you begin this chapter. (See the inside front cover for further information.)

© 2014, Andril Kondiuk. Used under license with Shutterstock, Inc.

Understanding Personality Types

Just as no two fingerprints or snowflakes are exactly alike, each person is a different and unique individual. Even with this uniqueness, however, we can make some general statements about personality. When we make generalizations, we are talking about averages. These averages can provide useful information about ourselves and other people, but it is important to remember that no individual is exactly described by the average. As you read through the following descriptions of personality types, keep in mind that we are talking about generalizations or beginning points for discussion and thoughtful analysis.

As you read through your personality description from Do What You Are and the information in this text, **focus on your personal strengths and talents**. Building on these personal strengths has several important benefits. It increases self-esteem and self-confidence, which contribute to your success and enjoyment of life. Building on your strengths provides the energy and motivation required to put in the effort needed to accomplish any worthwhile task. The assessment also identifies some of your possible weaknesses or "blind spots." Just be aware of these blind spots so that they do not interfere with your success. Being aware of your blind spots can even be used to your advantage. For example, some personality types thrive by working with people. A career that involves much public contact is a good match for this personality type, whereas choosing a career where public contact is limited can lead to job dissatisfaction. Knowing about your personality type can help you make the right decisions to maximize your potential.

Personality type has four dimensions:

1. Extraversion or Introversion

2. Sensing or Intuition

3. Thinking or Feeling

4. Judging or Perceiving

These dimensions of personality will be defined and examined in more depth in the sections that follow.

Extraversion or Introversion

The dimension of extraversion or introversion defines how we interact with the world and how our energy flows. In the general school population, 75 percent of students are usually extraverts and 25 percent are introverts.

Extraverts (E) focus their energy on the world outside themselves. They enjoy interaction with others and get to know a lot of different people. They enjoy and are usually good at communication. They are energized by social interaction and prefer being active. These types are often described as talkative and social.

Introverts (I) focus their energy on the world inside of themselves. They enjoy spending time alone to think about the world in order to understand it. Introverts prefer more limited social contacts, choosing smaller groups or one-on-one relationships. These types are often described as quiet or reserved.

We all use the introvert and extravert modes while functioning in our daily lives. Whether a person is an extravert or an introvert is a matter of preference, like being left- or right-handed. We can use our nondominant hand, but it is not as comfortable as using our dominant hand. We are usually more skillful in using the dominant hand. For example, introverts can learn to function well in social situations, but later may need some peace and quiet to recharge. On the other hand, social contact energizes the extravert.

One personality type is not better than the other: it is just different. Being an extravert is not better than being an introvert. Each type has unique gifts and talents that can be used in different occupations. An extravert might enjoy working in an occupation with lots of public contact, such as being a receptionist or handling public relations. An introvert might enjoy being an accountant or writer. However, as with all of the personality dimensions, a person may have traits of both types.

Introverts and Extraverts

The list below describes some qualities of introverts and extraverts. **For each pair of items,** quickly choose the phrase that describes you best and place a checkmark next to it. Remember that one type is not better than another. You may also find that you are a combination type and act like an introvert in some situations and an extravert in others. Each type has gifts and talents that can be used in choosing the best major and career for you. To get an estimate of your preference, notice which column has the most checkmarks.

Introvert (I)	Extravert (E)
_____ Energized by having quiet time alone	_____ Energized by social interaction
_____ Tend to think first and talk later	_____ Tend to talk first and think later
_____ Tend to think things through quietly	_____ Tend to think out loud
_____ Tend to respond slowly, after thinking	_____ Tend to respond quickly, before thinking
_____ Avoid being the center of attention	_____ Like to be the center of attention
_____ Difficult to get to know, private	_____ Easy to get to know, outgoing
_____ Have a few close friends	_____ Have many friends, know lots of people
_____ Prefer quiet for concentration	_____ Can read or talk with background noise
_____ Listen more than talk	_____ Talk more than listen
_____ View telephone calls as a distraction	_____ View telephone calls as a welcome break
_____ Talk to a few people at parties	_____ Talk to many different people at parties
_____ Share special occasions with one or a few people	_____ Share special occasions with large groups
_____ Prefer to study alone	_____ Prefer to study with others in a group
_____ Prefer the library to be quiet	_____ Talk with others in the library
_____ Described as quiet or reserved	_____ Described as talkative or friendly
_____ Work systematically	_____ Work through trial and error

Here are some qualities that describe the ideal work environment. Again, as you **read through each pair of items,** place a checkmark next to the work environment that you prefer.

Introvert (I)	Extravert (E)
_____ Work alone or with individuals	_____ Much public contact
_____ Quiet for concentration	_____ High-energy environment
_____ Communication one-on-one	_____ Present ideas to a group
_____ Work in small groups	_____ Work as part of a team
_____ Focus on one project until complete	_____ Variety and action
_____ Work without interruption	_____ Talk to others
_____ **Total** (from both charts above)	_____ **Total** (from both charts above)

Do these results agree with your personality assessment on the Do What You Are? If your results are the same, this is a good indication that your results are useful and accurate. Are there some differences with the results obtained from your personality assessment? If your results are different, this provides an opportunity for further reflection about your personality type. Here are a couple of reasons why your results may be different.

1. You may be a combination type with varying degrees of preference for each type.

2. You may have chosen your personality type on the Do What You Are based on what you think is best rather than what you truly are. Students sometimes do this because of the myth that there are good and bad personality types. It is important to remember that each personality type has strengths and weaknesses. By identifying strengths, you can build on them by choosing the right major and career. By being aware of weaknesses, you can come up with strategies to compensate for them to be successful.

Look at the total number of checkmarks for extravert and introvert on the two above charts. Do you lean toward being an introvert or an extravert? Remember that one type is not better than the other and each has unique gifts and talents. On the chart below, place an X on the line to indicate how much you prefer introversion or extraversion. If you selected most of the introvert traits, place your X somewhere on the left side. If you selected most of the extravert traits, place your X somewhere on the right side. If you are equally introverted and extraverted, place your X in the middle.

Introvert _____|_____ Extravert

Do you generally prefer introversion or extraversion? In the box below, write **I** for introversion or **E** for extraversion. If there is a tie between **E** and **I**, write **I**.

Notice that it is possible to be a combination type. At times you might prefer to act like an introvert, and at other times you might prefer to act like an extravert. It is beneficial to be able to balance these traits. However, for combination types, it is more difficult to select specific occupations that match this type

Journal Entry #1

Look at the results from Do What You Are and your own self-assessment above. Are you an introvert or an extravert or a combination of these two types? Can you give examples of how it affects your social life, school, or work? Write a paragraph about this preference.

Sensing or Intuition

The dimension of sensing or intuition describes how we take in information. In the general school population, 70 percent of students are usually sensing types and 30 percent are intuitive types.

Sensing (S) persons prefer to use the senses to take in information (what they see, hear, taste, touch, smell). They focus on "what is" and trust information that is concrete and observable. They learn through experience.

Intuitive (N) persons rely on instincts and focus on "what could be." While we all use our five senses to perceive the world, intuitive people are interested in relationships, possibilities, meanings, and implications. They value inspiration and trust their "sixth sense" or hunches. (Intuitive is designated as N so it is not confused with I for Introvert.)

We all use both of these modes in our daily lives, but we usually have a preference for one mode or the other. Again, there is no best preference. Each type has special skills that can be applied to the job market. For example, you would probably want your tax preparer to be a sensing type who focuses on concrete information and fills out your tax form correctly. An inventor or artist would probably be an intuitive type.

ACTIVITY

Sensing and Intuitive

Here are some qualities of sensing and intuitive persons. As you **read through each pair of items,** quickly place a checkmark next to the item that usually describes yourself.

Sensing (S)	INtuitive (N)
_____ Trust what is certain and concrete	_____ Trust inspiration and inference
_____ Prefer specific answers to questions	_____ Prefer general answers that leave room for interpretation
_____ Like new ideas if they have practical applications (if you can use them)	_____ Like new ideas for their own sake (you don't need a practical use for them)
_____ Value realism and common sense	_____ Value imagination and innovation
_____ Think about things one at a time and step by step	_____ Think about many ideas at once as they come to you
_____ Like to improve and use skills learned before	_____ Like to learn new skills and get bored using the same skills
_____ More focused on the present	_____ More focused on the future
_____ Concentrate on what you are doing	_____ Wonder what is next
_____ Do something	_____ Think about doing something
_____ See tangible results	_____ Focus on possibilities
_____ If it isn't broken, don't fix it	_____ There is always a better way to do it

Sensing (S)	INtuitive (N)
_____ Prefer working with facts and figures	_____ Prefer working with ideas and theories
_____ Focus on reality	_____ Use fantasy
_____ Seeing is believing	_____ Anything is possible
_____ Tend to be specific and literal (say what you mean)	_____ Tend to be general and figurative (use comparisons and analogies)
_____ See what is here and now	_____ See the big picture

Here are some qualities that describe the ideal work environment. Again, as you **read through each pair of items,** place a checkmark next to the work environment that you prefer.

Sensing (S)	INtuitive (N)
_____ Use and practice skills	_____ Learn new skills
_____ Work with known facts	_____ Explore new ideas and approaches
_____ See measurable results	_____ Work with theories
_____ Focus on practical benefits	_____ Use imagination and be original
_____ Learn through experience	_____ Freedom to follow your inspiration
_____ Pleasant environment	_____ Challenging environment
_____ Use standard procedures	_____ Invent new products and procedures
_____ Work step-by-step	_____ Work in bursts of energy
_____ Do accurate work	_____ Find creative solutions
_____ **Total** (from both charts above)	_____ **Total** (from both charts above)

Look at the two charts above and see whether you tend to be more sensing or intuitive. One preference is not better than another: it is just different. On the chart below, place an X on the line to indicate your preference for sensing or intuitive. Again, notice that it is possible to be a combination type with both sensing and intuitive preferences.

Sensing _____|_____Intuitive

Do you generally prefer sensing or intuition? In the box below, write **S** for sensing or **N** for intuitive. If there is a tie between **S** and **N**, write **N**.

Journal Entry #2

Look at the results from Do What You Are and your own self-assessment above. Are you a sensing, intuitive, or combination type? Can you give examples of how it affects your social life, school, or work? Write a paragraph about this preference.

Thinking or Feeling

The dimension of thinking or feeling defines how we prefer to make decisions. In the general school population, 60 percent of males are thinking types and 40 percent are feeling types. For females, 60 percent are feeling types and 40 percent are thinking types.

Thinking (T) individuals make decisions based on logic. They are objective and analytical. They look at all the evidence and reach an impersonal conclusion. They are concerned with what they think is right.

Feeling (F) individuals make decisions based on what is important to them and matches their personal values. They are concerned about what they feel is right.

We all use logic and have feelings and emotions that play a part in decision making. However, the thinking person prefers to make decisions based on logic, and the feeling person prefers to make decisions according to what is important to self and others. This is one category in which men and women often differ. Most women are feeling types, and most men are logical types. When men and women are arguing, you might hear the following:

Man: "I think that . . ."

Woman: "I feel that . . ."

By understanding these differences, it is possible to improve communication and understanding. Be careful with generalizations, since 40 percent of men and women would not fit this pattern.

When thinking about careers, a thinking type would make a good judge or computer programmer. A feeling type would probably make a good social worker or kindergarten teacher.

ACTIVITY

Thinking and Feeling

The following chart shows some qualities of thinking and feeling types. As you **read through each pair of items,** quickly place a checkmark next to the items that usually describe yourself.

Thinking (T)

_____ Apply impersonal analysis to problems

_____ Value logic and justice

_____ Fairness is important

_____ Truth is more important than tact

_____ Motivated by achievement and accomplishment

_____ Feelings are valid if they are logical or not

_____ Good decisions are logical

Feeling (F)

_____ Consider the effect on others

_____ Value empathy and harmony

_____ There are exceptions to every rule

_____ Tact is more important than truth

_____ Motivated by being appreciated by others

_____ Feelings are valid whether they make sense

_____ Good decisions take others' feelings into account

Thinking (T)

_____ Described as cool, calm, and objective

_____ Love can be analyzed

_____ Firm-minded

_____ More important to be right

_____ Remember numbers and figures

_____ Prefer clarity

_____ Find flaws and critique

_____ Prefer firmness

Feeling (F)

_____ Described as caring and emotional

_____ Love cannot be analyzed

_____ Gentle-hearted

_____ More important to be liked

_____ Remember faces and names

_____ Prefer harmony

_____ Look for the good and compliment

_____ Prefer persuasion

Here are some qualities that describe the ideal work environment. As you **read through each pair of items,** place a checkmark next to the items that usually describe the work environment that you prefer.

Thinking (T)

_____ Maintain business environment

_____ Work with people I respect

_____ Be treated fairly

_____ Fair evaluations

_____ Solve problems

_____ Challenging work

_____ Use logic and analysis

_____ **Total** (from both charts above)

Feeling (F)

_____ Maintain close personal relationships

_____ Work in a friendly, relaxed environment

_____ Be able to express personal values

_____ Appreciation for good work

_____ Make a personal contribution

_____ Harmonious work situation

_____ Help others

_____ **Total** (from both charts above)

While we all use thinking and feeling, what is your preferred type? Look at the charts above and notice whether you are more the thinking or feeling type. One is not better than the other. On the chart below, place an X on the line to indicate how much you prefer thinking or feeling.

Thinking _____|_____ Feeling

Do you generally prefer thinking or feeling? In the box below, write **T** for thinking or **F** for feeling. If there is a tie between **T** and **F**, write **F**.

[ ]

Journal Entry #3

Look at the results from Do What You Are and your own self-assessment above. Are you a thinking, feeling, or combination type? Can you give examples of how it affects your social life, school, or work? Write a paragraph about this preference.

Judging or Perceiving

The dimension of judging or perceiving refers to how we deal with the external world. In other words, do we prefer the world to be structured or unstructured? In the general school population, the percentage of each of these types is approximately equal.

Judging (J) types like to live in a structured, orderly, and planned way. They are happy when their lives are structured and matters are settled. They like to have control over their lives. **Judging does not mean to judge others.** *Think of this type as being orderly and organized.*

Perceptive (P) types like to live in a spontaneous and flexible way. They are happy when their lives are open to possibilities. They try to understand life rather than control it. **Think of this type as spontaneous and flexible.**

Since these types have very opposite ways of looking at the world, there is a great deal of potential for conflict between them unless there is an appreciation for the gifts and talents of both. In any situation, we can benefit from people who represent these very different points of view. For example, in a business situation, the judging type would be good at managing the money, while the perceptive type would be good at helping the business to adapt to a changing marketplace. It is good to be open to all the possibilities and to be flexible, as well as to have some structure and organization.

ACTIVITY

Judging and Perceptive

As you **read through each pair of items**, quickly place a checkmark next to the items that generally describe yourself.

Judging (J)

_____ Happy when the decisions are made and finished

_____ Work first, play later

_____ It is important to be on time

_____ Time flies

_____ Feel comfortable with routine

_____ Generally keep things in order

_____ Set goals and work toward them

_____ Emphasize completing the task

_____ Like to finish projects

_____ Meet deadlines

_____ Like to know what I am getting into

_____ Relax when things are organized

_____ Follow a routine

_____ Focused

_____ Work steadily

Perceptive (P)

_____ Happy when the options are left open; something better may come along

_____ Play first, do the work later

_____ Time is relative

_____ Time is elastic

_____ Dislike routine

_____ Prefer creative disorder

_____ Change goals as new opportunities arise

_____ Emphasize how the task is done

_____ Like to start projects

_____ What deadline?

_____ Like new possibilities and situations

_____ Relax when necessary

_____ Explore the unknown

_____ Easily distracted

_____ Work in spurts of energy

Here are some qualities that describe the ideal work environment. Again, as you **read through each pair of items**, place a checkmark next to the work environment that you prefer.

Judging (J)

_____ Follow a schedule

_____ Clear directions

_____ Organized work

_____ Logical order

_____ Control my job

_____ Stability and security

_____ Work on one project until done

_____ Steady work

_____ Satisfying work

_____ Like having high responsibility

_____ Accomplish goals on time

_____ Clear and concrete assignments

_____ **Total** (from both charts above)

Perceptive (P)

_____ Be spontaneous

_____ Minimal rules and structure

_____ Flexibility

_____ Many changes

_____ Respond to emergencies

_____ Take risks and be adventurous

_____ Juggle many projects

_____ Variety and action

_____ Fun and excitement

_____ Like having interesting work

_____ Work at my own pace

_____ Minimal supervision

_____ **Total** (from both charts above)

Look at the charts above and notice whether you are more the judging type (orderly and organized) or the perceptive type (spontaneous and flexible). We need the qualities of both types to be successful and deal with the rapid changes in today's world. On the chart below, place an X on the line to indicate how much you prefer judging or perceiving.

Judging _____|_____ Perceptive

Do you generally have judging or perceptive traits? In the box below, write **J** for judging or **P** for perceptive. If there is a tie between **J** and **P**, write **P**.

Journal Entry #4

Look at the results from Do What You Are and your own self-assessment above. Are you a judging, perceptive, or combination type? Can you give examples of how it affects your social life, school, or work? Write a paragraph about this preference.

"Knowing thyself is the height of wisdom."
Socrates

Summarize Your Results

Look at your results above and summarize them on this composite chart. Notice that we are all unique, according to where the Xs fall on the scale.

Extravert (E) _____|_____ Introvert (I)

Sensing (S) _____|_____ Intuitive (N)

Thinking (T) _____|_____ Feeling (F)

Judging (J) _____|_____ Perceptive (P)

Write the letters representing each of your preferences.

The above letters represent your estimated personality type based on your understanding and knowledge of self. It is a good idea to confirm that this type is correct for you by completing the online personality assessment, Do What You Are.

© 2014, Pavel L Photo and Video. Used under license with Shutterstock, Inc.

Personality Types

Test what you have learned by selecting the correct answer to the following questions.

1. A person who is energized by social interaction is a/an:

   a. introvert
   b. extravert
   c. feeling type

2. A person who is quiet and reserved is a/an:

   a. introvert
   b. extravert
   c. perceptive type

3. A person who relies on experience and trusts information that is concrete and observable is a/an:

   a. judging type
   b. sensing type
   c. perceptive type

4. A person who focuses on "what could be" is a/an:

   a. perceptive type
   b. thinking type
   c. intuitive type

5. A person who makes decisions based on logic is a/an:

   a. thinker
   b. perceiver
   c. sensor

6. A person who makes decisions based on personal values is a/an:

   a. feeling type
   b. thinking type
   c. judging type

7. The perceptive type:

   a. has extrasensory perception
   b. likes to live life in a spontaneous and flexible way
   c. always considers feelings before making a decision

8. The judging type likes to:

   a. judge others
   b. use logic
   c. live in a structured and orderly way

9. Personality assessments are an exact predictor of your best major and career.

   a. true
   b. false

10. Some personality types are better than others.

    a. true
    b. false

How did you do on the quiz? Check your answers: 1. b, 2. a, 3. b, 4. c, 5. a, 6. a, 7. b, 8. c, 9. b, 10. b

Personality and Preferred Work Environment

Knowing your personality type will help you to understand your preferred work environment and provide some insights into selecting the major and career that you would enjoy. Selecting the work environment that matches your personal preferences helps you to be energized on the job and to minimize stress. Understanding other types will help you to work effectively with co-workers. As you read this section, think about your ideal work environment and how others are different.

Extraverts are career generalists who use their skills in a variety of ways. They like variety and action in a work environment that provides the opportunity for social interaction. Extraverts communicate well and meet people easily. They like to talk while working and are interested in other people and what they are doing. They enjoy variety on the job and like to perform their work in different settings. They learn new tasks by talking with others and trying out new ideas. Extraverts are energized by working as part of a team, leading others in achieving goals, and having opportunities to communicate with others.

Introverts are career specialists who develop in-depth skills. The introvert likes quiet for concentration and likes to focus on a work task until it is completed. They need time to think before taking action. This type often chooses to work alone or with one other person and prefers written communication such as emails to oral communication or presentations. They learn new tasks by reading and reflecting and using mental practice. Introverts are energized when they can work in a quiet environment with few interruptions. They are stressed when they have to work in a noisy environment and do not have time alone to concentrate on a project.

The **sensing** type is realistic and practical and likes to develop standard ways of doing the job and following a routine. They are observant and interested in facts and finding the truth. They keep accurate track of details, make lists, and are good at doing precise work. This type learns from personal experience and the experience of others. They use their experience to move up the job ladder. Sensing types are energized when they are doing practical work with tangible outcomes where they are required to organize facts and details, use common sense, and focus on one project at a time. They are stressed when they have to deal with frequent or unexpected change.

The **intuitive** type likes to work on challenging and complex problems where they can follow their inspirations to find creative solutions. They like change and finding new ways of doing work. This type focuses on the whole picture rather than the details. The intuitive type is an initiator, promoter, and inventor of ideas. They enjoy learning a new skill more than using it. They often change careers to follow their creative inspirations. Intuitive types are energized by working in an environment where they can use creative insight, imagination, originality, and individual initiative. They are stressed when they have to deal with too many details or have little opportunity for creativity.

The **thinking** type likes to use logical analysis in making decisions. They are objective and rational and treat others fairly. They want logical reasons before accepting any new ideas. They follow policy and are often firm-minded and critical, especially when dealing with illogic in others. They easily learn facts, theories, and principles. They are interested in careers with money, prestige, or influence. Thinking types are energized when they are respected for their expertise and recognized for a job well done. They enjoy working with others who are competent and efficient. They become stressed when they work with people they consider to be illogical, unfair, incompetent, or overly emotional.

The **feeling** type likes harmony and the support of co-workers. They are personal, enjoy warm relationships, and relate well to most people. Feeling types know their personal values and apply them consistently. They enjoy doing work that provides a service to people and often do work that requires them to understand and analyze their own emotions and those of others. They prefer a friendly work environment and like to learn with others. They enjoy careers in which they can make a contribution to humanity. Feeling types are energized by working in a friendly, congenial, and supportive work environment. They are stressed when there is conflict in the work environment, especially when working with controlling or demanding people.

The **judging** type likes a work environment that is structured, settled, and organized. They prefer work assignments that are clear and definite. The judging type makes lists and plans to get the job done on time. They make quick decisions and like to have the work finished. They are good at doing purposeful and exacting work. They prefer to learn only the essentials that are necessary to do the job. This type carefully plans their career path. Judging types are energized by working in a predictable and orderly environment with clear responsibilities and deadlines. They become stressed when the work environment becomes disorganized or unpredictable.

The **perceptive** type likes to be spontaneous and go with the flow. They are comfortable in handling the unplanned or unexpected in the work environment. They prefer to be flexible in their work and feel restricted by structures and schedules. They are good at handling work which requires change and adaptation. They are tolerant and have a "live and let live" attitude toward others. Decisions are often postponed because this type wants to know all there is to know and explore all the options before making a decision. This type is often a career changer who takes advantage of new job openings and opportunities for change. Perceptive types are energized when the work environment is flexible and they can relax and control their own time. They are stressed when they have to meet deadlines or work under excessive rules and regulations.

Personality and Decision Making

Your personality type affects how you think and how you make decisions. Knowing your decision-making style will help you make good decisions about your career and personal life as well as work with others in creative problem solving. Each personality type views the decision-making process in a different way. Ideally, a variety of types would be involved in making a decision so that the strengths of each type could be utilized. As you read through the following descriptions, think about your personality type and how you make decisions as well as how others are different.

The **introvert** thinks up ideas and reflects on the problem before acting. The **extravert** acts as the communicator in the decision-making process. Once the decision is made, they take action and implement the decision. The **intuitive** type develops theories and uses intuition to come up with ingenious solutions to the problem. The **sensing** type applies personal experience to the decision-making process and focuses on solutions that are practical and realistic.

© 2014, Stephen Coburn. Used under license with Shutterstock, Inc.

The thinking and feeling dimensions of personality are the most important factors in determining how a decision is made. Of course, people use both thinking and feeling in the decision-making process, but tend to prefer or trust either thinking or feeling. Those who prefer **thinking** use cause-and-effect reasoning and solve problems with logic. They use objective and impersonal criteria and include all the consequences of alternative solutions in the decision-making process. They are interested in finding out what is true and what is false. They use laws and principles to treat everyone fairly. Once a decision is made, they are firm-minded, since the decision was based on logic. This type is often critical of those who do not use logic in the decision-making process. The **feeling** type considers human values and motives in the decision-making process (whether they are logical or not) and values harmony and maintaining good relationships. They consider carefully how much they care about each of the alternatives and how they will affect other people. They are interested in making a decision that is agreeable to all parties. Feeling types are tactful and skillful in dealing with people.

It is often asked if thinking types have feelings. They do have feelings, but use them as a criterion to be factored into the decision-making process. Thinking types are more comfortable when feelings are controlled and often think that feeling types are too emotional. Thinking types may have difficulties when they apply logic in a situation where a feeling response is needed, such as in dealing with a spouse. Thinking types need to know that people are important in making decisions. Feeling types need to know that behavior will have logical consequences and that they may need to keep emotions more controlled to work effectively with thinking types.

Judging and **perceptive** types have opposite decision-making strategies. The judging type is very methodical and cautious in making decisions. Once they have gone through the decision-making steps, they like to make decisions quickly so that they can have closure and finish the project. The perceptive type is an adventurer who wants to look at all the possibilities before making a decision. They are open-minded and curious and often resist closure to look at more options.

If a combination of types collaborates on a decision, it is more likely that the decision will be a good one that takes into account creative possibilities, practicality, logical consequences, and human values.

Understanding Your Personal Communication Style

Understanding your personality type can be helpful in improving your communication skills and establishing satisfying friendships, happy marriages, effective parenting skills, and good relationships in the workplace. Personality has a major impact on our style of communication. While we can make some generalizations about personality types, keep in mind that each individual is unique and may be a combination of the various types. For example, some people are a combination of introvert and extravert. The following descriptions will help you begin thinking about your own communication style and understanding others who are different. Remember that each personality type has positive and negative aspects. Knowledge of these differences can help individuals accentuate the positives and keep the negatives in perspective.

Introvert and Extravert Types

Extraverts are very social types who easily start conversations with strangers as well as friends. They know a lot of people and have many friends. They like going to parties and other social events and are energized by talking to people. They like to talk on the telephone and can read while watching TV, listening to music, or carrying on a conversation with someone else. They find talking easy and sometimes dominate the conversation. They find it more difficult to listen. They tend to talk first and think later, and sometimes regret that they have put their foot in their mouths.

In personal relationships, extraverts are fun to know and get along well with others. It is easy for them to make a date and do the talking. When extraverts are in conflict situations, they just talk louder and faster. They believe that the argument can be won if they can say just one more thing or provide more explanation. If there is a problem, extraverts want to talk about it right away. If they cannot talk about it, they become very frustrated. Extraverts enjoy occupations that provide opportunities for socialization.

The **introvert** is the opposite of the extravert. Introverts want to rehearse what they are going to say before they say it. They need quiet for concentration and enjoy peace and quiet. They have great powers of concentration and can focus their attention on projects for a long period of time. Because they tend to be quieter than extraverts, they are perceived as great listeners. Because they need time to think before talking, they often find it difficult to add their ideas to a conversation, especially when talking with extraverts. They often wish they could participate more in conversations. Because they are reserved and reflective, people often label the introvert as shy. In American society, introverts are the minority. There are three extraverts to every introvert. For this reason, the introvert is often pressured to act like an extravert. This can cause the introvert a great deal of anxiety.

The introvert often finds it difficult to start conversations or invite someone on a date. Introverts are often attracted to extraverts because they can relax and let the extravert do the talking. In conflict situations, the introverts are at a disadvantage. They will often withdraw from conflict because they need time to think about the situation and go over in their minds what to say. Introverts become stressed if they are faced with a conflict without advance notice. Introverts enjoy occupations that provide quiet for concentration.

Introverts and extraverts can improve their relationship by understanding each other and respecting their differences. The extravert can improve communication with the introvert by pausing to let the introvert have time to speak. He or she has to make a conscious effort to avoid monopolizing the conversation. Introverts can improve communication by making an effort to communicate. Introverts sometimes act like extraverts in social situations. Since this takes effort, they may need quiet time to relax and recharge after social events.

Imagine that two roommates are opposite types, extravert and introvert. The extravert enjoys talking and making noises. She will have guests, take telephone calls, and play music in the background while studying. These actions will cause the introvert to withdraw and leave the room to find a quiet place to study. These two roommates need to talk about their differences and do some compromising to get along with one another.

Communication Styles
• Introvert
• Extravert
• Sensing
• Intuitive
• Feeling
• Thinking
• Judging
• Perceptive

Sensing and Intuitive Types

Sensing types collect information through the senses. Their motto could be, "Seeing is believing." They are practical and realistic. They like communication to be exact and sequential. They want details and facts. They ask specific questions and want concrete answers. About 70 percent of the population of the United States is the sensing type. Sensing types enjoy occupations in which they can work step-by-step.

In a dating situation, the sensing type focuses on actual experience. A sensor will describe the date in terms of what his or her companion looked like, how the food tasted, how the music sounded, and the feelings involved. During the date, sensors may talk about concrete events such as people they have known, experiences they have had, and places they have visited. Sensing types are generally on time for the date and get irritated if the other person is late. In conflict situations, sensing types argue the facts. They often don't see the big issues because they are concentrating on the accuracy of the facts.

Intuitive types gather information from the senses and immediately look for possibilities, meanings, and relationships between ideas. They are often ingenious and creative. Sensing types often describe intuitives as dreamers who have their heads in the clouds. They represent about 30 percent of the population. Intuitive types enjoy occupations in which they can be creative.

In social situations such as dating, the intuitive person starts to fantasize and imagine what it is going to be like before it begins. The fantasies are often more exciting than the actual date. Conversations follow many different and creative trains of thought. Intuitive types are more likely to talk about dreams, visions, beliefs, and creative ideas, skipping from one topic to another. Sensing types sometimes have difficulty following the conversation. Intuitive types are less worried about being exactly on time. They believe that time is flexible and may not be on time for the date, much to the annoyance of sensing types. In conflict situations, intuitive types like to make broad generalizations. When sensing types remind them of the facts, they may accuse them of nitpicking.

Having both sensing and intuitive types in a relationship or business environment has many advantages, as long as these types can understand and appreciate one another. Sensing types need intuitive types to bring up new possibilities, deal with changes, and understand different perspectives. Intuitive types need sensing types to deal with facts and details.

Feeling and Thinking Types

Feeling types prefer to make decisions based on what they feel to be right or wrong based on their subjective values. They prefer harmony and are often described as tenderhearted. Other people's feelings are an important consideration in any decision they make. The majority of women (60 percent) are feeling types. In a conflict situation, feeling types take things personally. They prefer to avoid disagreements and will give in to reestablish a harmonious relationship. They enjoy harmonious working conditions in which everyone gets along with co-workers.

Thinking types are logical, detached, analytical, and objective and make decisions based on these characteristics. They like justice and clarity. The majority of men (60 percent) are thinking types. In a conflict situation, thinking types use logical arguments. They often get frustrated with feeling types and think they are too emotional. Thinking types enjoy analytical occupations such as business or engineering.

In a dating situation, the differences between feelers and thinkers can cause much misunderstanding and conflict. Thinking types strive to understand love and intimacy. Feeling types like to experience emotions. Thinking types process and analyze their feelings. For the thinker, love is to be analyzed. For the feeling types, love just happens.

Remember that while most women are feeling types and most men are thinking types, there are still 40 percent of women who are thinking types and 40 percent of men who are feeling types. Unfortunately, because of gender stereotyping, feeling-type men are often seen as less masculine and thinking-type women are seen as less feminine.

There is much to gain from understanding and appreciating the differences between feeling and thinking types. Feeling types need thinking types to analyze, organize, follow policy, and weigh the evidence. Thinking types need feeling types to understand how others feel and establish harmony in relationships or in a business environment.

Judging and Perceptive Types

Judging types prefer their environment to be structured, scheduled, orderly, planned, and controlled. Judging types even plan and organize their recreation time. They need events to be planned and organized in order to relax. They are quick to make decisions, and once the decisions are made, they find it difficult to change them. In the social scene, judging types schedule and plan the dates. When traveling, judging types carefully pack their suitcases using a list of essential items to make sure that nothing is forgotten. In conflict situations, judging types know that they are right. They tend to see issues in terms of right and wrong, good and bad, or black and white. It is difficult to negotiate with a judging type. Judging types enjoy occupations in which they can be organized and follow a routine.

Perceptive types are very much the opposite of the judging types. They prefer the environment to be flexible and spontaneous. Perceptive types find it difficult to make a decision and stick to it because it limits their flexibility. Perceptive types like to collect information and keep the options open. After all, something better might come along and they do not want to be restricted by a plan or schedule. In a social situation, these types are playful and easygoing. They provide the fun and find it easy to relax. They often feel controlled by judging types. In a conflict situation, this type sees many options to resolve the situation. They have trouble resolving conflicts because they keep finding many possible solutions. Perceptive types enjoy occupations that have variety and excitement.

The preference for judging or perceiving has the most potential for conflict between individuals. Judging types can drive perceptive types crazy with their need for schedules, planning, and organization. Perceptive types drive the judging types crazy with their spontaneous and easygoing nature. In spite of these differences, judging and perceptive types are often attracted to one another. Judging types need perceptive types to encourage them to relax and have fun. Perceptive types need judging types to help them be more organized and productive. These two types need understanding and appreciation of each other to have a good relationship. They also need excellent communication skills.

It is often asked whether two people should consider personality type in establishing relationships or choosing a marriage partner. There are two theories on this. One theory is that opposites attract. If two people have opposite personality types, they will have the potential for using the strengths of both types. For example, if one marriage partner is a judging type, this person can manage the finances and keep the family organized. The perceptive type can provide the fun and help the other to relax and enjoy life. A disadvantage is that opposite types have great potential for conflict. The conflict can be resolved by understanding the other type and appreciating different strengths the opposite type brings to the relationship. The relationship cannot work if one person tries to change the other. Good communication is essential in maintaining the relationship.

Another theory is that like types attract. If you have a relationship with another person of the same type, your basic preferences are similar. However, even matching types will be different depending on the strength of each preference. Communication is easier when two people have similar views of the world. One disadvantage is that the relationship can become predictable and eventually uninteresting.

Communication Style

Test what you have learned by selecting the correct answers to the following questions.

1. Extraverts can help introverts improve communication by

    a. clearly explaining their point of view.
    b. pausing to give the introvert time to think and respond.
    c. talking louder and faster.

2. In a dating situation, sensing types are likely to talk about

    a. concrete events such as the weather or personal experiences.
    b. dreams and visions.
    c. creative ideas.

3. In a conflict situation, feeling types

    a. use logic to analyze the situation.
    b. engage in debate based on logical arguments.
    c. take things personally.

4. Perceptive types

    a. find it difficult to make a decision and stick to it.
    b. tend to decide quickly in order to finish the project.
    c. find it easy to be on time and meet deadlines.

5. In choosing a marriage partner it is best to

    a. choose a person with the same personality.
    b. choose a person with the opposite personality.
    c. be aware of each other's personality type to appreciate each other.

How did you do on the quiz? Check your answers: 1. b, 2. a, 3. c, 4. a, 5. c

Personality and Time Management

How we manage our time is not just a result of personal habits: it is also a reflection of our personality type. Probably the dimension of personality type most connected to time management is the judging or perceptive trait. **Judging** types like to have things under control and live in a planned and orderly manner. **Perceptive** types prefer more spontaneity and flexibility. Understanding the differences between these two types will help you to better understand yourself and others.

Judging types are naturally good at time management. They often use schedules as a tool for time management and organization. Judging types plan their time and work steadily to accomplish goals. They are good at meeting deadlines and often put off relaxation, recreation, and fun. They relax after projects are completed. If they have too many projects, they find it difficult to find time for recreation. Since judging types like to have projects under control, there is a danger that projects will be completed too quickly and that quality will suffer. Judging types may need to slow down and take the time to do quality work. They may also need to make relaxation and recreation a priority.

Perceptive types are more open-ended and prefer to be spontaneous. They take time to relax, have fun, and participate in recreation. In working on a project, perceptive types want to brainstorm all the possibilities and are not too concerned about finishing projects. This type procrastinates when the time comes to make a final decision and finish a project. There is always more information to gather and more possibilities to explore. Perceptive types are easily distracted and may move from project to project. They may have several jobs going at once. These types need to try to focus on a few projects at a time in order to complete them. Perceptive types need to work on becoming more organized so that projects can be completed on time.

Research has shown that students who are judging types are more likely to have a higher grade point average in the first semester.[1] It has also been found that the greater the preference for intuition, introversion, and judgment, the better the grade point average.[2] Why is this true? Many college professors are intuitive types that use intuition and creative ideas. The college environment requires quiet time for reading and studying, which is one of the preferences of introverts. Academic environments require structure, organization, and completion of assignments. To be successful in an academic environment requires adaptation by some personality types. Extroverts need to spend more quiet time reading and studying. Sensing types need to gain an understanding of intuitive types. Perceptive types need to use organization to complete assignments on time.

© 2014, STILLFX. Used under license with Shutterstock, Inc.

Personality and Money

Does your personality type affect how you deal with money? Otto Kroeger and Janet Thuesen make some interesting observations about how different personality types deal with money.

- **Judging types (orderly and organized).** These types excel at financial planning and money management. They file their tax forms early and pay their bills on time.
- **Perceptive types (spontaneous and flexible).** These types adapt to change and are more creative. Perceivers, especially intuitive perceivers, tend to freak out as the April 15 tax deadline approaches and as bills become due.
- **Feeling types (make decisions based on feelings).** These types are not very money-conscious. They believe that money should be used to serve humanity. They are often attracted to low-paying jobs that serve others.[3]

In studying stockbrokers, these same authors note that ISTJs (introvert, sensing, thinking, and judging types) are the most conservative investors, earning a small but reliable return on investments. The ESTPs (extravert, sensing, thinking, perceptive types) and ENTPs (extravert, intuitive, thinking, perceptive types) take the biggest risks and earn the greatest returns.[4]

Journal Entry #5

Write a paragraph about how being a judging, perceptive, or combination type influences any of the following: how you manage your time, how you communicate with others, how you budget your money, or your preferred work environment. Remember that judging means orderly and organized, not judging other people; perceptive means spontaneous and flexible. How is this information useful in choosing your career or being successful in college?

Personality and Career Choice

While it is not possible to predict exactly your career and college major by knowing your personality type, it can be helpful in providing opportunities for exploration. Here are some general descriptions of personality types and preferred careers. Included are general occupational fields, frequently chosen occupations, and suggested majors. These suggestions about career selections are based on the general characteristics of each type and research that correlates personality type with choice of a satisfying career.[5] Read the personality descriptions and lists of careers and majors that match your personality type. Then continue your career exploration with the online career database in the Do What You Are personality assessment included with your textbook.

> "Choose a job you love, and you will never have to work a day in your life."
> Confucius

© 2014, iQoncept. Used under license with Shutterstock, Inc.

ISTJ

ISTJs are responsible, loyal, stable, practical, down-to-earth, hardworking, and reliable. They can be depended upon to follow through with tasks. They value tradition, family, and security. They are natural leaders who prefer to work alone, but can adapt to working with teams if needed. They like to be independent and have time to think things through. They are able to remember and use concrete facts and information. They make decisions by applying logic and rational thinking. They appreciate structured and orderly environments and deliver products and services in an efficient and orderly way.

General occupations to consider

business	education	health care
service	technical	military
law and law enforcement	engineering	management

Specific job titles

business executive	lawyer	electronic technician
administrator	judge	computer occupations
manager	police officer	dentist
real estate agent	detective	pharmacist
accountant	corrections officer	primary care physician
bank employee	teacher (math, trade,	nursing administrator
stockbroker	technical)	respiratory therapist
auditor	educational administrator	physical therapist
hairdresser	coach	optometrist
cosmetologist	engineer	chemist
legal secretary	electrician	military officer or
		enlistee

College majors

business	engineering	chemistry
education	computers	biology
mathematics	health occupations	vocational training
law		

ISTP

ISTPs are independent, practical, and easygoing. They prefer to work individually and frequently like to work outdoors. These types like working with objects and often are good at working with their hands and mastering tools. They are interested in how and why things work and are able to apply technical knowledge to solving practical problems. Their logical thinking makes them good troubleshooters and problem solvers. They enjoy variety, new experiences, and taking risks. They prefer environments with little structure and have a talent for managing crises. The ISTP is happy with occupations that involve challenge, change, and variety.

General occupations to consider

sales	technical	business and finance
service	health care	vocational training
corrections		

Specific job titles

sales manager	engineer	office manager
insurance agent	electronics technician	small business manager
cook	software developer	banker
firefighter	computer programmer	economist
pilot	radiologic technician	legal secretary
race car driver	exercise physiologist	paralegal

police officer	coach	computer repair
corrections officer	athlete	airline mechanic
judge	dental assistant/hygienist	carpenter
attorney	physician	construction worker
intelligence agent	optometrist	farmer
detective	physical therapist	military officer or enlistee

College majors

business	computers	health occupations
vocational training	biology	physical education
law		

ISFJ

ISFJs are quiet, friendly, responsible, hardworking, productive, devoted, accurate, thorough, and careful. They value security, stability, and harmony. They like to focus on one person or project at a time. ISFJs prefer to work with individuals and are very skillful in understanding people and their needs. They often provide service to others in a very structured way. They are careful observers, remember facts, and work on projects requiring accuracy and attention to detail. They have a sense of space and function that leads to artistic endeavors such as interior decorating or landscaping. ISFJs are most comfortable working in environments that are orderly, structured, and traditional. While they often work quietly behind the scenes, they like their contributions to be recognized and appreciated.

General occupations to consider

health care	education	artistic
social service	business	religious occupations
corrections	technical	vocational training

Specific job titles

nurse	social worker	counselor
physician	social services	secretary
medical technologist	administrator	cashier
dental hygienist	child care worker	accountant
health education	speech pathologist	personnel administrator
practitioner	librarian	credit counselor
dietician	curator	business manager
physical therapist	genealogist	paralegal
nursing educator	corrections worker	computer occupations
health administrator	probation officer	engineer
medical secretary	teacher (preschool,	interior decorator
dentist	grades 1–12)	home economist
medical assistant	guidance counselor	religious educator
optometrist	educational administrator	clergy
occupational therapist		

College majors

health occupations	education	graphics
biology	business	religious studies
psychology	engineering	vocational training
sociology	art	

ISFP

ISFPs are quiet, reserved, trusting, loyal, committed, sensitive, kind, creative, and artistic. They have an appreciation for life and value serenity and aesthetic beauty. These types are individualistic and generally have no desire to lead or follow; they prefer to work independently. They have a keen awareness of their environment and often have a special bond with children and animals. ISFPs are service-oriented and like to help others. They like to be original and unconventional. They dislike rules and structure and need space and freedom to do things in their own way.

General occupations to consider

artists	technical	business
health care	service	vocational training

Specific job titles

artist	recreation services	forester
designer	physical therapist	botanist
fashion designer	radiologic technician	geologist
jeweler	medical assistant	mechanic
gardener	dental assistant/hygienist	marine biologist
potter	veterinary assistant	teacher (science, art)
painter	veterinarian	police officer
dancer	animal groomer/trainer	beautician
landscape designer	dietician	merchandise planner
carpenter	optician/optometrist	stock clerk
electrician	exercise physiologist	store keeper
engineer	occupational therapist	counselor
chef	art therapist	social worker
nurse	pharmacy technician	legal secretary
counselor	respiratory therapist	paralegal

College majors

art	forestry	psychology
health occupations	geology	counseling
engineering	education	social work
physical education	business	vocational training
biology		

INFJ

INFJs are idealistic, complex, compassionate, authentic, creative, and visionary. They have strong value systems and search for meaning and purpose to life. Because of their strong value systems, INFJs are natural leaders or at least follow those with similar ideas. They intuitively understand people and ideas and come up with new ideas to provide service to others. These types like to organize their time and be in control of their work.

General occupations to consider

counseling	religious occupations	health care
education	creative occupations	social services
science	arts	business

Specific job titles

career counselor	director of religious	dental hygienist
psychologist	education	speech pathologist

teacher (high school or
    college English, art,
    music, social sciences,
    drama, foreign
    languages, health)
librarian
home economist
social worker
clergy

fine artist
playwright
novelist
poet
designer
architect
art director
health care administrator
physician
biologist

nursing educator
medical secretary
pharmacist
occupational therapist
human resources
    manager
marketer
employee assistance
    program
merchandise planner
environmental lawyer

College majors

psychology
counseling
education
art
music

drama
foreign languages
English
health occupations
social work

architecture
biology
business
law
science

INFP

INFPs are loyal, devoted, sensitive, creative, inspirational, flexible, easygoing, complex, and authentic. They are original and individualistic and prefer to work alone or with other caring and supportive individuals. These types are service-oriented and interested in personal growth. They develop deep relationships because they understand people and are genuinely interested in them. They dislike dealing with details and routine work. They prefer a flexible working environment with a minimum of rules and regulations.

General occupations to consider

creative arts
education

counseling
religious occupations

health care
organizational
    development

Specific job titles

artist
designer
writer
journalist
entertainer
architect
actor
editor
reporter
journalist
musician
graphic designer
art director

photographer
carpenter
teacher (art, drama,
    music, English, foreign
    languages)
psychologist
counselor
social worker
librarian
clergy
religious educator
missionary
church worker

dietician
psychiatrist
physical therapist
occupational therapist
speech pathologist
laboratory technologist
public health nurse
dental hygienist
physician
human resources
specialist
social scientist
consultant

College majors

art
music
graphic design
journalism
English

foreign languages
architecture
education
religious studies
psychology

medicine
health occupations
social work
counseling
business

INTJ

INTJs are reserved, detached, analytical, logical, rational, original, independent, creative, ingenious, innovative, and resourceful. They prefer to work alone and work best alone. They can work with others if their ideas and competence are respected. They value knowledge and efficiency. They enjoy creative and intellectual challenges and understand complex theories. They create order and structure. They prefer to work with autonomy and control over their work. They dislike factual and routine kinds of work.

General occupations to consider

business and finance	education	law
technical occupations	health care and medicine	creative occupations
science	architecture	engineering

Specific job titles

management consultant	astronomer	dentist
human resources planner	computer programmer	biomedical engineer
economist	biomedical researcher	attorney
international banker	software developer	manager
financial planner	network integration	judge
investment banker	specialist	electrical engineer
scientist	teacher (university)	writer
scientific researcher	school principal	journalist
chemist	mathematician	artist
biologist	psychiatrist	inventor
computer systems analyst	psychologist	architect
electronic technician	neurologist	actor
design engineer	physician	musician
architect		

College majors

business	physics	journalism
finance	education	art
chemistry	mathematics	architecture
biology	medicine	drama
computers	psychology	music
engineering	law	vocational training
astronomy	English	

INTP

INTPs are logical, analytical, independent, original, creative, and insightful. They are often brilliant and ingenious. They work best alone and need quiet time to concentrate. They focus their attention on ideas and are frequently detached from other people. They love theory and abstract ideas and value knowledge and competency. INTPs are creative thinkers who are not too interested in practical application. They dislike detail and routine and need freedom to develop, analyze, and critique new ideas. These types maintain high standards in their work.

General occupations to consider

planning and	technical	academic
development	professional	creative occupations
health care		

Specific job titles

computer software designer
computer programmer
research and development
systems analyst
financial planner
investment banker
physicist
plastic surgeon
psychiatrist
chemist
biologist
pharmaceutical researcher

pharmacist
engineer
electrician
dentist
veterinarian
lawyer
economist
psychologist
architect
psychiatrist
mathematician
archaeologist

historian
philosopher
college teacher
researcher
logician
photographer
creative writer
artist
actor
entertainer
musician
inventor

College majors

computers
business
physics
chemistry
biology
astronomy
medicine

philosophy
music
art
drama
engineering
psychology
architecture

mathematics
archaeology
history
English
drama
music
vocational training

ESTP

ESTPs have great people skills and are action-oriented, fun, flexible, adaptable, and resourceful. They enjoy new experiences and dealing with people. They remember facts easily and have excellent powers of observation that they use to analyze other people. They are good problem solvers and can react quickly in an emergency. They like adventure and risk and are alert to new opportunities. They start new projects but do not necessarily follow through to completion. They prefer environments without too many rules and restrictions.

General occupations to consider

sales
service
active careers
finance

entertainment
sports
health care

technical
trade
business

Specific job titles

marketing professional
firefighter
police officer
corrections officer
paramedic
detective
pilot
investigator
real estate agent
exercise physiologist
flight attendant
sports merchandise sales
stockbroker
financial planner
investor

insurance agent
sportscaster
news reporter
journalist
tour agent
dancer
bartender
auctioneer
professional athlete or coach
fitness instructor
recreation leader
optometrist
pharmacist
critical care nurse

dentist
carpenter
farmer
construction worker
electrician
teacher (trade, industrial, technical)
chef
engineer
surveyor
radiologic technician
entrepreneur
land developer
retail sales
car sales

College majors

business

physical education

health occupations

vocational training

education

English

journalism

ESTJ

ESTJs are loyal, hardworking, dependable, thorough, practical, realistic, and energetic. They value security and tradition. Because they enjoy working with people and are orderly and organized, these types like to take charge and be the leader. This personality type is often found in administrative and management positions. ESTJs work systematically and efficiently to get the job done. These types are fair, logical, and consistent. They prefer a stable and predictable environment filled with action and a variety of people.

General occupations to consider

managerial

sales

business

service

technical

agriculture

professional

military leaders

Specific job titles

retail store manager

fire department manager

small business manager

restaurant manager

financial or bank officer

school principal

sales manager

top-level manager in city/
    county/state
    government

management consultant

corporate executive

military officer or enlistee

office manager

purchasing agent

police officer

factory supervisor

corrections

insurance agent

detective

judge

accountant

nursing administrator

mechanical engineer

physician

chemical engineer

auditor

coach

public relations worker

cook

personnel or labor
    relations worker

teacher (trade, industrial,
    technical)

mortgage banker

College majors

business

business management

accounting

finance

small business
    management

engineering

agriculture

law

education

vocational training

ESFP

ESFPs are practical, realistic, independent, fun, social, spontaneous, and flexible. They have great people skills and enjoy working in environments that are friendly, relaxed, and varied. They know how to have a good time and make an environment fun for others. ESFPs have a strong sense of aesthetics and are sometimes artistic and creative. They often have a special bond with people or animals. They dislike structure and routine. These types can handle many activities or projects at once.

General occupations to consider

education

social service

food preparation

health care

entertainment

child care

business and sales

service

Specific job titles

child care worker
teacher (preschool,
  elementary school,
  foreign languages,
  mathematics)
athletic coach
counselor
library assistant
police officer
public health nurse
respiratory therapist
physical therapist
physician
emergency medical
  technician
dental hygienist
chef

medical assistant
critical care nurse
dentist
dental assistant
exercise physiologist
dog obedience trainer
veterinary assistant
travel or tour agent
recreation leader or
  amusement site worker
photographer
designer
film producer
musician
performer
actor

promoter
special events coordinator
editor or reporter
retail merchandiser
fund raiser
receptionist
real estate agent
insurance agent
sporting equipment sales
retail sales
retail management
waiter or waitress
cashier
cosmetologist
hairdresser
religious worker

College majors

education
psychology
foreign languages
mathematics
physical education
culinary arts

health occupations
art
design
photography
English
child development

journalism
drama
music
business
vocational training

ESFJ

ESFJs are friendly, organized, hardworking, productive, conscientious, loyal, dependable, and practical. These types value harmony, stability, and security. They enjoy interacting with people and receive satisfaction from giving to others. ESFJs enjoy working in a cooperative environment in which people get along well with each other. They create order, structure, and schedules and can be depended on to complete the task at hand. They prefer to organize and control their work.

General occupations to consider

health care
education
child care

social service
counseling

business
human resources

Specific job titles

medical or dental assistant
nurse
radiologic technician
dental hygienist
speech pathologist
occupational therapist
dentist
optometrist
dietician
pharmacist
physician

coach
administrator of
  elementary
  or secondary school
administrator of student
  personnel
child care provider
home economist
social worker
administrator of social
  services

sales representative
hairdresser
cosmetologist
restaurant worker
recreation or amusement
  site worker
receptionist
office manager
cashier
bank employee
bookkeeper

physical therapist
health education
   practitioner
medical secretary
teacher (grades 1–12,
   foreign languages,
   reading)

police officer
counselor
community welfare
   worker
religious educator
clergy

accountant
sales
insurance agent
credit counselor
merchandise planner

College majors

health occupations
biology
foreign languages
English

education
psychology
counseling
sociology

religious studies
business
vocational training
child development

ENFP

ENFPs are friendly, creative, energetic, enthusiastic, innovative, adventurous, and fun. They have great people skills and enjoy providing service to others. They are intuitive and perceptive about people. ENFPs are good at anything that interests them and can enter a variety of fields. These types dislike routine and detailed tasks and may have difficulty following through and completing tasks. They enjoy occupations in which they can be creative and interact with people. They like a friendly and relaxed environment in which they are free to follow their inspiration and participate in adventures.

General occupations to consider

creative occupations
marketing
education
environmental science

counseling
health care
religious services

social service
entrepreneurial business
arts

Specific job titles

journalist
musician
actor
entertainer
fine artist
playwright
newscaster
reporter
interior decorator
cartoonist
graphic designer
marketing
advertising

public relations
counselor
clergy
psychologist
teacher (health, special
   education, English, art,
   drama, music)
social worker
dental hygienist
nurse
dietician
holistic health practitioner
environmentalist

physical therapist
consultant
inventor
sales
human resources
   manager
conference planner
employment development
   specialist
restaurateur
merchandise planner
environmental attorney
lawyer

College majors

journalism
English
drama
art
graphic design

business (advertising,
   marketing, public
   relations)
counseling
psychology

religious studies
health occupations
law
vocational training

ENFJ

ENFJs are friendly, sociable, empathetic, loyal, creative, imaginative, and responsible. They have great people skills and are interested in working with people and providing service to them. They are good at building harmony and cooperation and respect other people's opinions. These types can find creative solutions to problems. They are natural leaders who can make good decisions. They prefer an environment that is organized and structured and enjoy working as part of a team with other creative and caring people.

General occupations to consider

religious occupations	counseling	health care
creative occupations	education	business
communications	human services	administration

Specific job titles

director of religious education	newscaster	social worker
minister	politician	home economist
clergy	editor	nutritionist
public relations	crisis counselor	speech pathologist
marketing	school counselor	occupational therapist
writer	vocational or career counselor	physical therapist
librarian	psychologist	optometrist
journalist	alcohol and drug counselor	dental hygienist
fine artist		family practice physician
designer	teacher (health, art, drama, English, foreign languages)	psychiatrist
actor		nursing educator
musician or composer		pharmacist
fundraiser	child care worker	human resources trainer
recreational director	college humanities professor	travel agent
TV producer		small business executive
		sales manager

College majors

religious studies	music	counseling
business (public relations, marketing)	journalism	sociology
art	English	health occupations
graphic design	foreign languages	business
drama	humanities	vocational training
	psychology	

ENTP

ENTPs are creative, ingenious, flexible, diverse, energetic, fun, motivating, logical, and outspoken. They have excellent people skills and are natural leaders, although they dislike controlling other people. They value knowledge and competence. They are lively and energetic and make good debaters and motivational speakers. They are logical and rational thinkers who can grasp complex ideas and theories. They dislike environments that are structured and rigid. These types prefer environments that allow them to engage in creative problem solving and the creation of new ideas.

General occupations to consider

creative occupations	law	health care
politics	business	architecture
engineering	science	education

Specific job titles

photographer
marketing professional
journalist
actor
writer
musician or composer
editor
reporter
advertising director
radio/TV talk show host
producer
art director
new business developer
architect

politician
political manager
political analyst
social scientist
psychiatrist
psychologist
engineer
construction laborer
research worker
electrician
lawyer
judge
corporate executive

computer professional
corrections officer
sales manager
speech pathologist
health education
practitioner
respiratory therapist
dental assistant
medical assistant
critical care nurse
counselor
human resources planner
educator

College majors

art
photography
journalism
drama
English
engineering
science

music
business (advertising,
   marketing,
   management,
   human resources)
architecture

political science
psychology
health occupations
computers
vocational training
education

ENTJ

ENTJs are independent, original, visionary, logical, organized, ambitious, competitive, hardworking, and direct. They are natural leaders and organizers who identify problems and create solutions for organizations. ENTJs are often in management positions. They are good planners and accomplish goals in a timely manner. These types are logical thinkers who enjoy a structured work environment where they have opportunity for advancement. They enjoy a challenging, competitive, and exciting environment in which accomplishments are recognized.

General occupations to consider

business
finance

management
health care

science
law

Specific job titles

executive
manager
supervisor
personnel manager
sales manager
marketing manager
human resources planner
corporate executive
college administrator
health administrator
small business owner
retail store manager

manager in city/county/
   state government
management trainer
school principal
bank officer
computer systems analyst
computer professional
credit investigator
mortgage broker
stockbroker
investment banker
economist

accountant
auditor
financial manager
real estate agent
lawyer, judge
consultant
engineer
corrections, probation
   officer
psychologist
physician

College majors

business management	computers	engineering
finance	law	psychology
economics	medicine	vocational training

Other Factors in Choosing a Major

Once you have completed a thorough self-assessment, you may still have several majors to consider. At this point, it is important to do some research on the outlook for a selected career in the future and the pay you would receive. Sometimes students are disappointed after graduation when they find there are few job opportunities in their chosen career field. Sometimes students graduate and cannot find jobs with the salary they had hoped to earn. It is important to think about the opportunities you will have in the future. If you have several options for a career you would enjoy, you may want to consider seriously the career that has the best outlook and pay.

According to the Bureau of Labor Statistics, fields with the best outlook include health care, computers, and new "green jobs" related to preserving the environment. The top-paying careers all require math skills and include the science, engineering, computer science, health care, and business fields. Only four percent of college graduates choose the engineering and computer science fields. Since there are fewer students in these majors, the salaries are higher. If you have a talent or interest in math, you can develop this skill and use it in high-paying careers.

© 2014, Maryna Pleshkun. Used under license with Shutterstock, Inc

Majors with Highest Earnings 2014*[6]

College Major	Beginning Median Salary	Mid-Career Median Salary
Petroleum Engineering	103,000	160,000
Actuarial Mathematics	58,700	120,000
Nuclear Engineering	67,600	117,000
Chemical Engineering	68,200	115,000
Aerospace Engineering	62,800	109,000
Electrical/Computer Engineering	64,300	106,000
Computer Science	59,800	102,000
Physics	53,100	101,000
Mechanical Engineering	60,900	99,700

(continued)

College Major	Beginning Median Salary	Mid-Career Median Salary
Materials Science & Engineering	62,700	99,500
Software Engineering	62,500	99,300
Statistics	52,500	98,900
Government	43,200	97,100
Economics	50,100	96,700
Applied Mathematics	52,800	96,200
Industrial Engineering	61,100	94,400
Management Information Systems	53,800	92,200
Biomedical Engineering	59,000	91,700
Civil Engineering	54,300	91,100
Environmental Engineering	49,400	89,800
Construction Management	51,500	88,800
Mathematics	49,400	88,800
Information Systems	51,900	87,200
Finance	49,200	87,100
Chemistry	44,100	84,100

*Includes bachelor's degrees only. Excludes medicine, law, and careers requiring advanced degrees.

Other Common Majors and Earnings 2014[7]

College Major	Beginning Median Salary	Mid-Career Median Salary
Marketing and Communications	40,200	77,600
Political Science	41,700	77,000
Architecture	41,900	75,800
Accounting	45,300	74,900
Business Administration	43,500	71,000
History	39,700	71,000
Biology	40,200	70,800
Health Sciences	38,400	70,500
Forestry	40,000	69,400
Journalism	38,100	67,700
Geography	40,800	67,200
Public Administration	40,600	66,900
English	38,700	65,200
Humanities	37,900	61,800
Psychology	36,300	60,700
Liberal Arts	36,600	60,500
Fashion Merchandising	39,100	59,100
Art History	36,900	59,000
Sociology	37,400	58,800
Criminal Justice	35,300	58,400
Fine Arts	37,400	58,200
Religious Studies	34,900	57,900
Education	37,400	55,200
Music	35,700	51,400

© 2014, Anson0618. Used under license with Shutterstock, Inc.

Top 15 Majors That Change the World*[8]

College Major	Beginning Median Salary	Mid-Career Median Salary
Nursing	55,400	71,700
Special Education	33,800	49,600
Medical Technology	48,900	60,500
Sports Medicine	39,300	57,400
Biomedical Engineering	59,000	91,700
Athletic Training	34,800	46,900
Social Work	33,000	46,600
Child and Family Studies	30,300	37,200
Biblical Studies	35,400	50,800
Dietetics	44,200	56,600
Molecular Biology	40,400	76,400
Health Care Administration	39,300	58,600
Elementary Education	32,200	45,300
Exercise Science	32,600	51,000
Public Health	35,900	56,500

*Based on an extensive survey by Payscale.com by asking college graduates, "Does your work make the world a better place to live?"

Career outlook includes salary as well as availability of employment. How much does the occupation pay? Will the occupation exist in the future, and will there be employment opportunities? Of course, you will want to prepare yourself for careers that pay well and have future employment opportunities. The following table lists the fastest-growing occupations, occupations with the highest salaries, and occupations with the largest job growth.

> "We act as though comfort and luxury were the chief requirements of life, when all that we need to make us really happy is something to be enthusiastic about."
> Charles Kingsley

Employment Projections 2008–2018[9]

10 Fastest-Growing Occupations	10 Industries with the Largest Wage and Salary Employment Growth	10 Occupations with the Largest Numerical Job Growth
Biomedical engineers	Management, scientific, technical	Registered nurses
Network systems and data communications analysts	Physicians	Home health aides
Home health aides	Computer systems design and related	Customer service representatives
Personal and home care aides	General merchandise stores	Food preparation workers
Financial examiners	Employment services	Personal and home care aides
Medical scientists	Local government	Retail salespersons
Physician assistants	Home health care services	Office clerks
Skin care specialists	Services for elderly and disabled	Accountants and auditors
Biochemists and biophysicists	Nursing care facilities	Nursing aides, orderlies
Athletic trainers	Full-service restaurants	Postsecondary teachers

> "Only passions, great passions, can elevate the soul to great things."
> Denis Diderot

Every career counselor can tell stories about students who ask, "What is the career that makes the most money? That's the career I want!" However, if you choose a career based on money alone, you might find it difficult and uninteresting for a lifetime of work. You might even find yourself retraining later in life for a job that you really enjoy. Remember that the first step is to figure out who you are and what you like. Then look at career outlook and opportunity. If you find your passion in a career that is in demand and pays well, you will probably be very happy with your career choice. If you find your passion in a career that offers few jobs and does not pay well, you will have to use your ingenuity to find a job and make a living. Many students happily make this informed choice and find a way to make it work.

Find Your Passion

© 2014, Iculig. Used under license with Shutterstock, Inc.

Mark Twain said, "The secret of success is making your vocation your vacation." Find what you like to do. Better yet, find your passion. If you can find your passion, it is easy to invest the time and effort necessary to be successful. Aviator Charles Lindbergh said, "It is the greatest shot of adrenaline to be doing what you've wanted to do so badly. You almost feel like you could fly without the plane."[10] We may not be as excited about our careers as Charles Lindbergh, but we can find careers that match our personalities and talents and provide meaning to our lives.

How do you know when you have found your passion? You have found your passion when you are doing an activity and you do not notice that the time is passing. The great painter Picasso often talked about how quickly time passed while he was painting. He said, "When I work, I relax; doing nothing or entertaining visitors makes me tired." Whether you are an artist, an athlete, a scientist, or a business entrepreneur, passion provides the energy needed to be successful. It helps you to grow and create. When you are using your talents to grow and create, you can find meaning and happiness in your life.

Psychologist Martin Seligman has written a book entitled *Authentic Happiness,* in which he writes about three types of work orientation: a job, a career, and a calling.[11] A job is what you do for the paycheck at the end of the week. Many college students have jobs to earn money for college. A career has deeper personal meaning. It involves achievement, prestige, and power. A calling is

defined as "a passionate commitment to work for its own sake."[12] When you have found your calling, the job itself is the reward. He notes that people who have found their calling are consistently happier than those who have a job or even a career. One of the ways that you know you have found your calling is when you are in the state of "flow." The state of "flow" is defined as "complete absorption in an activity whose challenges mesh perfectly with your abilities."[13] People who experience "flow" are happier and more productive. They do not spend their days looking forward to Friday. Understanding your personal strengths is the beginning step to finding your calling.

Seligman adds that any job can become a calling if you use your personal strengths to do the best possible job. He cited a study of hospital cleaners. Although some viewed their job as drudgery, others viewed the job as a calling. They believed that they helped patients get better by working efficiently and anticipating the needs of doctors and nurses. They rearranged furniture and decorated walls to help patients feel better. They found their calling by applying their personal talents to their jobs. As a result, their jobs became a calling.

Sometimes we wait around for passion to find us. That probably won't happen. The first step in finding your passion is to know yourself. Then find an occupation in which you can use your talents. You may be able to find your passion by looking at your present job and finding a creative way to do it based on your special talents. It has been said

(continued)

that there are no dead-end jobs, just people who cannot see the possibilities. Begin your search for passion by looking at your personal strengths and how you can apply them in the job market. If the job that you have now is not your passion, see what you can learn from it and then use your skills to find a career where you are more likely to find your passion.

> "Success is not the key to happiness; happiness is the key to success. If you love what you are doing, you will be successful."
>
> Anonymous

JOURNAL ENTRIES

Exploring Your Personality and Major

Go to http://www.collegesuccess1.com/JournalEntries.htm for Word files of the Journal Entries

Success over the Internet

Visit the *College Success Website* at http://www.collegesuccess1.com/

The *College Success Website* is continually updated with new topics and links to the material presented in this chapter. Topics include:

- Personality profiles
- Online personality assessments
- Personality types of famous people in history
- Personality types and relationships
- Personality types and marriage
- Personality and careers
- Personality and communication
- Choosing your major
- Topics just for fun

Contact your instructor if you have any problems in accessing the *College Success Website*.

Notes

1. Judith Provost and Scott Anchors, eds., *Applications of the Myers-Briggs Type Indicator in Higher Education* (Palo Alto, CA: Consulting Psychologists Press, 1991), 51.

2. Ibid., 49.

3. Otto Kroeger and Janet Thuesen, *Type Talk: The 16 Personality Types That Determine How We Live, Love and Work* (New York: Dell, 1989), 204.

4. Ibid.

5. Allen L. Hammer and Gerald P. Macdaid, *MBTI Career Report Manual* (CA: Consulting Psychologist Press, 1998), 57–89.

6. PayScale, "2013–14 College Salary Report," accessed September 2013, www.payscale.com/college-salary-report-2014/

7. Ibid

8. Ibid

9. U.S. Bureau Of Labor Statistics, "Overview of the 2008–18 Projection."

10. Quoted in Rob Gilbert, ed., *Bits and Pieces*, December 2, 1999.

11. Martin Seligman, *Authentic Happiness* (Free Press, 2002).

12. Martin Seligman, as reported by Geoffrey Cowley, "The Science of Happiness," *Newsweek*, September 16, 2002, 49.

13. Ibid.

Personality Preferences

Name _____ Date _____

Use the textbook and personality assessment to think about your personality type. Place an X on the scale to show your degree of preference for each dimension of personality.

Introvert _____|_____ Extravert

Sensing _____|_____ INtuitive

Thinking _____|_____ Feeling

Judging _____|_____ Perceptive

Write a key word or phrase to describe each preference.

Introvert

Extravert

Sensing

INtuitive

Thinking

Feeling

Judging

Perceptive

What careers are suggested by your personality assessment?

Was the personality assessment accurate and useful to you?

Name _____ Date _____

Read the chapter on personality before commenting on these scenarios. Keep in mind the theory that we are all born with certain personality types and there are no good or bad types. Each type has gifts and talents that can be used to be a successful and happy person. Relate your comments to the concepts in this chapter. Your instructor may have you do this exercise as a group activity in class.

Scenario 1 (Sensing vs. Intuitive): Julie is a preschool teacher. She assigns her class to draw a picture of a bicycle. Students share their pictures with the class. One of the students has drawn a bicycle with wings. Another student laughs at the drawing and says, "Bicycles don't have wings!" How should the teacher handle this situation?

Scenario 2 (Thinking vs. Feeling): John has the almost perfect girlfriend. She is beautiful, intelligent, and fun to be with. She only has one flaw: John thinks that she is too emotional and wishes she could be a little more rational. When his girlfriend tries to talk to him about emotional issues, he analyzes her problems and proposes a logical solution. His girlfriend doesn't like the solutions that John proposes. Should John find a new girlfriend?

Scenario 3 (Introvert vs. Extravert): Mary is the mother of two children, ages five (daughter) and eight (son). The five-year-old is very social and especially enjoys birthday parties. At the last party, she invited 24 girls and they all showed up at the party. Everyone had a great time. The eight-year-old is very quiet and spends his time reading, doing artwork, building models, and hanging out with his one best friend. Mary is concerned that her son does not have very many friends. She decides to have a birthday party for her son also. The only problem is that he cannot come up with a list of children to invite to the party. What should Mary do?

Scenario 4 (Judging vs. Perceptive): Jerry and Jennifer have just been married, and they love each other very much. Jennifer likes to keep the house neat and orderly and likes to plan out activities so that there are no surprises. Jerry likes creative disorder. He leaves his things all over the house. He often comes up with creative ideas for having fun. How can Jerry and Jennifer keep their good relationship going?

Name _____   Date _____

In the following scenarios, think about how personality type influences communication style. Knowing about your personality type and understanding opposite types can help to improve your communication. Your instructor may want to do this as a group activity in the classroom.

1. An introvert and an extravert are having an argument.

   How is the introvert likely to act?

   How is the extravert likely to act?

   How can the extravert improve communication?

   How can the introvert improve communication?

2. A sensing and an intuitive type are on a date.

   What is the sensing person likely to talk about?

   What is the intuitive type likely to talk about?

3. A thinking type and a feeling type are dating.

   When there are problems in the relationship, how is the thinking type likely to approach the problem?

   How will the feeling type approach the problem?

4. A judging type and a perceptive type are working on a group project.

What would the judging type contribute?

What would the perceptive type contribute?

What can be done to avoid conflict between these two different personality types?

CHAPTER 3

Learning Style and Intelligence

Learning Objectives

Read to answer these key questions:

- What is my learning style?

- What is the best learning environment for me?

- What are some specific learning strategies that match my learning style?

- How is learning style connected to personality type?

- What are some specific learning strategies that are based on personality type?

- How can I understand and adapt to my professor's personality type (or "psych out" the professor)?

- What kinds of intelligence do I have?

- How can I create my success?

- What is emotional intelligence and how can I use it to increase personal and career success?

Knowing about your learning style can help you to choose effective strategies for learning in school and on the job. Knowing about your preferred learning environment can help you increase productivity. Discovering your multiple intelligences will help you to gain an appreciation of your gifts and talents that can be used to develop your self-confidence, study effectively, and choose the career that is right for you.

What Is Learning Style?

Just as each individual has a unique personality, each individual has a unique learning style. It is important to remember that there are no good or bad learning styles. Learning style is simply your preferred way of learning. It is how you like to learn and how you learn best. By understanding your learning style, you can maximize your potential by choosing the learning techniques that work best for you. This chapter explores the many factors that determine how you learn best. Each individual also has a preferred learning environment. Knowing about your preferred learning environment and learning style helps you be more productive, increase achievement, be more creative, improve problem solving, make good decisions, and learn effectively. Personality type also influences how we learn. Knowing about how you learn best helps to reduce frustration and increase your confidence in learning.

© 2014, iQoncept. Used under license with Shutterstock, Inc.

Gary Price[1] developed the Productivity Environmental Preference Survey (PEPS) which is included in the textbook. He identified sixteen different elements of learning style and environmental factors that influence productivity and satisfaction in school and on the job. As you read the description of each of these elements, think about your preferences and place a checkmark next to them.

1. **Visual.** Some students learn through reading, observing, or seeing things.

    - Those who prefer visual learning benefit from pictures and reading.

    - Those who are not visual learners may dislike reading. If auditory learning is preferred, attend the lecture first to hear the lecturer talk about the subject and then do the reading. It is important to do the reading because not all the material is covered in the lecture.

2. **Design.** Some students study best in a more formal environment or less formal environment.

    - If you prefer a formal environment, sit in a straight chair and use a desk.

    - If you prefer an informal environment, sit on the sofa or a soft chair or on some pillows on the floor.

3. **Persistence.** Some students may finish what they start, whereas others have many things going on at once and may not finish what they started. Persistence may indicate whether or not you procrastinate in finishing tasks.

    - If you are persistent, you generally finish what you start.

    - If you lack persistence, you may get bored or easily distracted. You may find it easier to break tasks into small steps and work steadily toward completing assignments on time. Think about your college and career goals to increase motivation and persistence.

4. **Motivation.** Some students are self-motivated to learn, and others lack motivation.

    - If you are self-motivated, you usually like school and enjoy learning on your own.

    - If you lack motivation, think about your reasons for attending college and review the material in the motivation chapter in this book.

5. Time of day. Some students are most awake and learn easier early in the day while others are most awake and learn better in the afternoon or evening.

- If you are most alert in the morning, schedule your classes and learning for earlier in the day and your routine tasks for later in the day when you are tired.

- If you are most alert in the late afternoon or evening, schedule your classes and learning during that time.

6. Light. Some students prefer bright light for studying and others find bright light uncomfortable or irritating. Having the right light can help you to be more productive.

- If you prefer bright light, study near a window with light shining over your shoulder or invest in a good study lamp.

- If you prefer dim lights, sit away from direct sunlight or use a shaded light.

7. Intake. Some students like to eat or drink something while studying while others find eating or drinking to be distracting.

- If you prefer intake while learning, drink water and have nutritious snacks such a fruits and vegetables.

- Some students do not need intake to study.

8. Tactile. Some students prefer to touch the material or use a "hands-on" approach to learning while others do not need to touch what they are learning.

- Students who prefer tactile learning like manipulative and three-dimensional materials. They learn from working with models and writing. Taking notes is one of the best tactile learning strategies.

- Students who are not tactile learners can focus on visual or auditory strategies for learning.

9. Kinesthetic. Kinesthetic learning is related to tactile learning. Some students learn best by movement and experiencing what they are learning while other students do not use movement to learn.

- Students who prefer kinesthetic learning enjoy field trips, drama, and becoming physically involved with learning. For example, they can learn fractions by slicing an apple into parts. It is important to be actively involved in learning.

- Students who are not kinesthetic learners will use another preferred method of learning such as auditory or visual learning.

10. Structure. Some students prefer more or less structure. This preference may also be related to your personality type (judging or perceptive).

- Students who prefer more structure want the teacher to give details and directions about how to complete the assignment.

- Students who prefer less structure want the teacher to give assignments in which the students can choose the topic and organize the material on their own.

11. Authority. Some students are more or less independent learners.

- Some students prefer to have the professor or a tutor to guide learning. In the college environment, students may prefer traditional face-to-face classes.

- Others prefer to work on their own. In the college environment, students may prefer online classes or independent study.

12. **Mobility.** Some students like to move around frequently while studying while others can sit still for longer periods of time.

- If you prefer mobility, you may find it difficult to sit still for a long time. Take a break every 15–20 minutes to move around. When choosing an occupation, consider one that requires you to move around.

- If you don't need to move around while studying, a desk and chair are sufficient to help you concentrate on learning.

13. **Sound.** Some students need a quiet environment for study while others find it distracting if it is too quiet.

- If you prefer quiet, use the library or find another quiet place. If you cannot find a quiet place, sound-blocking earphones or earplugs may be helpful.

- If you study better with sound, play soft music or study in open areas. Use headphones for your music if you are studying with those who prefer quiet.

14. **Temperature.** Some students perform better in cool temperatures and others prefer warmer temperatures.

- If you prefer a warm environment, remember to bring your sweater or jacket. Sit near a window or other source of heat.

- If you prefer a cooler environment, study in a well-ventilated environment or even outside in the shade.

15. **Auditory.** Some students learn through listening and talking while others find it distracting.

- Those who prefer auditory learning find it easier to learn through lectures, audio materials, discussion, and oral directions.

- Those who do not prefer auditory learning may find their mind wandering during lectures and become confused by oral directions. It is helpful to read the material before the lecture and take notes during the lecture. Review the notes periodically to remember the material.

16. **Alone or with peers.** Some students prefer to study alone and others prefer to study in groups. This may be related to your personality type (introvert, extravert).

- You may find other people distracting and prefer to study alone. Find a private area to study.

- You may enjoy working in a group because talking with others helps you to learn.

Journal Entry #1

Review the 16 elements of learning style and environment in this chapter and in the PEPS learning style assessment included with this textbook. Write a paragraph about your ideal learning environment.

What are your strongest learning preferences?

What environment makes you most productive?

> "What I hear, I forget.
> What I see, I remember.
> What I do, I know."
> Chinese Proverb

Learning Techniques

It is important to connect specific learning strategies to your preferred learning style. Even if you have definite preferences, you can experiment with other styles to improve your learning. If you become frustrated with a learning task, first try a familiar technique that you have used successfully in the past. If that does not work, experiment with different ways of learning. If one technique does not work, try another. It is powerful to combine techniques. For example, it is a good idea to make pictures of what you want to remember (visual), recite the ideas you want to remember (auditory), and take notes (tactile).

The following are specific techniques for each type of learner. Underline or highlight techniques that are useful to you.

Auditory Learning Techniques

You like to learn by listening. You are good at listening to lectures, audio materials, and learning through discussions. You generally understand, comprehend, and remember oral instructions. Here are some auditory learning strategies that you might find useful.

© 2014, VLADGRIN. Used under license with Shutterstock, Inc.

- Before reading, skim through the textbook and look at the major headings. As you are reading, ask questions or say out loud what you think will be important to remember.
- Since you learn by listening, you may not think you need to take notes on college lectures. However, note taking is needed for review and long-term recall. Focus on writing down the key ideas in your notes and leave spaces to fill in the details. Immediately after the lecture, review your lecture notes to add details you heard in the lecture. To review your notes, read them aloud.
- To prepare for exams, rehearse or say information verbally. For example, while studying math, say the equations out loud.
- Use auditory tools for learning such as lectures, videos, discussions, and recordings.
- Work in a quiet area to avoid distractions.
- Make it a priority to attend lectures and participate in discussion sessions. Sit near the front of the classroom so that you can hear clearly. Ask questions in class.
- Discuss what you are learning with other students. Discuss what you are learning with a friend or form a study group where you can discuss what you are learning.
- Participate actively in class discussions.
- Use memory devices, rhymes, poems, rhythms, or music to remember what you are studying. For example, turn facts into a rap song or a musical jingle to aid in recall.
- Memorize key concepts by repeating them aloud.
- Read the textbook and any directions for assignments or tests out loud if possible. Hear the words or directions in your mind if you cannot read them aloud.
- When learning new or difficult material, begin with auditory learning techniques and then reinforce the learning with visual, kinesthetic, and tactile learning strategies according to your preferences.

Visual Learning Techniques

You learn best by reading, observing, and seeing things. You remember what you read and see.

- Use color to highlight the important points in the text while reading. Review the important points by looking at the highlighted passages again.
- Take notes and use underlining and highlighting in different colors to highlight the important points. Include flow charts, graphs, and pictures in your notes. Make summary sheets or mind maps to summarize or review your notes.
- Use pictures, diagrams, flow charts, maps, graphs, time lines, video, and multi-media to aid in learning and prepare for exams. Use flash cards to remember important details and facts.
- Sit in front of the class so you can carefully observe the professor. Copy what is written on the board.

- Organize your work area to avoid visual distractions.
- Create visual reminders to keep on track. Make lists on note pads or use sticky notes as reminders.
- Make a visual image of what you are learning. For example, while reading history, picture in your mind's eye what it would be like to live in that historical period.
- Before answering an essay question, picture the answer in your mind, create a mind map, or write a quick outline.
- Use outlines or mind maps to review for exams.
- When learning new or difficult material, begin with visual learning strategies and then reinforce your learning with audio, kinesthetic, and tactile learning strategies.
- Practice remembering what you hear for those situations where you cannot get the material or instructions in writing. Using mnemonic memory devices may be helpful in remembering what you hear.

Tactile Learning Techniques

You need to be involved in your learning by doing things with your hands and your sense of touch. You prefer to touch the material as you learn and you need "hands-on" kinds of activities, which will help you learn by doing.

- Try to select educational courses that allow you to "do" things. For example, take courses that involve science experiments, writing, practicing math problems, etc.
- As you are reading, mark or highlight the key ideas and review them to enhance recall. Writing a journal or making a summary sheet of key ideas will help you to remember what you have read.
- Attend lectures and take notes. The physical act of writing will help you to remember the important points in the lecture.
- To prepare for exams, use a mind map, outline or drawing to help you to remember.
- Use real objects to help you to learn. For example, in a physics class, if you are studying levers, create a simple lever and observe how it functions. If you are studying geography, use a globe or map to aid in studying.
- Keep your desk clear of distracting objects.
- Use flash cards to review for exams.
- When learning new or difficult material, begin with tactile learning strategies and then reinforce your learning with visual, auditory, and kinesthetic learning strategies according to your preferences.

Kinesthetic Learning Techniques

You learn better when you are able to move around while learning. You prefer to be active and it is important for you to be actively involved to remember. Here are some learning strategies for kinesthetic learners:

- Quickly skim through material before reading it in detail. As you are reading, think about how the material applies to your personal life. Underline the key ideas and review them to enhance recall.
- Writing a journal or make a summary sheet of key ideas to help you to remember what you have read.
- Take notes on lectures. You are more likely to remember what you have written down.

- To prepare for exams, use flashcards to learn detailed information and review them while walking around.
- Move while studying. For example, read while using your exercise bike or stair stepper.
- Use kinesthetic learning experiences such as drama, building, designing, visiting, interviewing, and going on field trips.
- Actively participate in discussions to increase motivation and recall.
- Use all of your senses (sight, touch, taste, smell, and hearing) to help you to remember. For example, when studying Spanish, picture yourself speaking the language, use flash cards you can touch to remember the vocabulary, imagine the smell of Mexican food, say the words out loud, and listen to recordings of the language.
- Actively participate in classroom exercises to involve yourself in learning and motivate yourself to learn.
- Avoid long classes if possible. For example, choose a class that meets one hour on Mondays, Wednesdays, and Fridays instead of three hours on Monday.
- If you have a choice on how to do your assignments, do a skit or create a video.
- Look for courses or majors with hands-on activities, labs, or field trips.
- Take frequent breaks and study in different locations.
- Use a study group to teach the material to someone else.
- Use bright colors to highlight reading material.
- If you find it helpful, listen to music while you are studying.
- Chew gum to stay alert while studying.
- To prepare for exams, write practice answers and essays. Break the material to be reviewed into small parts and review frequently.
- When learning new and difficult material, begin with kinesthetic learning strategies and then reinforce your learning with visual, tactile, and auditory techniques according to your preferences.

My Learning Strategies

If you are having difficulties learning some new material in college, list some strategies that you might try:

1. _____

2. _____

3. _____

4. _____

5. _____

_____

_____

_____

_____

_____

Developing Your E-Learning Style

There are many opportunities for learning online, including online courses, professional development, or learning for your personal life. Students who are independent learners or introverts who enjoy individual learning in a quiet place may prefer online learning. Students who prefer having a professor to guide learning with immediate feedback and extraverts who are energized by social interaction may prefer traditional classroom education. Because of work, family, and time constraints, online learning might be a convenient way to access education. No matter what your learning style, you are likely to be in situations where you may want to take advantage of online learning.

If you have never taken an online course, be aware of some of the myths of online learning. One of the most popular myths is than online courses are easier than traditional courses. Online courses cover the same content and are just as rigorous as traditional face-to-face courses. It is likely that your online course will require more writing; instead of responding verbally in discussions, you will have to write your answer. Online courses generally require the same amount of time as traditional courses. However, you will save time in commuting to class and have the added convenience of working on your class at any time or place where you can access the Internet.

Here are some suggestions for a successful e-learning experience.

© 2014, Naypong. Used under license with Shutterstock, Inc.

- The most important factor in online learning is to **log in regularly** and complete the work in a systematic way. Set goals for what you need to accomplish each week and do the work a step at a time. Get in the habit of regularly doing your online study, just as you would attend a traditional course each week.

- It is important to **carefully read the instructions** for the assignments and **ask for help** if you need it. Your online professor will not know when you need help.

- Begin your online work by getting familiar with the requirements and components of the course. Generally online courses have reading material, quizzes, discussion boards, chat rooms, assignments, and multimedia presentations. Make sure that you **understand all the resources, components, and requirements** of the course.

- **Have a backup plan** if your computer crashes or your Internet connection is interrupted. Colleges generally have computer labs where you can do your work if you have technical problems at home.

- Remember to **participate** in the online discussions or chats. It is usually part of your grade and a good way to learn from other students and apply what you have learned. The advantage of online communication is that you have time to think about your responses.

- **Check your grades** online to make sure you are completing all the requirements. Celebrate your success as you complete your online studies. Online learning becomes easier with experience.

Personality and Learning Preferences

Learning preferences are also connected to personality type. As a review, personality has four dimensions:

1. Extraversion or Introversion

2. Sensing or Intuition

3. Thinking or Feeling

4. Judging or Perceiving

What is your personality type? To review, read the following brief descriptions and think about your preferences:

Extraverts *focus their energy on the world outside themselves. They enjoy interaction with others and get to know a lot of different people. They enjoy and are usually good at communication. They are energized by social interaction and prefer being active. These types are often described as talkative and social.*

Introverts *focus their energy on the world inside of themselves. They enjoy spending time alone and think about the world in order to understand it. Introverts like more limited social contacts, preferring smaller groups or one-on-one relationships. These types are often described as quiet or reserved.*

Sensing *persons prefer to use the senses to take in information (what they see, hear, taste, touch, smell). They focus on "what is" and trust information that is concrete and observable. They learn through experience.*

INtuitive *persons rely on instincts and focus on "what could be." While we all use our five senses to perceive the world, the intuitive person is interested in relationships, possibilities, meanings, and implications. They value inspiration and trust their "sixth sense" or hunches. We all use our senses and intuition in our daily lives, but we usually have a preference for one mode or another.*

Thinking *individuals make decisions based on logic. They are objective and analytical. They look at all the evidence and reach an impersonal conclusion. They are concerned with what they think is right.*

Feeling *individuals make decisions based on what is important to them and matches their personal values. They are concerned about what they feel is right.*

Judging *types like to live in a structured, orderly, and planned way. They are happy when their lives are structured and matters are settled. They like to have control over their lives. Judging does not mean to judge others. Think of this type as orderly and organized.*

Perceptive *types like to live in a spontaneous and flexible way. They are happy when their lives are open to possibilities. They try to understand life rather than control it. Think of this type as spontaneous and flexible.*

ACTIVITY

Your Personality and Learning Style

Circle your personality type.

Extravert	or	Introvert
Sensing	or	Intuitive
Thinking	or	Feeling
Judging	or	Perceptive

Each personality type has a natural preference for how to learn. When learning something new, it may be easiest and most efficient to use the style that matches your personality type. It is also a good idea to experiment with using new techniques commonly used by other types. There is no learning style that

(continued)

works best in all situations. You may need to adapt your learning style based on the learning activity. As you look at the chart below, think about your personality type and learning preferences:

Learning Preferences Associated with Personality Types[2]

Extraversion	Introversion
Learn best when in action	Learn best by pausing to think
Value physical activity	Value reading
Like to study with others	Prefer to study individually
Say they're above average in verbal and interpersonal skills	Say they're below average in verbal expression
Say they need training in reading and writing papers	Say they need training in public speaking
Background sounds help them study	Need quiet for concentration
Want faculty who encourage discussion	Want faculty who give clear lectures

Sensing	INtuition
Seek specific information	Seek quick insights
Memorize facts	Use imagination to go beyond facts
Value what is practical	Value what is original
Follow instructions	Create their own directions
Like hands-on experience	Like theories to give perspective
Trust material as presented	Read between the lines
Want faculty who give clear assignments	Want faculty who encourage independent thinking

Thinking	Feeling
Want objective material to study	Want to be able to relate to the material personally
Logic guides learning	Personal values are important
Like to critique new ideas	Like to please instructors
Can easily find flaws in an argument	Can easily find something to appreciate
Learn by challenge and debate	Learn by being supported and appreciated
Want faculty who make logical presentations	Want faculty who establish personal rapport with students

Judging	Perceiving
Like formal instructions for solving problems	Like to solve problems informally
Value dependability	Value change
Plan work well in advance	Work spontaneously
Work steadily toward goals	Work impulsively with bursts of energy
Like to be in charge of events	Like to adapt to events
Drive toward closure (finish)	Stay open to new information
Want faculty to be organized	Want faculty to be entertaining and inspiring

Learning Strategies for Different Personality Types

Based on the above descriptions of learning preferences, the following learning strategies are suggested along with some cautions for each type. As you read these descriptions, think about those suggestions and cautions that apply to you.

© 2014, Monkey Business Images. Used under license with Shutterstock, Inc.

Extravert

1. Since extraverts learn best when talking, discuss what you have learned with others. Form a study group.

2. Extraverts like variety and action. Take frequent breaks and do something active during your break such as walking around.

3. *Caution!* You may become so distracted by activity and socialization that your studying does not get done.

Introvert

1. Since introverts like quiet for concentration, find a quiet place to study by yourself.

2. Plan to study for longer periods of time and in a way that minimizes interruptions. Turn off the phone or study in the library.

3. *Caution!* You may miss out on sharing ideas and the fun social life of college.

Sensing

1. Sensing types are good at mastering facts and details.

2. Think about practical applications in order to motivate yourself to learn. Ask, "How can I use this information?"

3. *Caution!* You may miss the big picture or general outline by focusing too much on the facts and details. Make a general outline to see the relationship and meaning of the facts.

Intuitive

1. Intuitive types are good at learning concepts and theories.

2. As you are reading, ask yourself, "What is the main point?"

3. *Caution!* Because this type focuses on general concepts and theories, they are likely to miss details and facts. To learn details, organize them into broad categories that have meaning for you.

Thinking

1. Thinking types are good at logic.

2. As you are reading, ask yourself, "What do I think of these ideas?" Discuss or debate your ideas with others.

3. Allow time to think and reflect on your studies.

4. If possible, pick instructors whom you respect and who are intellectually challenging.

5. *Caution!* Others may be offended by your logic and love of debate. Learn to respect the ideas of others.

Feeling

1. Feeling types need a comfortable environment in order to concentrate.

2. For motivation, search for personal meaning in your studies. Ask how the material affects you or others. Look for a supportive environment or study group.

3. Help others to learn.

4. When possible, choose classes that relate to your personal interests.

5. If possible, select instructors who get to know the students and establish a positive learning environment.

6. *Caution!* You may neglect studying because of time spent helping others or may find it difficult to pay attention to material that is not personally meaningful.

Judging

1. Judging types are orderly and organized. Find ways to organize the material to learn it easier.

2. If possible, select instructors who present material in an organized way.

3. Set goals and use a schedule to motivate yourself. This type is naturally good at time management.

4. Use a daily planner, calendar, or to-do list.

5. *Caution!* Being too structured and controlled may limit your creativity and cause conflict with others who are different. Judging types are sometimes overachievers who get stressed easily.

Perceptive

1. Perceptive students are good at looking at all the possibilities and keeping options open.

2. Allow enough time to be thorough and complete your work.

3. Keep learning fun and interesting.

4. Study in groups that have some perceptive types and some judging types. In this way, you can explore possibilities, have fun, and be organized.

5. *Caution!* Work on managing your time to meet deadlines. Be careful not to overextend yourself by working on too many projects at once.

Understanding Your Professor's Personality

Different personality types have different expectations of teachers.

- Extraverts want faculty who encourage class discussion.
- Introverts want faculty who give clear lectures.
- Sensing types want faculty who give clear assignments.
- Intuitive types want faculty who encourage independent thinking.
- Thinking types want faculty who make logical presentations.
- Feeling types want faculty who establish personal rapport with students.
- Judging types want faculty to be organized.
- Perceptive types want faculty to be entertaining and inspiring.

What can you do if your personality and the professor's personality are different? This is often the case. In a study reported by *Consulting Psychologist Press*, college faculty were twice as likely as students to be introverted intuitive types interested in abstractions and learning for its own sake.[3] College students are twice as likely as faculty to be extraverted sensing types who are interested in practical learning. There are three times more sensing and perceptive students than faculty. Faculty tend to be intuitive and judging types. Students expect faculty to be practical, fun, and flexible. Faculty tend to be theoretical and organized. In summary:

College faculty tend to be	College students tend to be
Introverted	Extraverted
Intuitive	Sensing
Judging	Perceptive

Of course, the above is not always true, but there is a good probability that you will have college professors who are very different from you. First, try to understand the professor's personality. This has been called "psyching out the professor." You can usually tell the professor's personality type on the first day of class by examining class materials and observing his or her manner of presentation. If you understand the professor's personality type, you will know what to expect. Next, try to appreciate what the professor has to offer. You may need to adapt your style to fit. If you are a perceptive type, be careful to meet the due dates of your assignments. Experiment with different study techniques so that you can learn the material presented.

"The wisest mind has something yet to learn."
George Santayana

"Tell me and I forget. Teach me and I remember. Involve me and I learn."
Benjamin Franklin

© 2014, Alexander Raths. Used under license with Shutterstock, Inc.

Journal Entry #3

How can you use your knowledge of personality type to understand your professor's teaching style and expectations? What should you do if your personality does not match the professor's personality? For example, if your professor is a judging type and you are a perceptive type, how can you adapt to be successful in this course?

QUIZ

Learning Style

Test what you have learned by selecting the correct answers to the following questions.

1. The best environment for learning

    a. matches your learning style.
    b. is a straight chair and a desk.
    c. includes music in the background.

2. Kinesthetic types learn best by

    a. listening to lectures.
    b. reading the textbook.
    c. taking notes and reviewing them.

3. If you become frustrated in learning, it is best to

    a. keep trying.
    b. take a long break.
    c. take a short break and then apply your preferred learning style.

4. Introverts would probably prefer

    a. studying quietly in the library.
    b. participating in a study group.
    c. learning through classroom discussions.

5. When working on a term paper, perceptive types would probably prefer

    a. organizing the project and completing it quickly.
    b. making a plan and finishing early.
    c. looking at all the possibilities and keeping their options open.

How did you do on the quiz? Check your answers: 1. a, 2. c, 3. c, 4. a, 5. c

Multiple Intelligences

In 1904, the French psychologist Alfred Binet developed the IQ test, which provided a single score to measure intelligence. This once widely used and accepted test came into question because it measured the intelligence of individuals in schools in a particular culture. In different cultures and different situations, the test was less valid. As an alternative to traditional IQ tests, Harvard professor Howard Gardner developed the theory of multiple intelligences. He looked at intelligence in a broader and more inclusive way than people had done in the past.

© 2014, VLADGRIN. Used under license with Shutterstock, Inc.

Howard Gardner observed famous musicians, artists, athletes, scientists, inventors, naturalists, and others who were recognized contributors to society to formulate a more meaningful definition of intelligence. He defined intelligence as **the human ability to solve problems or design or compose something valued in at least one culture**. His definition broadens the scope of human potential. He identified nine different intelligences: musical, interpersonal, logical-mathematical, spatial, bodily-kinesthetic, linguistic, intrapersonal, naturalist and existential. He selected these intelligences because they are all represented by an area in the brain and are valued in different cultures. His theory can help us to understand and use many different kinds of talents.

Within the theory of multiple intelligences, learning style is defined as intelligences put to work. These intelligences are measured by looking at performance in activities associated with each intelligence. A key idea in this theory is that most people can develop all of their intelligences and become relatively competent in each area. Another key idea is that these intelligences work together in complex ways to make us unique. For example, an athlete uses bodily-kinesthetic intelligence to run, kick, or jump. They use spatial intelligence to keep their eye on the ball and hit it. They also need linguistic and interpersonal skills to be good members of a team.

Developing intelligences is a product of three factors:

1. Biological endowment based on heredity and genetics

2. Personal life history

3. Cultural and historical background[4]

For example, Wolfgang Amadeus Mozart was born with musical talent (biological endowment). Members of his family were musicians who encouraged Mozart in music (personal life history). Mozart lived in Europe during a time when music flourished and wealthy patrons were willing to pay composers (cultural and historical background).

Each individual's life history contains **crystallizers** that promote the development of the intelligences and **paralyzers** that inhibit the development of the intelligences. These crystallizers and paralyzers often take place in early childhood. For example, Einstein was given a magnetic compass when he was four years old. He became so interested in the compass that he started on his journey of exploring the universe. An example of a paralyzer is being embarrassed or feeling humiliated about your math skills in elementary school so that you begin to lose confidence in your ability to do math. Paralyzers involve shame, guilt, fear, and anger and prevent intelligence from being developed.

"I have no special talent. I am only passionately curious."
Albert Einstein

Describing Your Multiple Intelligences

Below are some definitions and examples of the different intelligences. As you read each section, think positively about your intelligence in this area. Place a checkmark in front of each item that is true for you.

Musical

Musical intelligence involves hearing and remembering musical patterns and manipulating patterns in music. Some occupations connected with this intelligence include musician, performer, composer, and music critic. Place a checkmark next to each skill that you possess in this area.

_____ I enjoy singing, humming, or whistling.

_____ One of my interests is playing recorded music.

_____ I have collections of recorded music.

_____ I play or used to play a musical instrument.

_____ I can play the drums or tap out rhythms.

_____ I appreciate music.

_____ Music affects how I feel.

_____ I enjoy having music on while working or studying.

_____ I can clap my hands and keep time to music.

_____ I can tell when a musical note is off key.

_____ I remember melodies and the words to songs.

_____ I have participated in a band, chorus, or other musical group.

Look at the items you have checked above and summarize your musical intelligence.

_____

_____

_____

Interpersonal

Interpersonal intelligence is defined as understanding people. Occupations connected with this intelligence involve working with people and helping them, as in education or health care. Place a checkmark next to each skill that you possess in this area.

_____ I enjoy being around people.

_____ I am sensitive to other people's feelings.

_____ I am a good listener.

_____ I understand how others feel.

_____ I have many friends.

_____ I enjoy parties and social gatherings.

_____ I enjoy participating in groups.

_____ I can get people to cooperate and work together.

_____ I am involved in clubs or community activities.

_____ People come to me for advice.

_____ I am a peacemaker.

_____ I enjoy helping others.

Look at the items you have checked above and summarize your interpersonal intelligence.

_____

_____

_____

Logical-Mathematical

Logical-mathematical intelligence involves understanding abstract principles and manipulating numbers, quantities, and operations. Some examples of occupations associated with logical-mathematical intelligence are mathematician, tax accountant, scientist, and computer programmer. Place a checkmark next to each skill that you possess. Keep an open mind. People usually either love or hate this area.

_____ I can do arithmetic problems quickly.

_____ I enjoy math.

_____ I enjoy doing puzzles.

_____ I enjoy working with computers.

_____ I am interested in computer programming.

_____ I enjoy science classes.

_____ I enjoy doing the experiments in lab science courses.

_____ I can look at information and outline it easily.

_____ I understand charts and diagrams.

_____ I enjoy playing chess or checkers.

_____ I use logic to solve problems.

_____ I can organize things and keep them in order.

Look at the items you have checked above and summarize your logical-mathematical intelligence.

_____

_____

_____

(continued)

Spatial

Spatial intelligence involves the ability to manipulate objects in space. For example, a baseball player uses spatial intelligence to hit a ball. Occupations associated with spatial intelligence include pilot, painter, sculptor, architect, inventor, and surgeon. This intelligence is often used in athletics, the arts, or the sciences. Place a checkmark next to each skill that you possess in this area.

_____ I can appreciate a good photograph or piece of art.

_____ I think in pictures and images.

_____ I can use visualization to remember.

_____ I can easily read maps, charts, and diagrams.

_____ I participate in artistic activities (art, drawing, painting, photography).

_____ I know which way is north, south, east, and west.

_____ I can put things together.

_____ I enjoy jigsaw puzzles or mazes.

_____ I enjoy seeing movies, slides, or photographs.

_____ I can appreciate good design.

_____ I enjoy using telescopes, microscopes, or binoculars.

_____ I understand color, line, shape, and form.

Look at the items you have checked above and summarize your spatial intelligence.

_____

_____

_____

Bodily-Kinesthetic

Bodily-kinesthetic intelligence is defined as being able to use your body to solve problems. People with bodily-kinesthetic intelligence make or invent objects or perform. They learn by doing, touching, and handling. Occupations connected to this type of intelligence include athlete, performer (dancer, actor), craftsperson, sculptor, mechanic, and surgeon. Place a checkmark next to each skill that you possess in this area.

_____ I am good at using my hands.

_____ I have good coordination and balance.

_____ I learn best by moving around and touching things.

_____ I participate in physical activities or sports.

_____ I learn new sports easily.

_____ I enjoy watching sports events.

_____ I am skilled in a craft such as woodworking, sewing, art, or fixing machines.

_____ I have good manual dexterity.

_____ I find it difficult to sit still for a long time.

_____ I prefer to be up and moving.

_____ I am good at dancing and remember dance steps easily.

_____ It was easy for me to learn to ride a bike or skateboard.

Look at the items you checked above and describe your bodily-kinesthetic intelligence.

_____

_____

_____

Linguistic

People with linguistic intelligence are good with language and words. They have good reading, writing, and speaking skills. Linguistic intelligence is an asset in any occupation. Specific related careers include writing, education, and politics. Place a checkmark next to each skill that you possess in this area.

_____ I am a good writer.

_____ I am a good reader.

_____ I enjoy word games and crossword puzzles.

_____ I can tell jokes and stories.

_____ I am good at explaining.

_____ I can remember names, places, facts, and trivia.

_____ I'm generally good at spelling.

_____ I have a good vocabulary.

_____ I read for fun and relaxation.

_____ I am good at memorizing.

_____ I enjoy group discussions.

_____ I have a journal or diary.

Look at the items you have checked above and summarize your linguistic intelligence.

_____

_____

_____

Intrapersonal

Intrapersonal intelligence is the ability to understand yourself and how to best use your natural talents and abilities. Examples of careers associated with this intelligence include novelist, psychologist, or being self-employed. Place a checkmark next to each skill that you possess in this area.

_____ I understand and accept my strengths and weaknesses.

_____ I am very independent.

_____ I am self-motivated.

_____ I have definite opinions on controversial issues.

_____ I enjoy quiet time alone to pursue a hobby or work on a project.

_____ I am self-confident.

_____ I can work independently.

(continued)

_____ I can help others with self-understanding.

_____ I appreciate quiet time for concentration.

_____ I am aware of my own feelings and sensitive to others.

_____ I am self-directed.

_____ I enjoy reflecting on ideas and concepts.

Look at the items you have checked above and summarize your intrapersonal intelligence.

_____

_____

_____

Naturalist

The naturalist is able to recognize, classify, and analyze plants, animals, and cultural artifacts. Occupations associated with this intelligence include botanist, horticulturist, biologist, archeologist, and environmental occupations. Place a checkmark next to each skill you possess in this area.

_____ I know the names of minerals, plants, trees, and animals.

_____ I think it is important to preserve our natural environment.

_____ I enjoy taking classes in the natural sciences such as biology.

_____ I enjoy the outdoors.

_____ I take care of flowers, plants, trees, or animals.

_____ I am interested in archeology or geology.

_____ I would enjoy a career involved in protecting the environment.

_____ I have or used to have a collection of rocks, shells, or insects.

_____ I belong to organizations interested in protecting the environment.

_____ I think it is important to protect endangered species.

_____ I enjoy camping or hiking.

_____ I appreciate natural beauty.

Look at the items you have checked above and describe your naturalist intelligence.

_____

_____

_____

Existential

Existential intelligence is the capacity to ask profound questions about the meaning of life and death. This intelligence is the cornerstone of art, religion, and philosophy. Related occupations include minister, philosopher, psychologist, and artist. Place a checkmark next to each skill that you possess in this area.

_____ I often think about the meaning and purpose of life.

_____ I have strong personal beliefs and convictions.

_____ I enjoy thinking about abstract theories.

_____ I have considered being a philosopher, scientist, theologian, or artist.

_____ I often read books that are philosophical or imaginative.

_____ I enjoy reading science fiction.

_____ I like to work independently.

_____ I like to search for meaning in my studies.

_____ I wonder if there are other intelligent life forms in the universe.

Look at the items you have checked above and describe your existential intelligence.

_____

_____

Journal Entry #4

Look at the above charts and see where you have the most checkmarks. What do you think are your highest intelligences?

Build on Your Strengths

Consider your personal strengths when deciding on a career. People in each of the multiple intelligence areas have different strengths:

- Musical strengths include listening to music, singing, playing a musical instrument, keeping a beat, and recognizing musical patterns. People with this intelligence are "musical smart."

- Interpersonal strengths include communication skills, social skills, helping others, understanding other's feelings, and the ability to resolve conflicts. People with this intelligence are "people smart."

- Logical—mathematical strengths include math aptitude, interest in science, problem-solving skills, and logical thinking. People with this intelligence are "number/reasoning smart."

- Spatial strengths include visualization, understanding puzzles, navigation, visual arts, reading, and writing. People with this intelligence are "picture smart."

- Bodily-kinesthetic strengths include hand and eye coordination, athletics, dance, drama, cooking, sculpting, and learning by doing. People with this intelligence are "body smart."

- Linguistic strengths include good reading, writing, vocabulary, and spelling skills; good communication skills; being a good listener; having a good memory; and learning new languages easily. People with this intelligence are "word smart."

- Intrapersonal strengths include good self-awareness. They are aware of their feelings and emotions and are often independent and self-motivated to achieve. People with this intelligence are "self-smart."

- Naturalist strengths include exploring and preserving the environment and are very aware of natural surroundings. People with this intelligence are "nature smart."

- Existential strengths include reflecting on important questions about the universe, the purpose of life, and religious beliefs. People with this intelligence are "curiosity smart."

In what areas are you "smart?" _____

_____

© 2014, DeiMosz. Used under license with Shutterstock, Inc.

Some Careers and Multiple Intelligences

Circle any careers that seem interesting to you		
Musical	**Interpersonal**	**Logical–Mathematical**
disc jockey	cruise director	engineer
music teacher	mediator	accountant
music retailer	human resources	computer analyst
music therapist	dental hygienist	physician
recording engineer	nurse	detective
singer	psychologist	researcher
song writer	social worker	scientist
speech pathologist	administrator	computer programmer
music librarian	marketer	database designer
choir director	religious leader	physicist
music critic	teacher	auditor
music lawyer	counselor	economist
Spatial	**Bodily-Kinesthetic**	**Linguistic**
architect	athlete	journalist
artist	carpenter	writer
film animator	craftsperson	editor
mechanic	mechanic	attorney
pilot	jeweler	curator
webmaster	computer game designer	newscaster
interior decorator	firefighter	politician
graphic artist	forest ranger	speech pathologist
sculptor	physical therapist	translator
surveyor	personal trainer	comedian
urban planner	surgeon	historian
photographer	recreation specialist	librarian
		marketing consultant

Intrapersonal	Naturalist	Existential
career counselor	park ranger	counselor
wellness counselor	dog trainer	psychologist
therapist	landscaper	psychiatrist
criminologist	meteorologist	social worker
intelligence officer	veterinarian	ministry
entrepreneur	animal health technician	philosopher
psychologist	ecologist	artist
researcher	nature photographer	scientist
actor	wilderness guide	researcher
artist	anthropologist	motivational speaker
philosopher	environmental lawyer	human resources
writer	water conservationist	writer

Using Emotional Intelligence in Your Personal Life and Career

Emotional intelligence is related to interpersonal and intrapersonal intelligences. It is the ability to recognize, control, and evaluate your own emotions while realizing how they affect people around you. Emotional intelligence affects career and personal success because it is related to the ability to build good relationships, communicate, work as part of a team, concentrate, remember, make decisions, deal with stress, overcome challenges, deal with conflict, and empathize with others. Research has shown emotional intelligence can predict career success and that workers with high emotional intelligence are more likely to end up in leadership positions in which workers are happy with their jobs.

The premise of emotional intelligence is that you can be more successful if you are aware of your own emotions as well as the emotions of others. There are two aspects of emotional intelligence:

- Understanding yourself, your goals, intentions, responses, and behavior.
- Understanding others and their feelings.

Daniel Goleman has identified the five most important characteristics of emotional intelligence:[5]

1. **Self-Awareness**

   People with high emotional intelligence are aware of their emotions including strengths and weaknesses.

2. **Self-Regulation**

   This involves the ability to control emotions and impulses. Being impulsive can lead to careless decisions like attending a party the night before a final exam. Characteristics of self-regulation include comfort with change, integrity, and the ability to say no.

3. **Motivation**

   People with high emotional intelligence can defer immediate results for long-term success. For example, investing your time in education can lead to future career opportunities and income.

4. **Empathy**

   Empathy is the ability to understand the needs and viewpoints of others around you and avoiding stereotypes. It involves good listening skills that enhance personal relationships.

5. **Social Skills**

   People with good social skills are good team players and willing to help others to be successful.

   You can enhance your personal and career success by developing your emotional intelligence. Here are some tips for developing good relationships in your personal life and on the job.

   - Be empathetic when working with others by trying to put yourself in their place to understand different perspectives and points of view. Don't be quick to jump to conclusions or stereotype others.
   - Think about how your actions affect others. Always treat others as you would like to be treated.
   - Be open-minded and intellectually curious. Consider the opinions of others in a positive manner. Be willing to examine and change your mind-set.
   - Give others credit for their accomplishments in your personal life and in the workplace. When speaking about your own accomplishments, confidently state what you accomplished without trying to seek too much attention.
   - Evaluate your own strengths and weaknesses. Focus on your strengths, but be aware of the weaknesses and work to improve them. The personality assessment in the previous chapter helps you to understand your personal strengths and weaknesses.
   - Work on stress management by finding some stress reduction techniques that work for you. In stressful situations, it is helpful to remain calm and in control. Seek workable solutions without blaming others. Your college health services office often provides workshops on stress management.
   - Take a college course to improve verbal as well as nonverbal communication. When talking with others, focus on what they are saying rather than what you are going to say next. Learn how to make "I statements" that effectively communicate your thoughts without blaming others. Become aware of nonverbal communication which adds a significant dimension to communication.
   - Use humor to help you deal with challenges. Humor helps you to keep things in perspective, deal with differences, relax, and come up with creative solutions.
   - Deal with conflicts in a way that builds trust. Focus on win-win solutions that allow both parties to have their needs met.
   - Take responsibility for your actions. Admit when you make mistakes and work to improve the situation in the future.
   - Use critical thinking to analyze the pros and cons of the situation.
   - Be goal oriented and focus on the task and the steps needed to achieve your goals.
   - Be optimistic. Optimism leads to greater opportunities and results in better personal relationships.

Journal Entry #5

Comment on your emotional intelligence and how you can use it to be successful in your personal life and your career.

Multiple Intelligences

Test what you have learned by selecting the correct answers to the following questions.

1. Multiple intelligences are defined as

   a. the many parts of intelligence as measured by an IQ test.
   b. the ability to design something valued in at least one culture.
   c. the ability to read, write, and do mathematical computations.

2. The concept of multiple intelligences is significant because

   a. it measures the intelligence of students in schools.
   b. it does not use culture in measuring intelligence.
   c. it broadens the scope of human potential and includes all cultures.

3. Intelligences are measured by

   a. IQ tests.
   b. performance in activities related to the intelligence.
   c. performance in the classroom.

4. Each individual's life history contains crystallizers that

   a. promote the development of the intelligences.
   b. inhibit the development of the intelligences.
   c. cause the individual to be set in their ways.

5. Multiple intelligences include

   a. getting good grades in college.
   b. bodily kinesthetic skills.
   c. good test-taking skills.

How did you do on the quiz? Check your answers: 1. b, 2. c, 3. b, 4. a, 5. b

"The best years of your life are the ones in which you decide your problems are your own. You do not blame them on your mother, the ecology, or the president. You realize that you control your own destiny."

Albert Ellis

Create Your Success

We are responsible for what happens in our lives. We make decisions and choices that create the future. Our behavior leads to success or failure. Too often we believe that we are victims of circumstance. When looking at our lives, we often look for others to blame for how our lives are going:

- My grandparents did it to me. I inherited these genes.
- My parents did it to me. My childhood experiences shaped who I am.
- My teacher did it to me. He gave me a poor grade.
- My boss did it to me. She gave me a poor evaluation.
- The government did it to me. All my money goes to taxes.
- Society did it to me. I have no opportunity.

These factors are powerful influences in our lives, but we are still left with choices. Concentration camp survivor Viktor Frankl wrote a book, *Man's Search for Meaning,* in which he describes his experiences and how he survived his ordeal. His parents, brother, and wife died in the camps. He suffered starvation and torture. Through all of his sufferings and imprisonment, he still maintained that he was a free man because he could make choices.

We who lived in concentration camps can remember the men who walked through the huts comforting others, giving away their last piece of bread. They may have been few in number, but they offer sufficient proof that everything can be taken from a man but one thing: the last of the human freedoms—to choose one's attitude in any given set of circumstances, to choose one's own way. . . . Fundamentally, therefore, any man can, even under such circumstances, decide what shall become of him—mentally and spiritually. He may retain his human dignity even in a concentration camp.[6]

Viktor Frankl could not choose his circumstances at that time, but he did choose his attitude. He decided how he would respond to the situation.

He realized that he still had the freedom to make choices. He used his memory and imagination to exercise his freedom. When times were the most difficult, he would imagine that he was in the classroom lecturing to his students about psychology. He eventually did get out of the concentration camp and became a famous psychiatrist.

Hopefully none of you will ever have to experience the circumstances faced by Viktor Frankl, but we all face challenging situations. It is empowering to think that our behavior is more a function of our decisions than of our circumstances. It is not productive to look around and find someone to blame for your problems. Psychologist Abraham Maslow says that instead of blaming, we should see how we can make the best of the situation.

One can spend a lifetime assigning blame, finding a cause, "out there" for all the troubles that exist. Contrast this with the responsible attitude of confronting the situation, bad or good, and instead of asking, "What caused the trouble? Who was to blame?" asking, "How can I handle the present situation to make the best of it?"[7]

Author Stephen Covey suggests that we look at the word responsibility as "response-ability."[8] It is the ability to choose responses and make decisions about the future. When you are dealing with a problem, it is useful to ask yourself what decisions you made that led to the problem. How did you create the situation? If you created the problem, you can create a solution.

At times, you may ask, "How did I create this?" and find that the answer is that you did not create the situation. We certainly do not create earthquakes or hurricanes, for example. But we do create or at least contribute to many of the things that happen to us. Even if you did not create your circumstances, you can create your reaction to the situation. In the case of an earthquake, you can decide to panic or find the best course of action at the moment.

Stephen Covey believes that we can use our resourcefulness and initiative in dealing with most problems. When his children were growing up and they asked him how to solve a certain problem, he would say, "Use your R and I!" He meant resourcefulness and initiative. He notes that adults can use this R and I to get good jobs.

> *But the people who end up with the good jobs are the proactive ones who are solutions to problems, not problems themselves, who seize the initiative to do whatever is necessary, consistent with correct principles, to get the job done.*[9]

Use your resourcefulness and initiative to create the future that you want.

JOURNAL ENTRIES

Learning Style and Intelligence

Go to http://www.collegesuccess1.com/JournalEntries.htm for Word files of the Journal Entries

---

Success over the Internet

Visit the *College Success Website* at http://www.collegesuccess1.com/

The *College Success Website* is continually updated with new topics and links to the material presented in this chapter. Topics include:

- Learning style assessments
- Learning style and memory
- Learning style and personality type

Contact your instructor if you have any problems in accessing the *College Success Website*.

Notes

1. Gary E. Price, "Productivity Environmental Preference Survey," Price Systems, Inc., Box 1818, Lawrence, KS 66044-8818.

2. Modified and reproduced by special permission of the Publisher, Consulting Psychologist Press, Inc., Palo Alto, CA 94303, from *Introduction to Type in College* by John K. Ditiberio and Allen L. Hammer. Copyright 1993 by Consulting Psychologist Press, Inc. All rights reserved. Further reproduction is prohibited without the Publisher's written consent.

3. John K. Ditiberio and Allen L. Hammer, *Introduction to Type in College* (Palo Alto, CA: Consulting Psychologist Press, 1993), 7.

4. Howard Gardner, *Intelligence Reframed: Multiple Intelligences for the Twenty-First Century* (Boulder, CO: Basic Books, 1999).

5. Thomas Armstrong, *Multiple Intelligences in the Classroom* (Alexandria, VA: Association for Curriculum Development, 1994).

6. Viktor Frankl, *Man's Search for Meaning* (New York: Pocket Books, 1963), 104–5.

7. Quoted in Rob Gilbert, ed., *Bits and Pieces*, November 4, 1999.

8. Stephen Covey, *The Seven Habits of Highly Effective People* (New York: Simon and Schuster, 1989), 71.

9. Ibid., 75.

Learning Style Quiz

Name _____   Date _____

Read the following questions and circle the letter of the best answer for each in your opinion. There are no right or wrong answers in this quiz. Just circle what you usually prefer.

1. When learning how to use my computer, I prefer to
   a. read the manual first.
   b. have someone explain how to do it first.
   c. just start using the computer and get help if I need it.

2. When getting directions to a new location, it is easier to
   a. look at a map.
   b. have someone tell me how to get there.
   c. follow someone or have him or her take me there.

3. To remember a phone number, I
   a. look at the number and dial it several times.
   b. repeat it silently or out loud to myself several times.
   c. remember the number by the pattern pressed on the keypad, the tones of each number, or writing it down.

4. For relaxation, I prefer to
   a. read a book or magazine.
   b. listen to or play music.
   c. go for a walk or do something physical.

5. I am better at
   a. reading.
   b. talking.
   c. physical activities.

6. In school, I learn best by
   a. reading.
   b. listening.
   c. hands-on activities.

7. I tend to be a
   a. thinker.
   b. talker.
   c. doer.

8. When I study for a test, it works best when I
   a. read and picture the information in my head.
   b. read and say the ideas out loud or silently.
   c. highlight, write notes, and outline.

9. It is easier for me to remember
   a. faces.
   b. names.
   c. events.

10. On a Saturday, I would prefer to
    a. see a movie.
    b. go to a concert.
    c. participate in athletics or be outside.

11. In a college class, it is most important to have
    a. a good textbook with pictures, graphs, and diagrams.
    b. a good teacher who gives interesting lectures.
    c. hands-on activities.

12. It is easier for me to study by
    a. reading and reviewing the material.
    b. discussing the subject with others.
    c. writing notes or outlines.

13. When I get lost, I prefer to
    a. look at the map.
    b. call or ask for directions.
    c. drive around the area until I recognize familiar landmarks.

14. When cooking, I often
    a. look for new recipes.
    b. talk to others to get new ideas.
    c. just put things together and it generally comes out okay.

15. When assembling a new toy or piece of furniture, I usually
    a. read the instructions first.
    b. talk myself through each step.
    c. start putting it together and read the directions if I get stuck.

16. When solving a problem, it is more useful to
    a. read a bestselling book on the topic.
    b. talk over the options with a trusted friend.
    c. do something about it.

17. Which statement do you like the best?
    a. A picture is worth a thousand words.
    b. Talk to me and I can understand.
    c. Just do it.

18. When I was a child, my mother said I
    a. spent a lot of time reading, taking photos, or drawing.
    b. had lots of friends and was always talking to someone on the phone.
    c. was always taking things apart to see how they worked.

Score your quiz:

Number of A answers	_____	Visual Learner
Number of B answers	_____	Auditory Learner
Number of C answers	_____	Kinesthetic/Tactile Learner

What did you discover as a result of taking this quiz?

Learning Style Applications

Name _____ Date _____

How would you use the knowledge of your learning style to deal with the following college situations? Your instructor may use this exercise for a group activity and class discussion.

1. You have just been assigned a 10-page term paper.

2. You have to study for a challenging math test.

3. You have to write up a lab report for a biology class. It includes drawings of a frog you have dissected.

4. You are taking a required course for your major and it is taught by only one professor. You dislike this professor.

5. You are taking a business class and have been assigned a group project to design a small business. It is worth 50 percent of your grade.

6. You have signed up for an economics course and find it difficult to stay awake during the lecture.

7. You signed up for a philosophy course to meet a humanities requirement. The vocabulary in this course is unfamiliar.

8. As part of the final exam, you have to prepare a five-minute presentation for your art history class.

Crystallizers and Paralyzers

Name _____ Date _____

Complete the "Describing Your Multiple Intelligences" activity in this chapter before doing this exercise.

Each individual's life history contains **crystallizers** that promote the development of intelligences. Look at your highest scores on the multiple intelligences activity. List your highest scores below. Write down at least two crystallizers you experienced that may have helped you to develop these intelligences. For example, you may have been praised for your athletic skills and developed your bodily-kinesthetic intelligence.

My highest scores:

Crystallizers:

Each individual's life history also contains **paralyzers** that inhibit the development of intelligences. Look at your lowest scores on the multiple intelligences activity. Write down two paralyzers that may have discouraged you from developing this intelligence. For example, you may have been corrected many times during your piano lessons and given up learning the piano. Paralyzers often involve shame, guilt, fear, or anger.

My lowest scores:

Paralyzers:

How can you overcome some of your paralyzers if they are interfering with your success?

Are there some scores that you need to improve to accomplish your career and educational goals?

Based on the above analysis, write a discovery statement about what you have learned. I discovered that I . . . .

CHAPTER 4

Managing Time and Money

Learning Objectives

Read to answer these key questions:

- What are my lifetime goals?

- How can I manage my time to accomplish my goals?

- How much time do I need for study and work?

- How can I make an effective schedule?

- What are some time management tricks?

- How can I deal with procrastination?

- How can I manage my money to accomplish my financial goals?

- What are some ways to save money?

- How can I pay for my education?

- How can I use priorities to manage my time?

Success in college requires that you manage both time and money. You will need time to study and money to pay for your education. The first step in managing time and money is to think about the goals that you wish to accomplish in your life. Having goals that are important to you provides a reason and motivation for managing time and money. This chapter provides some useful techniques for managing time and money so that you can accomplish the goals you have set for yourself.

What Are My Lifetime Goals?

Setting goals helps you to establish what is important and provides direction for your life. Goals help you to focus your energy on what you want to accomplish. Goals are a promise to yourself to improve your life. Setting goals can help you turn your dreams into reality. Steven Scott, in his book *A Millionaire's Notebook*, lays out five steps in this process:

1. Dream or visualize.

2. Convert the dream into goals.

3. Convert your goals into tasks.

4. Convert your task into steps.

5. Take your first step, and then the next.[1]

As you begin to think about your personal goals in life, make your goals specific and concrete. Rather than saying, "I want to be rich," make your goal something that you can break into specific steps. You might want to start learning about money management or begin a savings plan. Rather than setting a goal for happiness, think about what brings you happiness. If you want to live a long and healthy life, think about the health habits that will help you to accomplish your goal. You will need to break your goals down into specific tasks to be able to accomplish them.

© 2014, winui. Used under license with Shutterstock, Inc.

Here are some criteria for successful goal setting:

1. **Is it achievable?** Do you have the skills, abilities, and resources to accomplish this goal? If not, are you willing to spend the time to develop the skills, abilities, and resources needed to achieve this goal?

2. **Is it realistic?** Do you believe you can achieve it? Are you positive and optimistic about this goal?

3. **Is it specific and measurable?** Can it be counted or observed? The most common goal mentioned by students is happiness in life. What is happiness, and how will you know when you have achieved it? Is happiness a career you enjoy, owning your own home, or a travel destination?

4. **Do you want to do it?** Is this a goal you are choosing because it gives you personal satisfaction, rather than meeting a requirement or an expectation of someone else?

5. **Are you motivated to achieve it?** What are your rewards for achieving it?

6. **Does the goal match your values?** Is it important to you?

7. **What steps do you need to take to begin?** Are you willing to take action to start working on it?

8. **When will you finish this goal?** Set a date to accomplish your goal.

> "A goal is a dream with a deadline."
>
> Napoleon Hill

Journal Entry #1

Write a paragraph about your lifetime goals. Use any of these questions to guide your thinking:

- What is your career goal? If you do not know what your career goal is, describe your preferred work environment. Would your ideal career require a college degree?

- What are your family goals? Are you interested in marriage and family? What would be your important family values?

- What are your social goals (friends, community, and recreation)?

- When you are older and look back on your life, what are the three most important life goals that you want to have accomplished?

A Goal or a Fantasy?

One of the best questions ever asked in my class was, "What is the difference between a goal and a fantasy?" As you look at your list of lifetime goals, are some of these items goals or fantasies? Think about this question as you read the following scenario:

When Linda was a college student, she was walking through the parking lot, noticed a beautiful red sports car, and decided that it would become a lifetime goal for her to own a similar car one day. However, with college expenses and her part-time job, it was not possible to buy the car. She would have to be content with the used car that her dad had given her so that she could drive to college. Years passed by, and Linda now has a good job, a home, and a family. She is reading a magazine and sees a picture of a similar red sports car. She cuts out this picture and tapes it to the refrigerator. After it has been on the refrigerator for several months, her children ask her why the picture is on the refrigerator. Linda replies, "I just like to dream about owning this car." One day, as Linda is driving past a car dealership, she sees the red sports car on display and stops in for a test drive. To her surprise, she decides that she does not like driving the car. It doesn't fit her lifestyle, either. She enjoys outdoor activities that would require a larger car. Buying a second car would be costly and reduce the amount of money that the family could spend on vacations. She decides that vacations are more important than owning the sports car. Linda goes home and removes the picture of the red sports car from the refrigerator.

© 2014, Natursports. Used under license with Shutterstock, Inc.

There are many differences between a goal and a fantasy. A fantasy is a dream that may or may not become a reality. A goal is something that we actually plan to achieve. Sometimes we begin with a fantasy and later it becomes a goal. A fantasy can become a goal if steps are taken to achieve it. In the preceding example, the sports car is a fantasy until Linda actually takes the car for a test drive. After driving the car, she decides that she really does not want it. The fantasy is sometimes better than the reality. Goals and fantasies change over a lifetime. We set goals, try them out, and change them as we grow and mature and find out what is most important in life. Knowing what we think is important, and what we value most, helps us make good decisions about lifetime goals.

What is the difference between a goal and a fantasy? A goal is something that requires action. Ask yourself if you are willing to take action on the goals you have set for yourself. Begin to take action by thinking about the steps needed to accomplish the goal. Then take the first step and continue. Change your goals if they are no longer important to you.

Journal Entry #2

Write a paragraph about how you will accomplish one of your important lifetime goals. Start your paragraph by stating an important goal from the previous journal entry. What is the first step in accomplishing this goal? Next, list some additional steps needed to accomplish it. How can you motivate yourself to begin taking these steps?

For example:

One of my important lifetime goals is _____. The first step in accomplishing this goal is . . . Some additional steps are . . . I can motivate myself to accomplish this goal by . . .

The ABCs of Time Management

Using the **ABCs of time management** is a way of thinking about priorities. Priorities are what you think is important. An **A priority** is a task that relates to your lifetime goal. For example, if my goal is to earn a college degree, studying becomes an A priority. This activity would become one of the most important tasks that I could accomplish today. If my goal is to be healthy, an A priority would be to exercise and plan a healthy diet. If my goal is to have a good family life, an A priority would be to spend time with family members. Knowing about your lifetime goals and spending time on those items that are most important to you will help you to accomplish the goals that you have set for yourself. If you do not spend time on your goals, you may want to look at them again and decide which ones are fantasies that you do not really value or want to accomplish.

A **B priority** is an activity that you have to do, but that is not directly related to your lifetime goal. Examples of B priorities might be getting out of bed, taking a shower, buying groceries, paying bills, or getting gas for the car. These activities are less important, but still are necessary for survival. If I do not put gas in the car, I cannot even get to school or work. If I do not pay the bills, I will soon have financial difficulties. While we often cannot postpone these activities in order to accomplish lifetime goals, we can learn efficient time management techniques to accomplish these tasks quickly.

A **C priority** is something that I can postpone until tomorrow with no harmful effect. For example, I could wait until tomorrow or another day to wash my car, do the laundry, buy groceries, or organize my desk. As these items are postponed, however, they can move up the list to a B priority. If I cannot see out of my car window or have no clean clothes to wear, it is time to move these tasks up on my list of priorities.

Have you ever been a victim of "**C fever**"? This is an illness in which we do the C activities first and do not get around to doing the A activities that are connected to lifetime goals. Tasks required to accomplish lifetime goals are often ones that are more difficult, challenge our abilities, and take some time to accomplish. These tasks are often more difficult than the B or C activities. The C activities can fill our time and exhaust the energy we need to accomplish the A activities. An example of C fever is the student who cleans the desk or organizes the CD collection instead of studying. C fever is doing the endless tasks that keep us from accomplishing goals that are really important to us. Why do we fall victim to C fever? C activities are often easy to do and give us a sense of accomplishment. We can see immediate progress without too much effort. I can wash my car and get a sense of accomplishment and satisfaction in my shiny clean car. The task is easy and does not challenge my intellectual capabilities.

© 2014, iQoncept. Used under license with Shutterstock, Inc.

Setting Priorities

To see how the ABCs of time management work, read the profile of Justin, a typical college student, below.

Justin is a 19-year-old college student who plans to major in physical therapy. He is athletic and values his good health. He cares about people and likes helping others. He has a part-time job working as an assistant in the gym, where he monitors proper use of the weightlifting machines. Justin is also a member of the soccer team and practices with the team every afternoon.

Here is a list of activities that Justin would like to do today. Label each task as follows:

A if it relates to Justin's lifetime goals

B if it is something necessary to do

C if it is something that could be done tomorrow or later

_____ Get up, shower, get dressed	_____ Study for biology test that is tomorrow
_____ Eat breakfast	_____ Meet friends for pizza at lunch
_____ Go to work	_____ Call girlfriend
_____ Go to class	_____ Eat dinner
_____ Visit with friends between classes	_____ Unpack gear from weekend camping trip
_____ Buy a new battery for his watch	_____ Watch football game on TV
_____ Go shopping for new gym shoes	_____ Play video games
_____ Attend soccer practice	_____ Do math homework
_____ Do weightlifting exercises	

While Justin is the only one who can decide how to spend his time, he can take some steps toward accomplishing his lifetime goal of being healthy by eating properly, exercising, and going to soccer practice. He can become a physical therapist by studying for the biology test and doing his math homework. He can gain valuable experience related to physical therapy by working in the gym. He cares about people and likes to maintain good relationships with others. Any tasks related to these goals are high-priority A activities.

What other activities are necessary B activities? He certainly needs to get up, shower, and get dressed. What are the C activities that could be postponed until tomorrow or later? Again, Justin needs to decide. Maybe he could postpone shopping for a new watch battery and gym shoes until the weekend. He would have to decide how much time to spend visiting with friends, watching TV, or playing video games. Since he likes these activities, he could use them as rewards for studying for the biology test and doing his math homework.

How to Estimate Study and Work Time

Students are often surprised at the amount of time necessary for study to be successful in college. A general rule is that you need to study two hours for every hour spent in a college class. A typical weekly schedule of a full-time student would look like this:

Typical College Schedule

> 15 hours of attending class
> +30 hours of reading, studying, and preparation
> 45 hours total

A full-time job involves working 40 hours a week. A full-time college student spends 45 hours or more attending classes and studying. Some students will need more than 45 hours a week if they are taking lab classes, need help with study and learning skills, or are taking a heavy course load.

Some students try to work full-time and go to school full-time. While some are successful, this schedule is extremely difficult.

The Nearly Impossible Schedule

> 15 hours attending class
> 30 hours studying
> +40 hours working
> 85 hours total

This schedule is the equivalent of having two full-time jobs! Working full-time makes it very difficult to find the time necessary to study for classes. Lack of study causes students to do poorly on exams and to doubt their abilities. Such a schedule causes stress and fatigue that make studying difficult. Increased stress can also lead to problems with personal relationships and emotional problems. These are all things that lead to dropping out of college.

Many students today work and go to college. Working during college can provide some valuable experience that will help you to find a job when you finish college. Working can teach you to manage your time efficiently and give you a feeling of independence and control over your own future. Many people need to work to pay for their education. A general guideline is to work no more than 20 hours a week if you plan to attend college full-time. Here is a workable schedule.

Part-Time Work Schedule

> 12 hours attending class
> 24 hours studying
> +20 hours working
> 56 hours total

A commitment of 56 hours a week is like having a full-time job and a part-time job. While this schedule takes extra energy and commitment, many students are successful with it. Notice that the course load is reduced to 12 hours. This schedule involves taking one less class per semester. The class missed can be made up in summer school, or the time needed to graduate can be extended. Many students take five years to earn the bachelor's degree because they work part-time. It is better to take longer to graduate than to drop out of college or to give up because of frustration. If you must work full-time, consider reducing your course load to one or two courses. You will gradually reach your goal of a college degree.

> "The key is not to prioritize what's on the schedule, but to schedule your priorities."
> Stephen Covey

> "When you do the things you have to do when you have to do them, the day will come when you can do the things you want to do when you want to do them."
> Zig Ziglar

Part-Time Student Schedule

     6 hours attending class
    12 hours studying
  +40 hours working
    58 hours total

Add up the number of hours you are attending classes, double this figure for study time, and add to it your work time, as in the above examples. How many hours of commitment do you have? Can you be successful with your current level of commitment to school, work, and study?

To begin managing your schedule, use the weekly calendar located at the end of this chapter to write in your scheduled activities such as work, class times, and athletics.

Schedule Your Success

If you have not used a schedule in the past, consider trying a schedule for a couple of weeks to see if it is helpful in completing tasks and working toward your lifetime goals. There are several advantages to using a schedule:

- It gets you started on your work.
- It helps you avoid procrastination.
- It relieves pressure because you have things under control.
- It frees the mind of details.
- It helps you find time to study.
- It eliminates the panic caused by doing things at the last minute.
- It helps you find time for recreation and exercise.

Once you have made a master schedule that includes classes, work, and other activities, you will see that you have some blanks that provide opportunities for using your time productively. Here are some ideas for making the most of your schedule:

1. Fill in your study times. Use the time immediately before class for previewing and the time immediately after class for reviewing. Remember that you need to study two hours or more for each hour spent in a college class.

© 2014, Caroline Eibl. Used under license with Shutterstock, Inc.

2. Break large projects such as a term paper or studying for a test into small tasks and begin early. Double your time estimates for completion of the project. Larger projects often take longer than you think. If you finish early, use the extra time for something fun.

3. Use the daylight hours when you are most alert for studying. It may take you longer to study if you wait until late in the day when you're tired.

4. Think about your day and see if you can determine when you are most alert and awake. Prime time differs with individuals, but it is generally earlier in the day. Use the prime time when you are most alert to accomplish your most challenging tasks. For example, do your math homework during prime time. Wash your clothes during nonprime time, when you are likely to be less alert.

5. Set priorities. Make sure you include activities related to your lifetime goals.

6. Allow time for sleep and meals. It is easier to study if you are well rested and have good eating habits.

7. Schedule your time in manageable blocks of an hour or two. Having every moment scheduled leads to frustration when plans change.

8. Leave some time unscheduled to use as a shock absorber. You will need unscheduled time to relax and to deal with unexpected events.

9. Leave time for recreation, exercise, and fun.

Return to the schedule at the end of this chapter. After you have written in classes, work times, and other scheduled activities, use the scheduling ideas listed earlier to write in your study times and other activities related to your lifetime goals. Leave some unscheduled time to provide flexibility in the schedule.

> "The only thing even in this world is the number of hours in a day. The difference in winning or losing is what you do with these hours."
>
> Woody Hayes

If You Dislike Schedules

Some personality types like more freedom and do not like the structure that a schedule provides. There are alternatives for those who do not like to use a schedule. Here are some additional ideas.

© 2014, iQoncept. Used under license with Shutterstock, Inc.

1. A simple and fast way to organize your time is to use a to-do list. Take an index card or small piece of paper and simply write a list of what you need to do during the day. You can prioritize the list by putting an A or star by the most important items. Cross items off the list as you accomplish them. A list helps you focus on what is important and serves as a reminder not to forget certain tasks.

2. Another idea is to use monthly or yearly calendars to write down important events, tasks, and deadlines. Use these calendars to note the first day of school, when important assignments are due, vacations, and final exams. Place the calendars in a place where they are easily seen.

3. Alan Lakein, who wrote a book titled *How to Get Control of Your Time and Your Life,* suggests a simple question to keep you on track.[2] Lakein's question is, "What is the best use of my time right now?" This question works well if you keep in mind your goals and priorities.

4. Use reminders and sticky notes to keep on track and to remind yourself of what needs to be done each day. Place the notes in a place where you will see them, such as your computer, the bathroom mirror, or the dashboard of your car.

5. Some families use their refrigerators as time management devices. Use the refrigerator to post your calendars, reminders, goals, tasks, and to-do lists. You will see these reminders every time you open the refrigerator.

6. Invent your own unique ideas for managing time. Anything will work if it helps to accomplish your goals.

Manage Your Time with a Web Application

There are thousands of new web applications available to organize your life. You can use a web application on your phone, laptop, computer, or other mobile device to:

- Create a to-do list or schedule.
- Send reminders when assignments are due.
- Organize your calendar and plan your tasks.
- Organize your study time and plan assignments.
- Avoid procrastination.
- Create a virtual assistant to keep you organized.

QUIZ

Time Management, Part I

Test what you have learned by selecting the correct answers to the following questions.

1. The most important difference between a goal and a fantasy is

   a. imagination.
   b. procrastination.
   c. action.

2. An A priority is

   a. related to your lifetime goals.
   b. something important.
   c. something you have to do.

3. A general rule for college success is that you must spend ___ hours studying for every hour spent in a college class.

   a. one
   b. four
   c. two

4. For a workable study schedule,

   a. fill in all the blank time slots.
   b. leave some unscheduled time to deal with the unexpected.
   c. plan to study late at night.

5. To complete a large project such as a term paper,

   a. break the project into small tasks and begin early.
   b. schedule large blocks of time the day before the paper is due.
   c. leave time for exercise, recreation, and fun before beginning on the project.

How did you do on the quiz? Check your answers: 1. c, 2. a, 3. c, 4. b, 5. a

---

Time Management Tricks

Life is full of demands for work, study, family, friends, and recreation. Time management tricks can help you get started on the important tasks and make the most of your time. Try the following techniques when you are feeling frustrated and overwhelmed.

Divide and Conquer

When large tasks seem overwhelming, think of the small tasks needed to complete the project and start on the first step. For example, suppose you have to write a term paper. You have to take out a paper and pencil, log onto your computer, brainstorm some ideas, go to the library to find information, think about your main ideas, and write the first sentence. Each of these steps is manageable. It's looking at the entire project that can be intimidating.

I once set out hiking on a mountain trail. When I got to the top of the mountain and looked down, I enjoyed a spectacular view and was amazed at how high I had climbed. If I had thought about how high the mountain was, I might not have attempted the hike. I climbed the mountain by taking it one step at a time. That's the secret to completing any large project: break it into small, manageable parts, then take the first step and keep going.

Learning a small part at a time is also easy and helps with motivation for learning. While in college, carry around some material that you need to study. Take advantage of five or ten minutes of time to study a small part of your material. In this way you make good use of your time and enhance memory by using distributed practice. Don't wait until you have large blocks of uninterrupted study time to begin your studies. You may not have the luxury of large blocks of time, or you may want to spend that time in other ways.

Time Management Tricks
• Divide and conquer
• Do the first small step
• 80/20 rule
• Aim for excellence, not perfection
• Make learning fun
• Take a break
• Study in the library
• Learn to say no

Do the First Small Step

The most difficult step in completing any project is the first step. If you have a challenging project to do, think of a small first step and complete that small step. Make the first step something that you can accomplish easily and in a short amount of time. Give yourself permission to stop after the first step. However, you may find that you are motivated to continue with the project. If you have a term paper to write, think about some small step you can take to get started. Log onto your computer and look at the blank screen. Start writing some ideas. Type the topic into a computer search engine and see what information is available. Go to the library and see what is available on your topic. If you can find some interesting ideas, you can motivate yourself to begin the project. Once you have started the project, it is easier to continue.

© 2014, iQoncept. Used under license with Shutterstock, Inc.

The 80/20 Rule

Alan Lakein is noted for many useful time management techniques. One that I have used over the years is the 80/20 rule. Lakein says, "If all items are arranged in order of value, 80 percent of the value would come from only 20 percent of the items, while the remaining 20 percent of the value would come from 80 percent of the items."[3] For example, if you have a list of ten items to do, two of the items on the list are more important than the others. If you were to do only the two most important items, you would have accomplished 80 percent of the value. If you are short on time, see if you can choose the 20 percent of the tasks that are the most valuable. Lakein noted that the 80/20 rule applies to many situations in life:

- 80 percent of file usage is in 20 percent of the files.
- 80 percent of dinners repeat 20 percent of the recipes.
- 80 percent of the washing is done on the 20 percent of the clothes worn most frequently.
- 80 percent of the dirt is on the 20 percent of the floor used most often.

Think about how the 80/20 rule applies in your life. It is another way of thinking about priorities and figuring out which of the tasks are C priorities. This prioritizing is especially important if you are short on time. The 80/20 rule helps you to focus on what is most important.

Aim for Excellence, Not Perfection

Are you satisfied with your work only if it is done perfectly? Do you put off a project because you cannot do it perfectly? Aiming for perfection in all tasks causes anxiety and procrastination. There are times when perfection is not necessary. Dave Ellis calls this time management technique "It Ain't No Piano."[4] If a construction worker bends a nail in the framing of a house, it does not matter. The construction worker simply puts in another nail. After all, "it ain't no piano." It is another matter if you are building a fine cabinet or finishing a piano. Perfection is more important in these circumstances. We need to ask: Is the task important enough to invest the time needed for perfection? A final term paper needs to be as perfect as we can make it. A rough draft is like the frame of a house that does not need to be perfect.

In aiming for excellence rather than perfection, challenge yourself to use perspective to see the big picture. How important is the project and how perfect does it need to be? Could your time be better invested accomplishing other tasks? This technique requires flexibility and the ability to change with different situations. Do not give up if you cannot complete a project perfectly. Do the best that you can in the time available. In some situations, if life is too hectic, you may need to settle for completing the project and getting it in on time rather than doing it perfectly. With this idea in mind, you may be able to relax and still achieve excellence.

Make Learning Fun by Finding a Reward

Time management is not about restriction, self-control, and deprivation. If it is done correctly, time can be managed to get more out of life and to have fun while doing it. Remember that behavior is likely to increase if followed by a reward. Think about activities that you find rewarding. In our time management example with Justin who wants to be a physical therapist, he could use many tasks as rewards for completing his studies. He could meet friends for pizza, call his girlfriend, play video games, or watch TV. The key idea is to do the studying first and then reward the behavior. Maybe Justin will not be able to do all of the activities we have mentioned as possible rewards, but he could choose what he enjoys most.

© 2014, carmen2011. Used under license with Shutterstock, Inc.

Studying first and then rewarding yourself leads to peace of mind and the ability to focus on tasks at hand. While Justin is out having pizza with his friends, he does not have to worry about work that he has not done. While Justin is studying, he does not have to feel that he is being deprived of having pizza with friends. In this way, he can focus on studying while he is studying and focus on having a good time while relaxing with his friends. It is not a good idea to think about having pizza with friends while studying or to think about studying while having pizza with friends. When you work, focus on your work and get it done. When you play, enjoy playing without having to think about work.

Take a Break

If you are overwhelmed with the task at hand, sometimes it is best to just take a break. If you're stuck on a computer program or a math problem, take a break and do something else. As a general rule, take a break of 10 minutes for each hour of study. During the break, do something totally different. It is a good idea to get up and move around. Get up and pet your cat or dog, observe your goldfish, or shoot a few baskets. If time is really at a premium, use your break time to accomplish other important tasks. Put your clothes in the dryer, empty the dishwasher, or pay a bill.

Study in the Library

If you are having difficulty with studying, try studying at school in the library. Libraries are designed for studying, and other people are studying there as well. It is hard to do something else in the library without annoying the librarian or other students. If you can complete your studying at school, you can go home and relax. This may be especially important if family, friends, or roommates at home easily distract you.

Learn to Say No Sometimes

Learn to say no to tasks that you do not have time to do. Follow your statement with the reasons for saying no: you are going to college and need time to study. Most people will understand this answer and respect it. You may need to say no to yourself as well. Maybe you cannot go out on Wednesday night if you have a class early on Thursday morning. Maybe the best use of your time right now is to turn off the TV or get off the Internet and study for tomorrow's test. You are investing your time in your future.

Dealing with Time Bandits

Time bandits are the many things that keep us from spending time on the things we think are important. Another word for a time bandit is a time waster. In college, it is tempting to do many things other than studying. We are all victims of different kinds of bandits.

© 2014, NorGal. Used under license with Shutterstock, Inc.

ACTIVITY

Put a checkmark next to the items that waste your time. Add your own personal time wasters at the end of the list.

_____ TV	_____ Phone	_____ Sleeping in
_____ Other electronic devices	_____ Household chores	_____ Shopping
_____ Daydreaming	_____ Roommates	_____ Being easily distracted
_____ Social networking	_____ Video games	_____ Studying at a bad time
_____ Saying yes when you mean no	_____ Partying	_____ Reading magazines
_____ Friends	_____ Children	_____ Studying in a distracting place
_____ Internet	_____ iPod	
_____ Social time	_____ Waiting time	_____ Movies
_____ Family	_____ Girlfriend, boyfriend, spouse	_____ Commuting time (travel)

List some of your personal time bandits here.

_____

_____

Here are some ideas for keeping time bandits under control:

- **Schedule time for other people.** Friends and family are important, so we do not want to get rid of them! Discuss your goal of a college education with your friends and family. People who care about you will respect your goals. You may need to use a Do Not Disturb sign at times. If you are a parent, remember that you are a role model for your children. If they see you studying, they are more likely to value their own education. Plan to spend quality time with your children and the people who are important to you. Make sure they understand that you care about them.

- **Remember the rewards.** Many of the time bandits listed above make good rewards for completing your work. Put the time bandits to work for you by studying first and then enjoying a reward. Enjoy the TV, Internet, iPod, video games, or phone conversations after you have finished your studies. Aim for a balance of work, study, and leisure time.

- **Use your prime time wisely.** Prime time is when you are most awake and alert. Use this time for studying. Use non-prime time for the time bandits. When you are tired, do household chores and shopping. If you have little time for household chores, you might find faster ways to do them. If you don't have time for shopping, you will notice that you spend less and have a better chance of following your budget.

- **Remind yourself about your priorities.** When time bandits attack, remind yourself of why you are in college. Think about your personal goals for the future. Remember that college is not forever. By doing well in college, you will finish in the shortest time possible.

- **Use a schedule.** Using a schedule or a to-do list is helpful in keeping you on track. Make sure you have some slack time in your schedule to handle unexpected phone calls and deal with the unplanned events that happen in life. If you cannot stick to your schedule, just get back on track as soon as you can.

Journal Entry #3

Write a paragraph about how you will manage your time to accomplish your goal of a college education. Use any of these questions to guide your thinking:

- What are your priorities?
- How will you balance school, work, and family/friends?
- What are some time management tools you plan to use?
- How can you deal with time bandits?

Dealing with Procrastination

Procrastination means putting off things until later. We all use delaying tactics at times. Procrastination that is habitual, however, can be self-destructive. Understanding some possible reasons for procrastination can help you use time more effectively and be more successful in accomplishing goals.

Why Do We Procrastinate?

There are many psychological reasons for procrastinating. Just becoming aware of these may help you deal with procrastination. If you have serious difficulty managing your time for psychological reasons, visit the counseling center at your college or university. Do you recognize any of these reasons for procrastination in yourself or others?

© 2014, bloomua. Used under license with Shutterstock, Inc.

- **Fear of failure.** Sometimes we procrastinate because we are afraid of failing. We see our performance as related to how much ability we have and how worthwhile we are as human beings. We may procrastinate in our college studies because of doubts about our ability to do the work. Success, however, comes from trying and learning from mistakes. There is a popular saying: falling down is not failure, but failing to get up or not even trying is failure.

- **Fear of success.** Most students are surprised to find out that one of the reasons for procrastination is fear of success. Success in college means moving on with your life, getting a job, leaving a familiar situation, accepting increased responsibility, and sometimes leaving friends behind. None of these tasks is easy. An example of fear of success is not taking the last step required to be successful. Students sometimes do not take the last class needed to graduate. Some good students do not show up for the final exam or do not turn in a major project. If you ever find yourself procrastinating on an important last step, ask yourself if you are afraid of success and what lies ahead in your future.

- **Perfectionism.** Some people who procrastinate do not realize that they are perfectionists. Perfectionists expect more from themselves than is realistic and more than others expect of themselves. There is often no other choice than to procrastinate because perfectionism is usually unattainable. Perfectionism generates anxiety that further hinders performance. Perfectionists need to understand that perfection is seldom possible. They need to set time limits on projects and do their best within those time limits.

- **Need for excitement.** Some students can only be motivated by waiting until the last minute to begin a project. These students are excited and motivated by playing a game of "Beat the Clock." They like living on the edge and the adrenaline rush of responding to a crisis. Playing this game provides motivation, but it does not leave enough time to achieve the best results. Inevitably, things happen at the last minute to make the game even more exciting and dangerous: the printer breaks, the computer crashes, the student gets ill, the car breaks down, or the dog eats the homework. These students need to start projects earlier to improve their chances of success. It is best to seek excitement elsewhere, in sports or other competitive activities.

- **Excellence without effort.** In this scenario, students believe that they are truly outstanding and can achieve success without effort. These students think that they can go to college without attending classes or reading the text. They believe that they can pass the test without studying. They often do not succeed in college the first semester, which puts them at risk of dropping out of school. They often return to college later and improve their performance by putting in the effort required.

- **Loss of control.** Some students fear loss of control over their lives and procrastinate to gain control. An example is students who attend college because others (such as parents) want them to attend. Procrastination becomes a way of gaining control over the situation by saying, "You can't make me do this." They attend college but accomplish nothing. Parents can support and encourage education, but students need to choose their own goals in life and attend college because it is an important personal goal.

Tips for Dealing with Procrastination

When you find yourself procrastinating on a certain task, think about the consequences. Will the procrastination lead to failing an exam or getting a low grade? Think about the rewards of doing the task. If you do well, you can take pride in yourself and celebrate your success. How will you feel when the task is completed? Will you be able to enjoy your leisure time without guilt about not doing your work? How does the task help you to achieve your lifetime goals?

Maybe the procrastination is a warning sign that you need to reconsider lifetime goals and change them to better suit your needs.

Procrastination Scenario

George is a college student who is on academic probation for having low grades. He is required to make a plan for improving his grades in order to remain in college. George tells the counselor that he is making poor grades because of his procrastination. He is an accounting major and puts off doing homework because he dislikes it and does not find it interesting. The counselor asks George why he had chosen accounting as a major. He replies that accounting is a major that is in demand and has a good salary. The counselor suggests that George consider a major that he would enjoy more. After some consideration, George changes his major to psychology. He becomes more interested in college studies and is able to raise his grades to stay in college.

Most of the time, you will reap benefits by avoiding procrastination and completing the task at hand. Jane Burka and Lenora Yuen suggest the following steps to deal with procrastination:

1. Select a goal.

2. Visualize your progress.

3. Be careful not to sabotage yourself.

4. Stick to a time limit.

5. Don't wait until you feel like it.

6. Follow through. Watch out for excuses and focus on one step at a time.

7. Reward yourself after you have made some progress.

8. Be flexible about your goal.

9. Remember that it does not have to be perfect.[5]

© 2014, iQoncept. Used under license with Shutterstock, Inc.

Time Management, Part II

Test what you have learned by selecting the correct answers to the following questions.

1. To get started on a challenging project,

   a. think of a small first step and complete it.
   b. wait until you have plenty of time to begin.
   c. wait until you are well rested and relaxed.

2. If you are completing a to-do list of 10 items, the 80/20 rule states that

   a. 80% of the value comes from completing most of the items on the list.
   b. 80% of the value comes from completing two of the most important items.
   c. 80% of the value comes from completing half of the items on the list.

3. It is suggested that students aim for

   a. perfection.
   b. excellence.
   c. passing.

4. Sometimes students procrastinate because of

   a. fear of failure.
   b. fear of success.
   c. all of the above.

5. Playing the game "Beat the Clock" when doing a term paper results in

   a. increased motivation and success.
   b. greater excitement and quality work.
   c. increased motivation and risk.

How did you do on the quiz? Check your answers: 1. a, 2. b, 3. b, 4. c, 5. c

Journal Entry #4

Write a paragraph about how you will avoid procrastination. Consider these ideas when thinking about procrastination: fear of failure, fear of success, perfectionism, need for excitement, excellence without effort, and loss of control. How will you complete your assignments on time?

Managing Your Money

To be successful in college and in life, you will need to manage not only time, but money. One of the top reasons that students drop out of college is that they cannot pay for their education or that they have to work so much that they do not have time for school. Take a look at your lifetime goals. Most students have a goal related to money, such as becoming financially secure or becoming wealthy. If financial security or wealth is one of your goals, you will need to begin to take some action to accomplish that goal. If you don't take action on a goal, it is merely a fantasy.

© 2014, ARENA Creative. Used under license with Shutterstock, Inc.

How to Become a Millionaire

Save regularly. Frances Leonard, author of *Time Is Money*, cites some statistics on how much money you need to save to become a millionaire.[6] You can retire with a million dollars by age 68 by saving the following amounts of money at various ages. These figures assume a 10 percent return on your investment.

> At age 22, save $87 per month
> At age 26, save $130 per month
> At age 30, save $194 per month
> At age 35, save $324 a month

Notice that the younger you start saving, the less money is required to reach the million-dollar goal. (And keep in mind that even a million dollars may not be enough money to save for retirement.) How can you start saving money when you are a student struggling to pay for college? The answer is to practice money management techniques and to begin a savings habit, even if the money you save is a small amount to buy your books for next semester. When you get that first good job, save 10 percent of the money. If you are serious about becoming financially secure, learn about investments such as real estate, stocks and bonds, and mutual funds. Learning how to save and invest your money can pay big dividends in the future.

Think thrifty. Money management begins with looking at your attitude toward money. Pay attention to how you spend your money so that you can accomplish your financial goals such as getting a college education, buying a house or car, or saving for the future. The following example shows how one woman accomplished her financial goals through being thrifty. Amy Dacyczyn, author of *The Tightwad Gazette*, says, "A lot of people get a thrill out of buying things. Frugal people get a rush from the very act of saving. Saving can actually be fun—we think of it almost as a sport."[7] She noticed that people were working harder and harder for less and less. Amy Dacyczyn had the goals of marriage, children, and a New England farmhouse to live in. She wanted to stay home and take care of her six children instead of working. In seven years, she was able to accomplish her goals with her husband's income of $30,000 a year. During this time, she saved $49,000 for the down payment on a rural farmhouse costing $125,000. She also paid cash for $38,000 worth of car, appliance, and furniture purchases while staying at home with her children. How did she do this? She says that she just started paying attention to how she was spending her money.

To save money, Amy Dacyczyn made breakfast from scratch. She made oatmeal, pancakes, and muffins instead of purchasing breakfast cereals. She saved $440 a year in this way. She purchased the family clothing at yard sales. She thought of so many ideas to save money that she began publishing *The Tightwad Gazette* to share her money-saving ideas with others. At $12 per subscription, she grosses a million dollars a year!

Challenge yourself to pay attention to how you spend your money, and make a goal of being thrifty in order to accomplish your financial goals. With good money management, you can work less and have more time for college and recreational activities.

> **Managing Your Money**
> - Monitor your spending
> - Prepare a budget
> - Beware of credit and interest
> - Watch spending leaks

Budgeting: The Key to Money Management

It is important to control your money, rather than letting your money control you. One of the most important things that you can do to manage your money and begin saving is to use a budget. A budget helps you become aware of how you spend your money and will help you make a plan for how you would like to spend your money.

Monitor how you spend your money. The first step in establishing a workable budget is to monitor how you are actually spending your money at the present time. For one month, keep a list of purchases with the date and amount of money spent for each. You can do this on a sheet of paper, on your calendar, on index cards, or on a money management application for your phone. If you write checks for items, include the checks written as part of your money monitor. At the end of the month, group your purchases in categories such as food, gas, entertainment, and credit card payments, and add them up. Doing this will yield some surprising results. For example, you may not be aware of just how much it costs to eat at a fast-food restaurant or to buy lunch or coffee every day.

© 2014, koya979. Used under license with Shutterstock, Inc.

Prepare a budget. One of the best tools for managing your money is a budget. At the end of this chapter, you will find a simple budget sheet that you can use as a college student. After you finish college, update your budget and continue to use it. Follow these three steps to make a budget:

1. Write down your income for the month.
2. List your expenses. Include tuition, books, supplies, rent, telephone, utilities (gas, electric, water, cable TV, internet), car payments, car insurance, car maintenance (oil, repairs), parking fees, food, personal grooming, clothes, entertainment, savings, credit card payments, loan payments, and other bills. Use your money monitor to discover how you are spending your money and include categories that are unique to you.
3. Subtract your total expenses from your total income. You cannot spend more than you have. Make adjustments as needed.

Beware of credit and interest. College students are often tempted to use credit cards to pay for college expenses. This type of borrowing is costly and difficult to repay. It is easy to pull out a plastic credit card and buy items that you need and want. Credit card companies earn a great deal of money from credit cards. Jane Bryant Quinn gives an example of the cost of credit cards.[8] She says that if you owe $3,000 at 18 percent interest and pay the minimum payment of $60 per month, it will take you 30 years and 10 months to get out of debt! Borrowing the $3,000 would cost about $22,320 over this time! If you use a credit card, make sure you can pay it off in one to three months. It is good to have a credit card in order to establish credit and to use in an emergency.

Watch those spending leaks. We all have spending problem areas. Often we spend small amounts of money each day that add up to large spending leaks over time. For example, if you spend $3 on coffee each weekday for a year, this adds up to $780 a year! If you eat lunch out each weekday and spend $8 for lunch, this adds up to $2,080 a year. Here are some common areas for spending leaks:

- Fast food and restaurants
- Entertainment and vacations
- Clothing
- Miscellaneous cash
- Gifts

© 2014, Andrey Armyagov. Used under license with Shutterstock, Inc.

To identify your spending problem areas, write down all of your expenditures for one month. Place a three-by-five card in your wallet or use your phone to monitor your cash expenditures. At the end of the month, organize your expenditures into categories and total them up. Then ask yourself if this is how you want to spend your money.

Need More Money?

You may be tempted to work more hours to balance your budget. Remember that to be a full-time college student, it is recommended that you work no more than 20 hours per week. If you work more than 20 hours per week, you will probably need to decrease your course load. Before increasing your work hours, see if there is a way you can decrease your monthly expenses. Can you make your lunch instead of eating out? Can you get by without a car? Is the item you are purchasing a necessity, or do you just want to have it? These choices are yours.

1. **Check out financial aid.** All students can qualify for some type of financial aid. Visit the Financial Aid Office at your college for assistance. Depending on your income level, you may qualify for one or more of the following forms of aid.

   - **Loans.** A loan must be paid back. The interest rate and terms vary according to your financial need. With some loans, the federal government pays the interest while you are in school.

   - **Grants.** A grant does not need to be repaid. There are both state and federal grants based on need.

   - **Work/study.** You may qualify for a federally subsidized job depending on your financial need. These jobs are often on campus and provide valuable work experience for the future.

   The first step in applying for financial aid is to fill out the Free Application for Federal Student Aid (FAFSA). This form determines your eligibility for financial aid. You can obtain this form from your college's financial aid office or over the Internet at www .fafsa.ed.gov.

   Here are some other financial aid resources that you can obtain from your financial aid office or over the Internet.

   - **Student Guide.** The Student Guide, published by the U.S. Department of Education, describes in detail the kinds of financial aid available and eligibility requirements; it is available over the Internet at http://studentaid.ed.gov/resources.

   - **How to apply for financial aid.** Learn how to apply for federal financial aid and scholarships at www.finaid.org.

2. **Apply for a scholarship.** Applying for a scholarship is like having a part-time job, only the pay is often better, the hours are flexible, and you can be your own boss. For this part-time job, you will need to research scholarship opportunities and fill out applications. There are multitudes of scholarships available, and sometimes no one even applies for them. Some students do not apply for scholarships because they think that high grades and financial need are required. While many scholarships are based on grades and financial need, many are not. Any person or organization can offer a scholarship for any reason they want. For example, scholarships can be based on hobbies, parent's occupation, religious background, military service, and personal interests, to name a few.

   There are several ways to research a scholarship. As a first step, visit the financial aid office on your college campus. This office is staffed with persons knowledgeable about researching and applying for scholarships. Organizations or persons wishing to fund scholarships often contact this office to advertise opportunities.

   You can also research scholarships through your public or college library. Ask the reference librarian for assistance. You can use the Internet to research scholarships as well. Use any search engine such as Google.com and simply type in the keyword scholarships. The following websites index thousands of scholarships:

   - The Federal Student Aid Scholarship site is located at http://studentaid.ed.gov/ types/grants-scholarships/finding-scholarships
   - fastweb.com
   - college-scholarships.com
   - http://www.scholarships.com/
   - collegenet.com/mach25
   - studentscholarshipsearch.com
   - collegeboard.com/paying

© 2014, mangostock. Used under license with Shutterstock, Inc.

To apply for scholarships, start a file of useful material usually included in scholarship applications. You can use this same information to apply for many scholarships.

- Three current letters of recommendation
- A statement of your personal goals
- A statement of your financial need
- Copies of your transcripts
- Copies of any scholarship applications you have filled out

Be aware of scholarship scams. You do not need to pay money to apply for a scholarship. No one can guarantee that you will receive a scholarship. Use your college scholarship office and your own resources to research and apply for scholarships.

The Best Ideas for Becoming Financially Secure

Financial planners provide the following ideas as the best ways to build wealth and independence.[9] If you have financial security as your goal, plan to do the following:

1. **Use a simple budget to track income and expenses.** Do not spend more than you earn.

2. **Have a financial plan.** Include goals such as saving for retirement, purchasing a home, paying for college, or taking vacations.

3. **Save 10 percent of your income.** As a college student, you may not be able to save this much, but plan to do it as soon as you get your first good-paying job. If you cannot save 10 percent, save something to get in the habit of saving. Save to pay for your tuition and books.

4. **Don't take on too much debt.** Be especially careful about credit cards and consumer debt. Credit card companies often visit college campuses and offer high-interest credit cards to students. It is important to have a credit card, but pay off the balance each month. Consider student loans instead of paying college fees by credit card.

5. **Don't procrastinate.** The earlier you take these steps toward financial security, the better.

Tips for Managing Your Money

Keeping these guidelines in mind can help you to manage your money.

- Don't let friends pressure you into spending too much money. If you can't afford something, learn to say no.
- Keep your checking account balanced or use online banking so you will know how much money you have.
- Don't lend money to friends. If your friends cannot manage their money, your loan will not help them.
- Use comparison shopping to find the best prices on the products that you buy.
- Get a part-time job while in college. You will earn money and gain valuable job experience.
- Don't use shopping as a recreational activity. When you visit the mall, you will find things you never knew you needed and will wind up spending more money than intended.
- Make a budget and follow it. This is the best way to achieve your financial goals.

Do What Is Important First

The most important thing you can do to manage time and money is to spend it on what is most important. Manage time and money to help you live the life you want. How can you do this? Author Stephen Covey wrote a book titled *The Seven Habits of Highly Effective People.* One of the habits is "Put first things first." Covey suggests that in time management, the "challenge is not to manage our time but to manage ourselves."[10]

How can you manage yourself? Our first thoughts in answering this question often involve suggestions about willpower, restriction, and self-control. Schedules and budgets are seen as instruments for self-control. It seems that the human spirit resists attempts at control, even when we aim to control ourselves. Often the response to control is rebellion. With time and money management, we may not follow a schedule or budget. A better approach to begin managing yourself is to know your values. What is important in your life? Do you have a clear mental picture of what is important? Can you describe your values and make a list of what is important to you? With your values and goals in mind, you can begin to manage both your time and your money.

When you have given some thought to your values, you can begin to set goals. When you have established goals for your life, you can begin to think in terms of what is most important and establish your priorities. Knowing your values is essential in making decisions about how to invest your time and money. Schedules and budgets are merely tools for helping you accomplish what you have decided is important. Time and money management is not about restriction and control, but about making decisions regarding what is important in your life. If you know what is important, you can find the strength to say no to activities and expenditures that are less important.

As a counselor, I have the pleasure of working with many students who have recently explored and discovered their values and are highly motivated to succeed. They are willing to do what is important first. I recently worked with a young couple who came to enroll in college. They brought their young baby with them. The new father was interested in environmental engineering. He told me that in high school, he never saw a reason for school and did just the minimum needed to get by. He was working as a construction laborer and making a living, but did not see a future in the occupation. He had observed an environmental engineer who worked for the company and decided that was what he wanted for his future. As he looked at his new son, he told me that he needed to have a better future for himself and his family.

He and his wife decided to do what was important first. They were willing to make the sacrifice to attend school and invest the time needed to be successful. The father planned to work during the day and go to school at night. Later, he would go to school full-time and get a part-time job in the evening. His wife was willing to get a part-time job also, and they would share in taking care of the baby. They were willing to manage their money carefully to accomplish their goals. As they left, they added that their son would be going to college as well.

How do you get the energy to work all day, go to school at night, and raise a family? You can't do it by practicing self-control. You find the energy by having a clear idea of what you want in your life and focusing your time and resources on the goal. Finding what you want to do with your life is not easy either. Many times people find what they want to do when some significant event happens in their lives.

Begin to think about what you want out of life. Make a list of your important values and write down your lifetime goals. Don't forget about the people who are important to you, and include them in your priorities. Then you will be able to do what is important first.

> "Fathers send their sons to college either because they went to college or because they didn't."
>
> L. L. Henderson

Journal Entry #5

What is your plan for managing your money? Consider these ideas when thinking about your plan: monitoring how you spend your money, using a budget, applying for financial aid and scholarships, saving money, and spending money wisely.

JOURNAL ENTRIES

Managing Time and Money

Go to http://www.collegesuccess1.com/JournalEntries.htm for Word files of the Journal Entries

Success over the Internet

Visit the *College Success Website* at http://www.collegesuccess1.com/

The *College Success Website* is continually updated with new topics and links to the material presented in this chapter. Topics include:

- Suggestions for time management
- How to overcome procrastination
- How to deal with perfectionism
- Goal setting
- Goal setting in sports
- Goal setting and visualization
- Scholarship websites
- Recognizing scholarship scams
- Financial aid websites

Ask your instructor if you need any assistance in accessing the *College Success Website.*

Notes

1. Steven K. Scott, *A Millionaire's Notebook*, quoted in Rob Gilbert, Editor, *Bits & Pieces*, November 4, 1999, 15.

2. Alan Lakein, *How to Get Control of Your Time and Your Life* (New York: Peter H. Wyden, 1973).

3. Ibid., 70–71.

4. Dave Ellis, *Becoming a Master Student* (Boston: Houghton Mifflin, 1998).

5. Jane Burka and Lenora Yuen, *Procrastination* (Reading, MA: Addison-Wesley, 1983).

6. Frances Leonard, *Time Is Money* (Addison-Wesley), cited in the *San Diego Union Tribune*, October 14, 1995.

7. Amy Dacyczyn, *The Tightwad Gazette II* (Villard Books), cited in the *San Diego Union Tribune*, February 20, 1995.

8. Jane Bryant Quinn, "Money Watch," *Good Housekeeping*, November 1996, 80.

9. Robert Hanley, "Breaking Bad Habits," *San Diego Union Tribune*, September 7, 1992.

10. Stephen R. Covey, *The Seven Habits of Highly Effective People* (New York: Simon and Schuster, 1990), 150.

My Lifetime Goals: Brainstorming Activity

Name _____ Date _____

1. Think about the goals that you would like to accomplish in your life. At the end of your life, you do not want to say, "I wish I would have _____." Set a timer for five minutes and write whatever comes to mind about what you would like to do and accomplish over your lifetime. Include goals in these areas: career, personal relationships, travel, and financial security or any area that is important to you. Write down all your ideas. The goal is to generate as many ideas as possible in five minutes. You can reflect on which ones are most important later. You may want to do this as part of a group activity in your class.

Look over the ideas you wrote above and highlight or underline the goals that are most important to you.

2. Ask yourself what you would like to accomplish in the next five years. Think about where you want to be in college, what you want to do in your career, and what you want to do in your personal life. Set a timer and write whatever comes to mind in five minutes. The goal is to write down as many ideas as possible.

Again, look over the ideas you wrote and highlight or underline the ideas that are most important to you.

3. What goals would you like to accomplish in the next year? What are some steps that you can begin now to accomplish your lifetime goals? Consider work, study, leisure, and social goals. Set your timer for five minutes and write down your goals for the next year.

Review what you wrote and highlight or underline the ideas that are most important to you. When writing your goals, include fun activities as well as taking care of others.

Looking at the items that you have highlighted or underlined, make a list of your lifetime goals using the form that follows. Make sure your goals are specific enough so that you can break them into steps you can achieve.

Name _____ Date _____

Using the ideas that you brainstormed in the previous exercise, make a list of your lifetime goals. Make sure your goals are specific and concrete. Begin with goals that you would like to accomplish over a lifetime. In the second section, think about the goals you can accomplish over the next one to three years.

Long-Term Goals (lifetime goals)

Short-Term Goals (one to three years)

What are some steps you can take now to accomplish intermediate and long-term goals?

Successful Goal Setting

Name _____ Date _____

Look at your list of lifetime goals. Which one is most important? Write the goal here:

Answer these questions about the goal you have listed above.

1. What skills, abilities, and resources do you have to achieve this goal? What skills, abilities, and resources will you need to develop to achieve this goal?

2. Do you believe you can achieve it? Write a brief positive statement about achieving this goal.

3. State your goal in specific terms that can be observed or counted. Rewrite your goal if necessary.

4. Write a brief statement about how this goal will give you personal satisfaction.

5. How will you motivate yourself to achieve this goal?

6. What are your personal values that match this goal?

7. List some steps that you will take to accomplish this goal.

8. When will you finish this goal?

9. What roadblocks will make this goal difficult to achieve?

10. How will you deal with these roadblocks?

Weekly College Schedule

Name _____   Date _____

Copy the following schedule to use in future weeks or design your own schedule. Fill in this schedule and try to follow it for at least one week. First, fill in scheduled commitments (classes, work, activities). Next, fill in the time you need for studying. Put in some tasks related to your lifetime goals. Leave some blank time as a shock absorber to handle unexpected activities.

Time	Monday	Tuesday	Wednesday	Thursday	Friday	Saturday	Sunday
7 A.M.							
8							
9							
10							
11							
Noon							
1 P.M.							
2							
3							
4							
5							
6							
7							
8							
9							
10							
11							

Weekly To-Do Chart

Name _____ Date _____

Using a to-do list is an easy way to remind yourself of important priorities each day. This chart is divided into three areas representing types of tasks that college students need to balance: academic, personal, and social.

Weekly To-Do List

	Monday	Tuesday	Wednesday	Thursday	Friday
Academic					
Personal					
Social					

Study Schedule Analysis

Name _____ Date _____

Before completing this analysis, use the schedule form to create a master schedule. A master schedule blocks out class and work times as well as any regularly scheduled activities. Looking at the remaining time, write in your planned study times. It is recommended that you have two hours of study time for each hour in class. For example, a three-unit class would require six hours of study time. A student with 12 units would require 24 hours of study time. You may need more or fewer hours, depending on your study skills, reading skills, and difficulty of courses.

1. How many units are you enrolled in?

2. How many hours of planned study time do you have?

3. How many hours do you work each week?

4. How many hours do you spend in relaxation/social activities?

5. Do you have time planned for exercise?

6. Do you get enough sleep?

7. What are some of your time bandits (things that take up your time and make it difficult to accomplish your goals)?

Write a few discovery statements about how you use your time.

8. Are you spending enough time to earn the grades you want to achieve? Do you need to spend more time studying to become successful?

9. Does your work schedule allow you enough time to study?

10. How can you deal with your time bandits?

11. How can you use your time more effectively to achieve your goals?

Name _____ Date _____

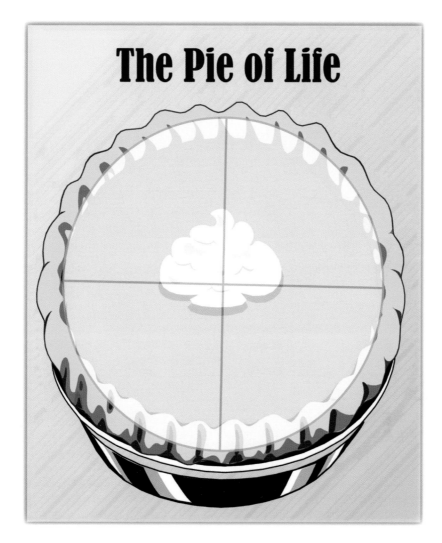

This circle represents 24 hours. Each piece is six hours. Draw a slice of pie to represent how much time you spend on each of these activities in a typical day: sleeping, attending classes, studying, work, family, friends, and other activities.

Thinking about your values is the first step in setting goals. How you spend your time determines whether you will accomplish these goals. Are you using your time to accomplish your goals? Make some intention statements for the future on how you want to spend your time.

I intend to:

The College Student's Tightwad Gazette

Name _____ Date _____

List five ideas for saving money that could be included in a publication called *The College Student's Tightwad Gazette*.

1. _____

2. _____

3. _____

4. _____

5. _____

Get together with other students in the class and come up with five additional ideas that college students can use to save money or increase income.

1. _____

2. _____

3. _____

4. _____

5. _____

List five ways that college students can have fun without spending much money.

1. _____

2. _____

3. _____

4. _____

5. _____

Budgeting for College

Name _____   Date _____

Before you complete this budget, monitor your expenses for one month. Write down all expenditures and then divide them into categories that have meaning for you. Then complete the following budget and try to follow it for at least two months. Do this exercise on your own, since it is likely to contain private information.

College Student Monthly Budget

Monthly income for _____ (month)

Income from job _____

Money from home _____

Financial aid _____

Other _____

Total Income [ ]

Budgeted Monthly Expenses:	Actual Monthly Expenses:

Total Budgeted [ ]   **Total Actual**

Total Income [ ]   **Minus Total Budgeted** [ ]   **Equals** [ ]

CHAPTER 5

Improving Memory and Reading

Learning Objectives

Read to answer these key questions:

- How does the memory work?

- Why do we forget?

- How can I remember what I study?

- What are some memory tricks?

- How can I apply memory techniques to reading?

- What is a reading system for college texts?

- What are some ways to improve reading speed and comprehension?

- Why is positive thinking a key to remembering and reading?

L earning how to improve your memory and remember what you read will be a great asset in college, on the job, and in life in general. This chapter describes how memory works and provides some practical techniques for improving your memory. Once you understand how memory works, you can apply these techniques to remembering what you read. Positive thinking will help you be successful in remembering and reading effectively.

Improving Your Memory

How Does the Memory Work?

Understanding how the memory works provides the framework for effective study techniques. There are three stages of memory: **sensory register, short-term memory,** and **long-term memory.** Understanding these stages of memory will help you learn how to store information in your long-term memory, which lasts a lifetime.

- **Sensory register.** The first stage of memory is called sensory register. It is the initial moment of perception. This stage of memory lasts less than a second and is used to record sensory experience (what you see, hear, taste, touch, or do). It is like a quickly fading snapshot of what your senses perceive. The purpose of the sensory register is to allow the brain to process information and to focus on relevant information. To remember information for more than a second, it must be transferred to short-term memory.

- **Short-term memory (STM).** Paying attention to the information you have perceived in the sensory register transfers the information to STM. STM is temporary and limited, lasting only about half a minute. The information must be rehearsed or renewed for longer storage. STM records what we see, hear, feel, taste, or touch. Information is best stored in STM through recitation or mentally talking to ourselves. If the information is not repeated, it is very quickly lost. For example, when you meet a person for the first time, the person's name is often quickly forgotten because it is only stored in short-term memory. The purpose of STM is to ponder the significance of the stimuli we have received, detect patterns, and decide if the information is important enough to remember.

   Grouping together or chunking bits of information can increase the limited capacity of STM. George Miller of Harvard University found that the optimum number of chunks or bits of information that we can hold in STM is five to nine.[1] For example, we remember telephone numbers of seven digits by using a hyphen to separate the numbers into two more easily remembered chunks. We divide our Social Security numbers into three chunks for easier recall.

   According to George Miller's research, we often use the "Magical Number Seven" technique to remember material. It is much easier to remember material that is grouped in chunks of seven or less. You can find many examples of groups of seven used to enhance memory. There are seven days of the week and seven numbers in your driver's license and license plate. There are also seven dwarfs, seven deadly sins, and seven wonders of the world!

- **Long-term memory (LTM).** Long-term memory has a large capacity and is used to store information more permanently. You will want to use your LTM to store important information that you want to be able to recall at a later date. Most psychologists agree that once information is in LTM, it is there forever. Although the information is available, the problem becomes how to access it. Think of LTM as a library in which many available books are stored. If the books in the library are randomly stored, retrieval of information becomes extremely difficult. If the books are properly stored and indexed, we can find them more easily.

How are long-term memories formed? Short-term memories become long-term through repetition or meaningful association. Creating long-term memories takes some purposeful action. We are motivated to take some purposeful action to remember if the information has some survival value. When we touch a hot stove, this memory moves from sensory register to short-term memory and then is stored in long-term memory to avoid injury in the future. In an academic setting, we must convince ourselves of the survival value of what we are learning. Is the information needed to pass a test, to be successful in a career, or for personal reasons? If so, it is easier to take the action required to store information in long-term memory. Emotions such as fear, anger, or joy are also involved in the storing of memories. In the hot stove example, fear elevates the importance of the memory and helps us to store it in long-term memory. In the educational setting, an interest or joy in learning helps to store information in long-term memory.

In summary, when you are trying to store information in your memory, the first step is receiving information through the five senses to store in the sensory register, similar to entering data in a computer through the use of a keyboard. This takes less than a second. The next step involves paying attention to the sensory stimulus in order to transfer it to STM for the purpose of seeing patterns and judging significance or importance. Information only stays in STM for 30 seconds or less unless rehearsed or repeated. If you decide that the information is likely to be on a test and you need to remember it, you must organize the material in a meaningful way or repeat it to store the information in LTM. Information must be stored in LTM in order for you to remember it permanently. Effective techniques for storing information in LTM will be presented later in this chapter.

How Does the Memory Work?

Sensory Register	Initial moment of perception	Lasts less than a second
STM Short Term Memory	Temporary and limited	Lasts less than 30 seconds
LTM Long Term Memory	Permanent storage of information	Lasts forever, although you may lose access through disuse

Figure 5.1 Short-Term Memory and Long-Term Memory

Why Do We Forget?

Is it true that we never forget? Material that is stored in the sensory register is forgotten in less than one second. Material stored in STM is forgotten in 30 seconds unless rehearsed or repeated. We do not forget material stored in LTM, but we can lose access to the information, similar to when a book is filed incorrectly in the library. The book is in the library, but we cannot find it.

© 2014, Edyta Pawlowska. Used under license with Shutterstock, Inc.

Examining the following lists of items frequently forgotten or remembered can give us insight into why forgetting or losing access occurs.

We frequently forget these things:

- Unpleasant experiences
- Names of people, places, or things
- Numbers and dates
- What we have barely learned
- Material we do not fully understand
- What we try to remember when embarrassed, frustrated, tired, or ill
- Material we have learned by cramming
- Ideas or theories that conflict with our beliefs

We tend to remember these things:

- Pleasant experiences
- Material that is important to us
- What we have put an effort into learning
- What we have reviewed or thought about often
- Material that is interesting to us
- Muscular skills such as riding a bike
- What we had an important reason to remember
- Items we discuss with others
- Material that we understand
- Frequently used information

Theories of Forgetting

An understanding of theories of forgetting is also helpful in developing techniques for effective study and learning. There are many theories about why we forget or lose access to information stored in LTM.

1. **I forgot.** If you forget a name, number, or fact, you might just say, "I forgot." The information was stored in STM and never made it to LTM. Have you ever been introduced to a person and really not listened to his or her name? You didn't forget it. You never learned it.

2. **The mental blur.** If you are studying and don't understand the material, you will not remember it.

3. **The decay theory.** If you do not use information, you lose access to it, just as weeds grow over a path that is seldom used.

4. **Interference theory.** New memories interfere with old memories, and old memories interfere with new memories. Interference is especially likely when the memories are similar. For example, when I meet my students in the hallway, it is difficult to remember which class they are in because I have several similar classes.

5. **Reactive interference.** We tend not to remember ideas or subjects that we dislike.

6. **Reconstruction theory.** What we remember becomes distorted over time. Our personal biases affect what we remember.

7. **Motivated forgetting.** We choose to remember pleasant experiences and to forget unpleasant experiences.

Minimizing Forgetting

Herman Ebbinghaus (1850–1909), a German psychologist and pioneer in research on forgetting, described a curve of forgetting.[2] He invented nonsense syllables such as WUX, CAZ, BIJ, and ZOL. He chose these nonsense syllables so that there would be no meaning, associations, or organizations that could affect the memory of the words. He would learn these lists of words and measure forgetting over time. The following is a chart of time and forgetting of nonsense syllables.

Time	Percent Forgotten
After 20 minutes	47
After 1 day	62
After 2 days	69
After 15 days	75
After 31 days	78

> "Just as iron rusts from disuse, even so does inaction spoil the intellect."
> Leonardo da Vinci

We can draw three interesting conclusions from examining these figures. First, **most of the forgetting occurs within the first 20 minutes**. Immediate review, or at least review during the first 20 minutes, would prevent most of the forgetting. Second, forgetting slows down over time. The third conclusion is that forgetting is significant after 31 days. Fortunately, we do not need to memorize nonsense syllables. We can use meaning, associations, organization, and proper review to minimize forgetting.

Review is important in transferring information from short-term to long-term memory. You can also minimize forgetting over time through the proper use of review.[3] Let's assume that you spend 45 minutes studying and learning something new. The optimum schedule for review would look like this:

After 10 minutes	Review for 5 minutes
After 1 day	Review for 5 minutes
After 1 week	Review for 3 minutes
After 1 month	Review for 3 minutes
After 6 months	Review for 3 minutes

Memorization Tips

- Meaningful organization
- Visualization
- Recitation
- Develop an interest
- See the big picture first
- Intend to remember
- Learn small amounts frequently
- Basic background
- Relax

Improving Your Memory

Test what you have learned by circling the letters of the correct answers to the following questions.

1. Information is stored permanently in the

    a. sensory register.
    b. short-term memory (STM).
    c. long-term memory (LTM).

2. You never forget.

    a. False.
    b. True.
    c. This is true only if the information is stored properly in long-term memory.

3. According to Ebbinghaus, the greatest rate of forgetting occurs

    a. within the first 20 minutes.
    b. within the first day.
    c. within the first 15 days.

4. If you do not review information stored in long-term memory, you will

    a. still remember it because it is in long-term memory.
    b. probably lose access to the information.
    c. lose the information forever.

5. The best way to review is

    a. in a 45-minute study session.
    b. in a 20-minute study session.
    c. in three- to five-minute study sessions spaced out over time.

How did you do on the quiz? Check your answers: 1. c, 2. c, 3. a, 4. b, 5. c

By spending about 20 minutes in review time, you can remember 90 to 100 percent of the material. The short periods of review are much easier to accomplish than spending larger periods of review. Make good use of your time by having material for review immediately available. When you have three to five minutes available, review some material that you have learned previously. You will be improving access to material stored in long-term memory, and you will be able to easily recall the information for an exam or for future use in your career.

> "Today I will do what others won't, so I can accomplish what others can't."
>
> Jerry Rice

How Can I Remember What I Study?

Based on the above theories of memory and forgetting, here are some practical suggestions for storing information in LTM. Information stored in LTM can be retrieved for tests in college and for success in your career and personal life.

Meaningful Organization

There is no better method of memory improvement than imposing your own form of personal organization on the material you are trying to remember. Psychologists have even suggested that your intelligence quotient (IQ) may be related to how well you have organized material you learned in the past. When learning new material, cluster facts and ideas into categories that are meaningful to you.

Magical Number Seven

Remember George Miller's Magical Number Seven Theory? It is more efficient to limit the number of categories to seven or less, although you can have subcategories. Examine the following list of words.

goat	horse	cow
carrot	cat	lettuce
banana	tomato	pig
celery	orange	peas
cherry	apple	strawberry

Look at the list for one minute. Then look away from the list and write down all the words you can recall. Record the number of words you remembered: _____

Note that the following lists are divided into categories: animals, crops, and tropical fruits.

animals	crops	tropical fruits
lion	wheat	banana
giraffe	beans	kiwi
kangaroo	corn	mango
coyote	hay	guava
bear	oats	orange

Look at the above list for one minute. Then look away from the list and write down the words you recall. Record the number of words you remembered: _____

You probably remembered more from the second list because the list is organized into categories. Notice that there are only five words in each category. Remember that it is easier to remember lists with seven items or less. If these words have some meaning for you, it is easier to remember them. A farmer from the Midwest would probably have an easier time remembering the crops. A person from Hawaii would probably remember the list of tropical fruits. We also tend to remember unusual items and the first and last items on the list. If you need to memorize a list, pay more attention to the mundane items and the items in the middle of the list.

Visualization

Another very powerful memorization technique is visualization. The right side of the brain specializes in visual pictures and the left side in verbal functions. If you focus on the words only, you are using only half of your brain. If you can focus on the words and accompany them with pictures, you are using your brain in the most efficient way. Advertisers use pictures as powerful influences to motivate you to purchase their products. You can use the same power of visualization to enhance your studying. While you are studying history, picture what life would be like in that time period. In engineering, make pictures in your mind or on paper to illustrate scientific principles. Challenge yourself to see the pictures along with the words. Add movement to your pictures, as in a video. During a test, relax and recall the pictures.

© 2014, scyther5. Used under license with Shutterstock, Inc.

Recitation

Although scientists are still researching and learning how the memory works and how information is stored, we do know that recitation, rehearsal, and reviewing the ideas are powerful techniques for learning. Memories exist in the brain in the form of a chemical neural trace. Some researchers think that it takes about four or five seconds for this neural trace to be established in LTM. It is through recitation that we keep the ideas in our mind long enough to store them in LTM. Often students say they cannot remember the material that they have just read. The reason for this problem is not a lack of intelligence, but rather a simple lack of rehearsal. If information obtained through reading is stored in STM, it is very quickly forgotten. Say aloud or to yourself the material you want to remember. This process takes about five seconds.

Applying the recitation technique can help you remember names. When you are introduced to someone, first pay attention to make sure that you have heard the name correctly. Ask the person to repeat their name if necessary. Repeat the name out loud or in your mind. Say something like, "Glad to meet you, *Lydia*." Say the name silently to yourself five times to establish the neural trace. If possible, make a visual connection with the name. If the person's name is Frank, you might picture a hot dog, for example. Thinking about the name or reviewing it will help to access the name in the future.

Remember that most of the forgetting occurs in the first 20 minutes after learning something. Reviewing the material within 20 minutes is the fastest and most effective way to remember it. You will also need to review the information you have stored in LTM periodically so it is more accessible. This periodic review can be done effectively in three to five minutes.

Develop an Interest

We tend to remember what interests us. People often have phenomenal memories when it comes to sports, automobiles, music, stamp collecting, or anything they consider fun or pursue as a hobby. Find something interesting in your college studies. If you are not interested in what you are studying, look for something interesting or even pretend that you are interested. Reward yourself for studying by doing something enjoyable.

Attitude has a significant impact on memory. Approaching your studies with a positive attitude will help you to find something interesting and make it easier to remember. In addition, the more you learn about a topic, the more interesting it becomes. Often we judge a subject as boring because we know nothing about it.

Another way to make something interesting is to look for personal meaning. How can I use this information in my future career? Does the information relate to my personal experience in some way? How can I use this information? What is the importance of this information? And finally, is this information likely to be on the test?

© 2014, Zurijeta. Used under license with Shutterstock, Inc.

See the Big Picture First

Imagine looking at a painting one inch at a time. It would be difficult to understand or appreciate a painting in this way. College students often approach reading a textbook in the same way. They focus on the small details without first getting an idea of the main points. By focusing on the details without looking at the main points, it is easy to get lost.

The first step in reading is to skim the chapter headings to form a mental outline of what you will be learning. Then read for detail. Think of the mind as a file cabinet or a computer. Major topics are like folders in which we file detailed information. When we need to find or access the information, we think of the major topic and look in the folder to find the details. If we put all of our papers into the file drawer without organization, it is difficult to find the information we need. Highlight or underline key ideas to focus on the main points and organize what you are learning.

Be selective and focus on key ideas to increase learning efficiency. Herman Ebbinghaus studied the length of time needed to remember series of six nonsense syllables and 12 nonsense syllables.[4] We might assume that it would take twice as long to remember 12 syllables as it would six syllables. Ebbinghaus found that it took 15 times longer to memorize 12 syllables. The Magic Number Seven Theory seems to apply to the number of items that can be memorized efficiently.

Does this mean that we should try to remember only seven or less ideas in studying a textbook chapter? No—it is most efficient to identify seven or fewer key ideas and then cluster less important ideas under major headings. In this way, you can remember the key ideas in the chapter you are studying. The critical thinking required by this process also helps in remembering ideas and information.

Intend to Remember

Tell yourself that you are going to remember. If you think you won't remember, you won't remember. This step also relates to positive thinking and self-confidence and will take some practice to apply. Once you have told yourself to remember, apply some of the above techniques such as organizing, visualizing, and reciting. If you intend to remember, you will pay attention, make an effort to understand, and use memory techniques to strengthen your memory.

One practical technique that involves intent to remember is the memory jogger. This involves doing something unusual to jog or trigger your memory. If you want to be sure to remember your books, place your car keys on the books. Since you cannot go anywhere without your keys, you will find them and remember the books too. Another application is putting your watch on your right hand to remember to do something. When you look at your left hand and notice that the watch is not there, the surprise will jog your memory for the item you wish to recall. You can be creative with this technique and come up with your own memory joggers.

Distribute the Practice

Learning small amounts of material and reviewing frequently are more effective than a marathon study session. One research study showed that a task that took 30 minutes to learn in one day could be learned in 22 minutes if spread over two days. This is almost a 30 percent increase in efficiency.[5]

If you have a list of vocabulary words or formulas to learn, break the material into small parts and frequently review each part for a short period of time. Consider putting these facts or figures on index cards to carry with you in your purse or pocket. Use small amounts of time to quickly review the cards. This technique works well because it prevents fatigue and helps to keep motivation high. One exception to the distributed practice rule is creative work such as writing a paper or doing an art project, where a longer time period is needed for creative inspiration and immediate follow-through.

A learning technique for distributed practice is summed up in the acronym **SAFMEDS**, which stands for Say All Fast for one Minute Each Day and Shuffle.[6] With this technique, you can easily and quickly learn 100 or more facts. To use this technique, prepare flash cards that contain the material to be learned (vocabulary, foreign language words, numbers, dates, places, names, formulas). For example, if you are learning Spanish, place the Spanish word on one side of the card and the English word on the other side. Just writing out the flash cards is an aid to learning and is often sufficient for learning the material. Once the cards are prepared, *say* the Spanish word and see if you can remember what it means in English. Look at the back of the card to see if your answer is correct. Do this with *all* of the cards as *fast* as you can for *one minute each day*. Then *shuffle* the cards and repeat the process the next day.

It is important that you do this activity quickly. Don't worry if you do not know the answer. Just flip each card over, quickly look at the answer, and put the cards that you missed into a separate pile. At the end of the minute, count the number of cards you answered correctly. You can learn even faster if you take the stack of cards you missed and practice them quickly one more time. Shuffling the cards helps you to remember the actual meanings of the words, instead of just the order in which they appear. In the case of the Spanish cards, turn the cards over and say each English word to see if you can remember the equivalent word in Spanish. Each day, the number of correct answers will increase, and you will have a concrete measure of your learning. Consider this activity as a fun and fast-moving game to challenge yourself.

Create a Basic Background

You remember information by connecting it to things you already know. The more you know, the easier it is to make connections that make remembering easier. You will even find that it is easier to remember material toward the end of a college class because you have established a basic background at the beginning of the semester. With this in mind, freshman-level courses will be the most difficult in college because they form the basic background for your college education. College does become easier as you establish this basic background and practice effective study techniques.

You can enhance your basic background by reading a variety of books. Making reading a habit also enhances vocabulary, writing, and spelling. College provides many opportunities for expanding your reading horizons and areas of basic knowledge.

Relax While Studying

The brain works much better when it is relaxed. As you become more confident in your study techniques, you can become more relaxed. Here are some suggestions to help you relax during study time.

- Use distributed practice to take away some of the pressure of learning; take breaks between periods of learning. Give yourself time to absorb the material.
- Plan ahead so that you do not have to cram. Waiting until the last minute to study produces anxiety that is counterproductive.
- If you are anxious, try a physical activity or relaxation exercise before study sessions. For example, imagine a warm, relaxing light beginning at the feet and moving slowly up the body to the top of the head. Feel each part of the body relax as the light makes contact with it. You will find other relaxation techniques in Chapter 12.
- If you are feeling frustrated, it is often a good idea to stop and come back to your studies later. You may gain insight into your studies while you are more relaxed and doing something else. You can often benefit from a fresh perspective.

Using Mnemonics and Other Memory Tricks

Memory tricks can be used to enhance your memory. These memory tricks include acrostics, acronyms, peg systems, and loci systems. These systems are called *mnemonics*, from the Greek word *mneme* which means "to remember."

Mnemonic devices are very effective. A research study by Gerald R. Miller found that students who used mnemonic devices improved their test scores by up to 77 percent.[7] Mnemonics are effective because they help to organize material. They have been used throughout history, in part as a way to entertain people with amazing memory feats.

Mnemonics are best used for memorizing facts. They are not helpful for understanding or thinking critically about the information. Be sure to memorize your mnemonics carefully and review them right before exam time. Forgetting the mnemonic or a part of it can cause major problems.

© 2014, Lightspring. Used under license with Shutterstock, Inc.

Acrostics

Acrostics are creative rhymes, songs, poems, or sentences that help us to remember. Maybe you previously learned some of these in school.

- Continents: Eat an Aspirin after a Nighttime Snack (Europe, Antarctica, Asia, Africa, Australia, North America, South America)
- Directions of the compass: Never Eat Sour Watermelons (North, East, South, West)
- Geological ages: Practically Every Old Man Plays Poker Regularly (Paleocene, Eocene, Oligocene, Miocene, Pliocene, Pleistocene, Recent)
- Guitar Strings: Eat All Dead Gophers Before Easter (E, A, D, G, B, E)
- Oceans: I Am a Person (Indian, Arctic, Atlantic, Pacific)
- Metric system in order: King Henry Drinks Much Dark Chocolate Milk (Kilometer, hectometer, decameter, meter, decimeter, centimeter, millimeter)
- Notes on the treble clef in music: Every Good Boy Does Fine (E, G, B, D, F)
- Classification in biology: Kings Play Cards on Fairly Good Soft Velvet (Kingdom, Phylum, Class, Order, Family, Genus, Species, Variety)

Memorization Tricks
• Acrostics
• Acronyms
• Peg systems
• Loci systems
• Visual clues
• Say it aloud
• Have a routine
• Write it down

An effective way to invent your own acrostics is to first identify key ideas you need to remember, underline these key words or write them down as a list, and think of a word that starts with the first letter of each idea you want to remember. Rearrange the words if necessary to form a sentence. The more unusual the sentence, the easier it is to remember.

In addition to acrostics, there are many other creative memory aids:

- Days in each month: Thirty days hath September, April, June, and November. All the rest have 31, except February which has 28 until leap year gives it 29.
- Spelling rules: *i* before *e* except after *c*, or when sounding like *a* as in neighbor and weigh.
- Numbers: Can I remember the reciprocal? To remember the reciprocal of pi, count the letters in each word of the question above. The reciprocal of pi = .3 1 8 3 10

Mnemonics become more powerful when used with visualization. For example, if you are trying to remember the planets, use a mnemonic and then visualize Saturn as a hula-hoop dancer to remember that it has rings. Jupiter could be a king with a number of maids to represent its moons.

Acronyms

Acronyms are commonly used as shortcuts in our language. The military is especially fond of using acronyms. For example, NASA is the acronym for the National Aeronautics and Space Administration. You can invent your own acronyms as a memory trick. Here are some common ones that students have used:

- The colors of the spectrum: Roy G. Biv (red, orange, yellow, green, blue, indigo, violet)
- The Great Lakes: HOMES (Huron, Ontario, Michigan, Erie, Superior)
- The stages of cell division in biology: IPMAT (interphase, prophase, metaphase, and telophase)

To make your own acronym, list the items you wish to remember. Use the first letter of each word to make a new word. The word you make can be an actual word or an invented word.

Peg Systems

Peg systems start with numbers, typically 1 to 100. Each number is associated with an object. The object chosen to represent each number can be based on rhyme or on a logical association. The objects are memorized and used with a mental picture to recall a list. There are entertainers who can have the audience call out a list of 100 objects and then repeat all of the objects through use of a peg system. Here is an example of a commonly used peg system based on rhyme:

One	Bun	Six	Sticks
Two	Shoe	Seven	Heaven
Three	Tree	Eight	Gate
Four	Door	Nine	Wine
Five	Hive	Ten	Hen

For example, if I want to remember a grocery list consisting of milk, eggs, carrots, and butter, I would make associations between the peg and the item I want to remember. The more unusual the association is, the better. I would start by making a visual connection between *bun*, my peg word, and *milk*, the first item on the list. I could picture dipping a bun into a glass of milk for a snack. Next I would make a connection between *shoe* and *eggs*. I could picture eggs being broken into my shoe as a joke. Next I would picture a *tree* with orange *carrots* hanging from it and then a *door* with *butter* dripping from the doorknob. The technique works because of the organization provided by the pegs and the power of visualization.

There are many variations of the peg system. One variation is using the letters of the alphabet instead of numbers. Another variation is to visualize objects and put them in a stack, one on top of the other, until you have a great tottering tower, like a totem pole telling a story. Still another variation is to use your body or your car as a peg system. Using our example of the grocery list above, visualize balancing the milk on your head, carrying eggs in your hands, having carrots tied around your waist and smearing butter on your feet. Remember that the more unusual the pictures, the easier they are to remember.

Loci Systems

Loci or location systems use a series of familiar places to aid the memory. The Roman orators often used this system to remember the outline of a speech. For example, the speaker might connect the entry of a house with the introduction, the living room with the first main point, and each part of the speech with a different room. Again, this technique works through organization and visualization.

Another example of using a loci system to remember a speech or dramatic production is to imagine a long hallway. Mentally draw a picture of each topic or section you need to remember, and then hang each picture on the wall. As you are giving your speech or acting out your part in the play, visualize walking down the hallway and looking at the pictures on the wall to remind yourself of the next topic. For multiple topics, you can place signs over several hallway entrances labeling the contents of each hallway.

Visual Clues

Visual clues are helpful memory devices. To remember your books, place them in front of the door so you will see them on your way to school. To remember to take your finished homework to school, put it in your car when you are done. To remember to fill a prescription, put the empty bottle on the front seat of your car. Tie a bright ribbon on your backpack to remind you to attend a meeting with your study group. When parking your car in the mall, look around and notice landmarks such as nearby stores or row numbers. When you enter a large department store, notice the items that are near the door you entered. Are you worried that you left the iron on? Tie a ribbon around the handle of the iron each time you turn it off or unplug it. To find out if you have all the items you need to go skiing, visualize yourself on the ski slope wearing all those items.

Say It Aloud

Some people are auditory learners and can remember items by repeating them out loud. For example, if you want to remember where you hid your diamond ring; say it out loud a few times. Then reinforce the memory by making a visual picture of where you have hidden the ring. You can also use your auditory memory by making a rhyme or song to remember something. Commercials use this technique all the time to try to get you to remember a product and purchase it.

Have a Routine

Do you have a difficult time trying to remember where you left your keys, wallet, or purse? Having a routine can greatly simplify your life and help you to remember. As you enter your house, hang your keys on a hook each time. Decide where you will place your wallet or purse and put it in the same place each time. When I leave for work, I have a mental checklist with four items: keys, purse, glasses, and cell phone.

Write It Down

One of the easiest and most effective memory techniques is to simply write something down. Make a grocery list or to-do list, send yourself an email, or tape a note to your bathroom mirror or the dashboard of your car.

Remembering Names

Many people have difficulty remembering names of other people in social or business situations. The reason we have difficulty in remembering names is that we do not take the time to store the name properly in our memories. When we first meet someone, we are often distracted or thinking about ourselves. We are trying to remember our own names or wondering what impression we are making on the other person.

To remember a name, first make sure you have heard the name correctly. If you have not heard the name, there is no way you can remember it. Ask the person to repeat his or her name or check to see if you have heard it correctly. Immediately use the name. For example, say "It is nice to meet you, *Nancy*." If you can mentally repeat the name about five times, you have a good chance of remembering it. You can improve the chances of remembering the name if you can make an association. For example, you might think, "She looks like my daughter's friend Nancy." Some people remember names by making a rhyme such as "fancy Nancy."

Journal Entry #2

Review the memory tricks explained in this chapter: acrostics, acronyms, peg systems, loci systems, visual clues, say it aloud, have a routine, write it down, and remembering names. List and briefly explain at least three memory tricks you are willing to try, and give examples of how you would use each of the three memory tricks you select.

Optimize Your Brain Power

The mind can be strengthened and remain healthy throughout life. Scientists have studied a group of nuns from Mankato, Minnesota, who have lived long lives and suffer less from dementia and brain diseases than the general population. These nuns have lived a long time because they do not drink to excess or smoke. They have kept their minds healthy into old age by staying mentally active. They keep active by discussing current events, playing cards, practicing math problems, and doing crossword puzzles. Arnold Scheibel, head of the UCLA Brain Institute, gives the following suggestions for strengthening your mind.

- Do jigsaw and crossword puzzles.
- Play a musical instrument.
- Fix something. The mental challenge stimulates the brain.
- Participate in the arts. Draw or paint something.
- Dance. Exercise and rhythm are good for the brain.
- Do aerobic exercise. This promotes blood flow to the brain.
- Meet and interact with interesting people.
- Read challenging books.
- Take a college class.[8]

Doing these kinds of activities can actually stimulate the development of neurons and nerve connections in the brain so that the brain functions more efficiently. The good news is that you can do this at any age.

Besides doing mental exercises to strengthen your brain, you can take other actions to keep your brain healthy. Here are some ideas:

1. **Do aerobic exercise.** Exercise improves the flow of oxygen to the brain. The brain needs oxygen to function. Researchers have just found that the human brain can grow new nerve cells by putting subjects on a three-month aerobic workout regimen. It was interesting to note that these new nerve cells could be generated at any age and are important in reversing the aging process and delaying the onset of Alzheimer's disease or other cognitive disorders.[9] For optimum health and learning, it is important to exercise the body as well as the mind.

2. **Get enough rest.** Nobel laureate Francis Crick, who studies the brain at the Salk Institute, proposes that the purpose of sleep is to allow the brain to "take out the trash." Sleep provides time for the brain to review the events of the day and to store what is needed and discard what is not worth remembering. During sleep, the brain sorts memories and stores significant ones in long-term memory. Studies have shown that when humans and lab animals are taught a new task and deprived of sleep, they do not perform the task the next day as well as non-sleep-deprived subjects.[10]

3. **Eat a balanced, low-fat diet.** The brain needs nutrients, vitamins, and minerals to be healthy. Low-fat diets have been shown to improve mental performance.[11]

4. **Eat proteins and carbohydrates.** Proteins are the building blocks of neurotransmitters that increase mental activity. Carbohydrates provide energy and are the building blocks of neurotransmitters that have a calming effect.[12]

5. **Drink caffeine in moderation.** Caffeine can make you feel stressed, making it difficult to think.

6. **Don't abuse drugs or alcohol.** These substances kill brain cells and change brain chemistry.

7. **Use safety gear.** Wear a seat belt when driving and a helmet when biking or skating to reduce head injuries.

Journal Entry #3

What is your plan for keeping your brain healthy throughout life? Include some of these ideas: diet, exercise, music, art, games, fixing something, challenging your brain, social contacts, and continued learning.

Improving Your Reading

Myths about Reading

Effective reading techniques are crucial to college success. The level and quantity of reading expected in college may be greatly increased over what you have experienced in the past. The following are some myths about reading that cause problems for many college students.

1. **"If I read a chapter, I should remember what I read."** Many students say that they read the chapter, but "it goes in one ear and out the other." After such a frustrating experience, students often conclude that they cannot read well or are not intelligent

© 2014, Vitchanan Photography. Used under license with Shutterstock, Inc.

enough to succeed in college. If you just read the chapter, you have stored it in short-term memory, which lasts about 30 seconds. Reading a chapter takes a lot of effort. You want to make sure the effort you have invested pays off by storing the material in long-term memory. You can then retrieve the information in the future, as well as pass exams. Material is stored in long-term memory through rehearsal or review. Without review, you will not remember.

2. **"I do not need to read if I go to class."** The role of the college professor is to supplement material in the text and increase student understanding of the material. Some professors do not even cover topics contained in the text and consider it the student's responsibility to learn textbook material. If you do not read the text, you may miss out on important material that is not presented during class. Reading the text also helps you understand the material that the professor presents.

3. **"Practice makes perfect."** Students think that if they keep reading the way they are reading, their reading will get better. The truth is that "perfect practice makes perfect." If you are reading in a way that enhances memory, you will get better and better. Success in college reading may mean learning some new reading habits. You will learn about effective reading habits in this chapter.

4. **"Learn the facts that will be on the test."** Focusing on details without looking at the big picture can slow down learning and lead to frustration. If you start with the big picture or outline, then it is easier to learn the details.

A Study System for Reading a College Text: SQ4R

There are many systems for reading a college textbook. All successful systems involve ways to store information in long-term memory: recognizing major points, organizing material to be learned, reviewing, intending to remember, and critical thinking about reading. The crucial step in transferring information to long-term memory is rehearsal, reviewing, or reciting. You need to keep information in your mind for five to 5 seconds in order for it to be stored in long-term memory. The **SQ4R system (Survey, Question, Read, Recite, Review, Reflect)** is a simple and effective way to store information in long-term memory. This system was derived from an information-processing theory developed by Francis P. Robinson in 1941 for use by military personnel attending college during World War II. Since that time, the system has been used by many colleges to teach students effective study skills. The system can be broken down into three steps.

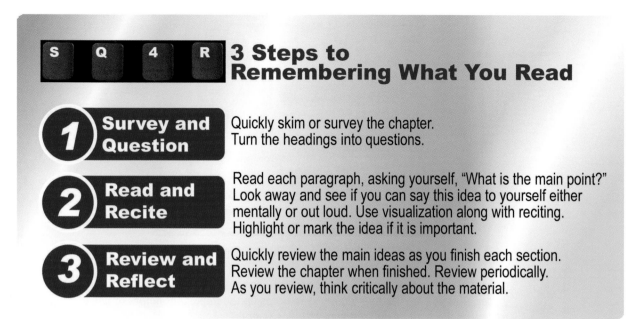

Figure 5.2 The SQ4R System for reading a college textbook.

Step 1: Survey and Question. The first step is to survey and question the chapter before you begin reading. Read the title and first paragraph or introduction to the chapter and then look quickly through the chapter, letting your eyes glide across bold headings, diagrams, illustrations, and photos. Read the last paragraph or summary of the chapter. This process should take five minutes or less for a typical chapter in a college textbook.

While you are surveying the chapter, ask yourself questions. Take each major heading in the chapter and turn it into a question. For example, in this section of the book you might ask: What is a system for reading a college text? Why do I need a system? What is SQ4R? What is the first step of SQ4R? You can also ask some general questions as you survey the chapter: What is the main point? What will I learn? Do I know something about this? Can I find something that interests me? How can I use this? Does this relate to something said in class? What does this mean? Is this a possible test question? Asking questions will help you to become an active reader and to find some personal meaning in the content that will help you remember it. If you at least survey and question the relevant textbook material before you go to class, you will have the advantage of being familiar with some of the key ideas to be discussed.

There are several benefits to taking this first step:

- This is the first step in rehearsal for storage of information into long-term memory.
- The quick survey is a warmup for the brain, similar to an athlete's warmup before exercise.
- A survey step is also good practice for improving your reading speed.
- Reading to answer questions increases comprehension, sparks interest, and has the added bonus of keeping you awake while reading.

If you want to be able to read faster, improve your reading comprehension, and increase retention of your reading material, practice the survey and question step before you begin your detailed reading.

> "The important thing is to not stop questioning."
> Albert Einstein

Step 2: Read and recite. The second step in reading a text is to read and recite. Read each paragraph and look for the most important point or topic sentence. If the point is important, highlight or underline it. You might use different colors to organize the ideas. You can also make a notation or outline in the margin of the text if the point is especially significant, meaningful, useful, or likely to appear on an exam. A picture, diagram, or

© 2014, George Dolgikh. Used under license with Shutterstock, Inc.

chart drawn in the margin is a great way to use visualization to improve retention of the material. If you are reading online, take notes on the important points or use cut and paste to collect the main ideas in a separate document.

Next, look away and see if you can say the main point to yourself either silently or out loud. Reciting is even more powerful if you combine it with visualization. Make a video in your head to illustrate what you are learning. Include color, movement, and sound if possible. Reciting is crucial to long-term memory storage. It will also keep you awake. Beginning college students will find this step a challenge, but practice makes it a habit that becomes easier and easier.

If you read a paragraph or section and do not understand the main point, try these techniques:

1. **Notice any vocabulary or technical terms that are unfamiliar.** Look up these words in a dictionary or in the glossary at the back of the book. Use index cards; write the words on one side and the definition on the other side. Use the SAFMEDS technique (Say All Fast in one Minute Each Day Shuffle) discussed earlier in this chapter. You are likely to see these vocabulary words on quizzes and exams.

2. **Read the paragraph again.** Until you get into the habit of searching for the main point, you may need to reread a paragraph until you understand. If this does not work, reread the paragraphs before and after the one you do not understand.

3. **Write a question in the margin and ask your instructor or tutor to explain.** College instructors have office hours set aside to assist students with questions, and faculty are generally favorably impressed with students who care enough to ask questions. Most colleges offer tutoring free of charge.

4. **If you are really frustrated, put your reading away and come back to it later.** You may be able to relax and gain some insight about the material.

5. **Make sure you have the proper background for the course.** Take the introductory course first.

6. **Assess your reading skills.** Colleges offer reading assessments, and counselors can help you understand your skill level and suggest appropriate courses. Most colleges offer reading courses that can help you to be successful in college.

7. **If you have always had a problem with reading, you may have a learning disability.** A person with a learning disability is of average or higher-than-average intelligence, but has a problem that interferes with learning. Most colleges offer assessment that can help you understand your learning disability and tutoring that is designed to help you to compensate for the disability.

Step 3: Review and reflect. The last step in reading is to review and reflect. After each section, quickly review what you have highlighted or underlined. Again, ask questions. How can I use this information? How does it relate to what I already know? What is most important? What is likely to be on the exam? Is it true? Learn to think critically about the material you have learned.

When you finish the chapter, quickly (in a couple of minutes) look over the highlights again. This last step, review and reflect, is another opportunity for rehearsal. At this point, you have stored the information in long-term memory and want to make sure that you can access the information again in the future. Think of this last step as a creative step in which you put the pieces together, gain an understanding, and begin to think of how you can apply your new knowledge to your personal life. This is the true reward of studying.

Review is faster, easier, and more effective if done immediately. As discussed previously in this chapter, most forgetting occurs in the first 20 minutes after exposure to new information. If you wait 24 hours to review, you will probably have forgotten 80 percent of the material and will have to spend a longer time in review. Review periodically to make sure that you can access the material easily in the future, and review again right before the test.

As you read about the above steps, you may think that this process takes a lot of time. Remember that it is not how much you read, but how you read that is important. In reality, the SQ4R technique is a time-saver in that you do not have to reread all the material before the test. You just need to quickly review information that is stored in long-term memory. Rereading can be purely mechanical and consume your time with little payoff. Rather than rereading, spend your time reciting the important points. With proper review, you can remember 80 to 90 percent of the material.

In his book *Accelerated Learning*, Colin Rose states that you can retain 88 percent of the material you study using the following review schedule.[13] He also notes that the rate of retention using this schedule is four times better than the expected curve of forgetting.

1. Review immediately within 30 seconds.

2. Review after a few minutes.

3. Review after one hour.

4. Review a day later after an overnight rest.

5. Review after a week.

6. Review after one month.

Suggestions for review schedules vary, but the key point is that review is most effective when it is done in short sessions spaced out over time.

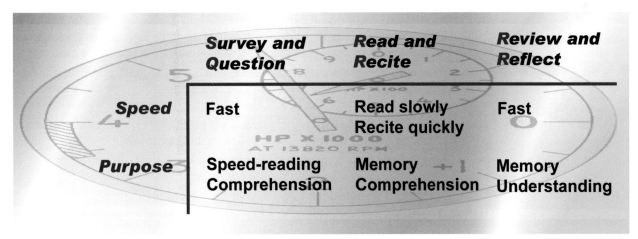

	Survey and Question	Read and Recite	Review and Reflect
Speed	Fast	Read slowly Recite quickly	Fast
Purpose	Speed-reading Comprehension	Memory Comprehension	Memory Understanding

Figure 5.3 This chart summarizes the speed and purpose of each SQ4R step.

Online Reading Strategies

To read efficiently, you will need some reading strategies for the vast amount of online material you will use in college and in everyday life. First, determine your purpose for reading. If you are reading for entertainment, to interact with others, or to find needed information, quickly scan the material to see if it meets your needs. Look for bulleted lists, menu bars, highlighted words, and headers; read only what suits your purpose. Avoid getting lost on your search by using browser tools such as favorites/bookmarks or the history, which is a list of the pages you have visited before. Use multiple browser windows to compare or synthesize information. To avoid eyestrain while reading online, be sure to take breaks and look away from the screen. It is important to get up and stretch periodically.

If you are study reading for an online course, first scan the material for key words. Then carefully read each section and summarize what you have learned. If you cannot do this, reread the section. If you are an auditory learner, you can repeat to yourself what you have learned, either silently or aloud. If you are a kinesthetic learner who learns by the hands-on approach, take notes on the important points. You can save time by opening a separate document in a new window and cutting and pasting the important points into your notes. Be sure to include the source of the material, so that you can use it in writing papers or find the material again. As in reading print material, use some techniques to assure good comprehension: as you read each section, visualize what you are reading, ask questions, and think critically about the material.

Journal Entry #4

Describe a system for college reading. Include these ideas: survey, question, read, recite, review, and reflect.

Guidelines for Marking Your Textbook

Marking your textbook can help you pick out what is important, save time, and review the material. It is a great way to reinforce your memory and help you access the material you have learned. In high school, you were given the command, "Thou shalt not mark in thy book!" College is different. You have paid for the book and need to use it as a tool. Even if you plan to sell your book, you can still mark it up. Here are some guidelines for marking your book:

- Underline or mark the key ideas in your text. You don't have to underline complete sentences; just underline enough to make sense when you review your markings. This technique works especially well for kinesthetics or tactile learners. If reading online, use the highlighter tool to mark the main points and then cut and paste the main points into a separate document.
  - Aim for marking or highlighting about 20 percent of the most important material. If you mark too much of your reading, it will be difficult to review the main points.
  - Read each paragraph first. Ask yourself, "What is the main point?" Highlight or mark the main point if it is important. Not every paragraph has a main point that needs to be marked.
  - Use other marks to help you organize what you have read. Write in numbers or letters and use different colors to help you organize ideas.
  - Most college texts have wide margins. Use these margins to write down questions, outlines, or key points to remember.
  - Learn to be brief, fast, and neat in your marking or highlighting.
  - If you are tempted to mark too much, use the double system of first underlining with a pencil as much as you want and then using a highlighter to pick out the most important 20 percent of the material in the chapter.

© 2014, SnowWhiteimages. Used under license with Shutterstock, Inc.

- Use different kinds of marks and symbols, such as the following:
  - Single or double underlines
  - Brackets around an important paragraph
  - Numbers or letters to organize points
  - Circles or squares to make important words stand out
  - An asterisk or star in the margin for a very important idea
  - A question mark next to something you do not understand
  - "DEF" in the margin to point out a definition
  - Use your imagination to come up with your own symbols
- Learn to recognize organizing patterns in your reading. These patterns will help you to pick out and mark the important ideas.
  - **The listing pattern.** Identify and mark the items in the list. Use numbers and letters to identify the parts of a list.
  - **The sequence pattern.** This pattern presents a list in a certain order. Note the items in the list and the order by using numbers or letters.
  - **The definition pattern.** Circle the word being defined. Underline the definition.
  - **The comparison/contrast pattern.** This pattern explains similarities or differences. Underline or mark these.
  - **The cause/effect pattern.** This pattern describes the reasons things happen. Underline or mark the cause and the effect.
- Quickly review the important points after you have marked each section. Quickly review again when you have finished the chapter. If you review within 20 minutes, the review will be faster and easier.

Reading for Speed and Comprehension

In *How to Read for Speed and Comprehension,* Gordon Wainwright suggests using different gears, or speeds, when reading for different purposes.[14] Understanding these four gears can be helpful for college students.

1. **Studying.** In this gear, the maximum reading speed is about 200 words per minute. It is used for material that is difficult or unfamiliar, such as a college textbook. For this material, a high quality of retention is required. It involves the steps described in SQ4R.

2. **Slow reading.** In this gear, reading speed ranges from 150 to 300 wpm. It is used for material that is fairly difficult when a good quality of retention is desired.

3. **Rapid reading.** In rapid reading, speeds range from 300 to 800 wpm. It is used for average or easy material. Use this gear for review of familiar material.

4. **Skimming.** Skimming is a type of very fast reading, done at 800 to 1000 wpm. With practice, it is possible to skim at 2000 to 3000 wpm. Using this technique, the eyes glide quickly down the page looking for specific information. Not every group of words or line is read. The eyes focus quickly on key ideas, bold headings, and titles. The purpose is to get a quick overview of the important ideas in the material.

Different reading speeds are used for different purposes. In college reading, it is more important to have good comprehension and retention than speed. However, we all live busy lives, and many college students today try to combine study, work, family, and social life. Learning to read faster is important to survival. You can learn to read faster by practicing skimming as a first step in reading. The next step is to slow down, look for the major points, and rehearse them so that they are stored in long-term memory. Using the SQ4R study technique described above will guide you through the process so that you can remember what you read.

Improving Reading

Test what you have learned by circling the letters of the correct answers to the following questions.

1. If you have read the chapter and can't remember what you have read,

   a. read the chapter again.
   b. remember to select important points and review them.
   c. the material is stored in long-term memory.

2. When you start reading a new textbook,

   a. begin with chapter one.
   b. focus on the details you will need to remember.
   c. skim over the text to get a general idea of what you will be reading.

3. The first step in reading a chapter in a college textbook is to

   a. survey and question.
   b. read and recite.
   c. review and reflect.

4. As you are reading each paragraph in a college textbook, it is most important to

   a. read quickly.
   b. identify the main point and recite it.
   c. focus on the details first.

5. When marking a college textbook, it is recommended to mark about

   a. 50%.
   b. 30%.
   c. 20%.

How did you do on the quiz? Check your answers: 1. b, 2. c, 3. a, 4. b, 5. c

What to Do If Your Reading Goes in One Ear and Out the Other

1. **Silence your inner critic.**
   If you have always told yourself that you are a poor reader or hate reading, these thoughts make it difficult to read. Think positively and tell yourself that with some effort, you can read and understand. Focus on what you can do, rather than what you can't do.

2. Look for the key ideas and underline them.

3. **Try visualization.**
   Make a mental picture or video with the material you are reading.

4. **Look for personal meaning.**
   Can you relate the material to your life in any way?

5. Do a quick scan of the material to find some major points and then reread the material closely.

6. Try talking to the text as you read it. Ask questions. Why is this important? Do you know anything about this? Do you agree or disagree? Do you think it is a good or bad idea? Can you use this information in the future? Can you find something interesting in the text? Challenge the material and think critically about it. Make humorous remarks. Imagine yourself in the situation. What would it be like and what would you do? You can write your comments in the text or do this silently in your head.

© 2014, wavebreakmedia. Used under license with Shutterstock, Inc.

Improving Reading Concentration

Hank Aaron said that what separates the superstar from the average ballplayer is that the superstar concentrates just a little longer. Athletes are very aware of the power of concentration in improving athletic performance. Coaches remind athletes to focus on the ball and to develop good powers of concentration and visualization. Being able to concentrate on your reading helps you to study more efficiently.

It is important to have a regular place for studying that has all the needed materials. You will need a table or desk with space for a computer, space for writing, and a comfortable chair. Keep a good supply of writing materials, computer supplies, and reference materials. To minimize fatigue and eyestrain, good lighting is essential. It is best to have an overhead light and a lamp. Place the lamp to your left if you are right-handed. In this way, you will not be writing in a shadow. Do the reverse if you are left-handed. If you have space, use two lamps with one placed on each side. Eliminate glare by using a lampshade. Study lamps often come with a deflector on the bottom of the lampshade that further eliminates glare. Lighter colors on your desk and wall also help to eliminate glare and fatigue.

In setting up your regular place for studying, keep in mind your environmental preferences as identified by your PEPS learning style inventory. Consider these factors:

- Do you need a quiet environment to focus on your studies?
- Do you prefer bright or dim light?
- Do you prefer a warm or cool environment?
- Do you prefer learning by yourself or with others?
- Do you study best in the morning or the afternoon?

Having and using a well-equipped and comfortable study place reduces external distractions. Internal distractions are many and varied and may be more difficult to manage. Internal distractions include being hungry, tired, or ill. It is a good idea to eat and be well rested before reading any course material. If you are ill, rest and get well. Study when you feel better. Many internal distractions are mental, such as personal problems, worrying about grades, lack of interest or motivation, frustration, or just daydreaming.

Here are some ideas for dealing with internal mental distractions while reading.

1. **Become an active reader.** Read to answer questions. Search for the main idea. Recite or re-say the main idea in your mind. Reflect and think critically about the material you are reading. Mark or highlight the text. Visualize what you are reading.

2. **Remind yourself of your purpose for reading.** Think of your future college and career goals.

> **Improving Reading Concentration**
>
> 1. Become an active reader
> 2. Remember your purpose
> 3. Use daydreaming to relax
> 4. Plan to deal with worry
> 5. Break tasks into small parts

© 2014, Diego Cervo. Used under license with Shutterstock, Inc.

3. **Give yourself permission to daydream.** If you like to daydream, give yourself permission to daydream as a break from your studies. Come back to your studies with a more relaxed attitude.

4. **Plan to deal with worry.** Worry is not a very good motivator and it interferes with memory. Take some positive action to deal with problems that cause you to worry. If you are worried about your grades, what can you do right now to improve your chances of making better grades? See a college counselor if worrying about personal problems interferes with studying.

5. **Break the task into small parts.** If the task seems overwhelming, break it into small parts and do the first part. If you have 400 pages to read in 10 days, read 40 pages each day. Make a schedule that allows time to read each day until you have accomplished your goal. Use distributed practice in your studies. Study for a short time each day rather than holding a marathon study session before the test.

Reading Strategies for Different Subjects

While the SQ4R technique is a good general strategy for reading textbook material, there are steps that you will need to add depending on the subject area you are studying.

Math

1. Make sure you have the proper prerequisites or background courses before you begin your math class.

2. When skimming a math book, keep in mind that many of the topics will be unfamiliar to you. You should be able to understand the first few pages and build your knowledge from there. If all the concepts are familiar to you, you may be taking a class that you do not need.

3. It is not enough to read and understand mathematical concepts. Make sure that you add practice to your study system when studying math. Practice gives you the self-confidence to relax when working with math.

4. It is helpful to read over your math book before you go to class so that you will know what areas need special attention.

5. Focus on understanding the math problems and concepts rather than on memorizing problems.

6. Do not get behind in your math studies. You need to understand the first step before you can go on to the next.

7. Ask for help as soon as you have difficulties.

Science

1. In science classes, the scientific method is used to describe the world. The scientific method relies on questioning, observing, hypothesizing, researching, and analyzing. You will learn about theories and scientific principles. Highlight or mark theories, names of scientists, definitions, concepts, and procedures.

2. Understand the scientific principles and use flash cards to remember details and formulas.

3. Study the charts, diagrams, tables, and graphs. Draw your own pictures and graphs to get a visual picture of the material.

4. Use lab time as an opportunity to practice the theories and principles that you have learned.

Social and Behavioral Sciences

1. Social and behavioral scientists focus on principles of behavior, theories, and research. Notice that there are different theories that explain the same phenomena. Highlight, underline, and summarize these theories in your own words.

2. When looking at the research, ask yourself what the point of the research was, who conducted the research, when the research was completed, what data was collected, and what conclusions were drawn.

3. Think of practical applications of theories.

4. Use flash cards to remember details.

Literature Courses

When taking a course in literature, you will be asked to understand, appreciate, interpret, evaluate, and write about the literature.

1. Underline the names of characters and write plot summaries.

2. Write notes about your evaluation of literary works.

3. Make flash cards to remember literary terms.

4. Write down important quotes or note page numbers on a separate piece of paper so that you don't have to go back and find them later when you are writing about a work.

Foreign Language Courses

Foreign language courses require memorization and practice.

1. Distribute the practice. Practice a small amount each day. It is not possible to learn everything at once.

2. Complete the exercises as a way to practice and remember.

3. Study out loud.

4. Practice speaking the language with others.

5. Use flash cards to remember vocabulary.

6. Make charts to practice verb conjugations.

7. Ask for help if you do not understand.

8. Learn to think in the foreign language. Translating from English causes confusion because the structures of languages are different.

> "Whatever the mind of man can conceive and believe, it can achieve."
> Napoleon Hill

KEYS TO SUCCESS

Positive Thinking

You can improve your memory and your reading (as well as your life) by using positive thinking. Positive thinking involves two aspects: thinking about yourself and thinking about the world around you. When you think positively about yourself, you develop confidence in your abilities and become more capable of whatever you are attempting to do. When you think positively about the world around you, you look for possibilities and find interest in what you are doing.

Golfer Arnold Palmer has won many trophies, but places high value on a plaque on his wall with a poem by C.W. Longenecker:

If you think you are beaten, you are.
If you think you dare not, you don't.
If you like to win but think you can't,
It's almost certain that you won't.

(continued)

Life's battles don't always go
To the stronger woman or man,
But sooner or later, those who win
Are those who think they can.[15]

Success in athletics, school, or any other endeavor begins with positive thinking. To remember anything, you first have to believe that you can remember. Trust in your abilities. Then apply memory techniques to help you to remember. If you think that you cannot remember, you will not even try. To be a good reader, you need to think that you can become a good reader and then work toward learning, applying, and practicing good reading techniques.

The second part of positive thinking involves thinking about the world around you. If you can convince yourself that the world and your college studies are full of interesting possibilities, you can start on a journey of adventure to discover new ideas. It is easier to remember and to read if you can find the subject interesting. If the topic is interesting, you will learn more about it. The more you learn about a topic, the more interesting it becomes, and you are well on your way in your journey of discovery. If you tell yourself that the task is boring, you will struggle and find the task difficult. You will also find it difficult to continue.

You can improve your reading through positive thinking. Read with the intent to remember and use reading techniques that work for you. We remember what interests us, and having a positive attitude helps us to find something interesting. To find something interesting, look for personal meaning. How can I use this information? Does it relate to something I know? Will this information be useful in my future career? Why is this information important? Write down your personal goals and remind yourself of your purpose for attending college. You are not just completing an assignment: you are on a path to discovery.

To be successful in college and to remember what you read, start with the belief that you can be successful. Anticipate that the journey will be interesting and full of possibilities. Enjoy the journey!

© 2014, Anson0618. Used under license with Shutterstock, Inc.

Journal Entry #5

How can you use positive thinking to improve memory, reading, and success in college? Use any of these questions to guide your thinking:

- How can you improve your memory or reading with positive thinking?
- How can I think positively about myself?
- How can I think positively about my college experience?
- What is the connection between belief and success?
- How can positive thinking make college more fun?

Improving Memory and Reading

Go to http://www.collegesuccess1.com/JournalEntries.htm for Word files of the Journal Entries

Success over the Internet

Visit the *College Success Website* at http://www.collegesuccess1.com/

The *College Success Website* is continually updated with new topics and links to the material presented in this chapter. Topics include:

- Memory techniques
- Reading strategies
- How to concentrate
- How to highlight a textbook
- Speed reading
- How to study science
- Study groups
- Examples of mnemonics

Contact your instructor if you need assistance in accessing the *College Success Website.*

Notes

1. G. A. Miller, "The Magical Number Seven, Plus or Minus Two: Some Limits on Our Capacity for Processing Information," *Psychological Review* 63 (March 1956): 81–97.

2. Colin Rose, *Accelerated Learning* (New York: Dell Publishing, 1985), 33–36.

3. Ibid., 50–51.

4. Walter Pauk, *How to Study in College* (Boston: Houghton Mifflin, 1989), 96–97.

5. Rose, *Accelerated Learning*, 34.

6. Adapted from Paul Chance, *Learning and Behavior* (Pacific Grove, CA: Brooks/Cole, 1979), 301.

7. Pauk, *How to Study in College,* 108.

8. Daniel Golden, "Building a Better Brain," *Life Magazine,* July 1994, 63–70.

9. Mary Carmichael, "Stronger, Faster, Smarter," *Newsweek,* March 26, 2007, 38–46.

10. Scott LaFee, "A Chronic Lack of Sleep Can Lead to the Big Sleep," *San Diego Union Tribune,* October 8, 1997.

11. Randy Blaun, "How to Eat Smart," *Psychology Today,* May/June 1996, 35.

12. Ibid.

13. Rose, *Accelerated Learning*, 51.

14. Gordon R. Wainwright, *How to Read for Speed and Comprehension* (NJ: Prentice-Hall, 1977), 100–101.

15. Rob Gilbert, ed., *Bits and Pieces* (Fairfield, NJ: The Economics Press, 1998), Vol. R, No. 40, p. 12.

Scenarios

Name _____ Date _____

Review the main ideas on improving memory and reading. Based on these ideas, how would you be successful in the following situations? You may want to do this as a group activity in your class.

1. You just read the assigned chapter in economics and cannot remember what you read. It went in one ear and out the other.

2. In your anatomy and physiology class, you are required to remember the scientific names for 100 different muscles in the body.

3. You signed up for a philosophy class because it meets general education requirements. You are not interested in the class at all.

4. You have a midterm in your literature class and have to read 400 pages in one month.

5. You must take American history to graduate from college. You think that history is boring.

6. You have been introduced to an important business contact and would like to remember his/her name.

7. You are enrolled in an algebra class. You continually remind yourself that you have never been good at math. You don't think that you will pass this class.

8. You have noticed that your grandmother is becoming very forgetful. You want to do whatever is possible to keep your mind healthy as you age.

Memory Test

Name _____ Date _____

Part 1. Your professor will read a list of 15 items. Do not write them down. After listening to this list, see how many you can remember and write them here.

1.	6.	11.
2.	7.	12.
3.	8.	13.
4.	9.	14.
5.	10.	15.

After your professor has given you the answers, write the number of words you remembered: _____

Part 2. Your professor will discuss memory techniques that you can use to improve your test scores and then will read another list. Again, do not write the words down, but try to apply the recommended techniques. Write as many words as you can remember.

1.	6.	11.
2.	7.	12.
3.	8.	13.
4.	9.	14.
5.	10.	15.

How many words did you remember this time? _____

Name _____ Date _____

Join with a group of students in your class to invent some acrostics and acronyms.

Acrostics

Acrostics are creative rhymes, songs, poems, or sentences that help us to remember. To write an acrostic, think of a word that starts with the same letter as each idea you want to remember. Sometimes you can rearrange the words if necessary to form a sentence. At other times, it is necessary to keep the words in order. The more unusual the sentence, the easier it is to remember.

> **Example:** Classification in biology: Kings Play Cards on Fairly Good Soft Velvet (Kingdom, Phylum, Class, Order, Family, Genus, Species, Variety)

Create an acrostic for the planets in the solar system. Keep the words in the same order as the planets from closest to the sun to farthest from the sun.

Mercury, Venus, Earth, Mars, Jupiter, Saturn, Uranus, Neptune, Pluto

_____

_____

_____

Acronyms

To make your own acronym, list the items you wish to remember. Use the first letter of each word to make a new word. The new word you invented can be an actual word or an invented word.

> **Example:** The Great Lakes: HOMES (Huron, Ontario, Michigan, Erie, and Superior)

The following are the excretory organs of the body. Make an acronym to remember them. Rearrange the words if necessary.

intestines, liver, lungs, kidneys, skin

_____

_____

_____

Write down any acrostics or acronyms that you know. Share them with your group.

Check Your Textbook Reading Skills

Name _____ Date _____

As you read each of the following statements, mark your response using this key:

1   I seldom or never do this.

2   I occasionally do this, depending on the class.

3   I almost always or always do this.

_____   **1.** Before I read the chapter, I quickly skim through it to get main ideas.

_____   **2.** As I skim through the chapter, I form questions based on the bold printed section headings.

_____   **3.** I read with a positive attitude and look for something interesting.

_____   **4.** I read the introductory and summary paragraphs in the chapter before I begin reading.

_____   **5.** As I read each paragraph, I look for the main idea.

_____   **6.** I recite the main idea so I can remember it.

_____   **7.** I underline, highlight, or take notes on the main ideas.

_____   **8.** I write notes or outlines in the margin of the text.

_____   **9.** After reading each section, I do a quick review.

_____   **10.** I quickly review the chapter immediately after reading it.

_____   **11.** During or after reading, I reflect on how the material is useful or meaningful to me.

_____   **12.** I read or at least skim the assigned chapter before I come to class.

_____   **13.** I have planned reading time in my weekly schedule.

_____   **14.** I generally think positively about my reading assignments.

_____   **Total points**

Check your score.
42–36   You have excellent college reading skills.
35–30   You have good skills, but can improve.
29–24   Some changes are needed.
23–14   Major changes are needed.

Becoming an Efficient College Reader

Name _____ Date _____

1. Based on your responses to the reading skills checklist on the previous page, list some of your good reading habits.

2. Based on this same checklist, what are some areas you need to improve?

3. Review the material on SQ4R and reading for speed and comprehension. Write five intention statements about how you plan to improve your reading. I intend to . . .

4. Review the material on how to concentrate while reading. List some ideas that you can use.

Surveying and Questioning a Chapter

Name _____   Date _____

Using the *next chapter* assigned in this class or any other class, answer these questions. Again, challenge yourself to do this activity quickly. Can you finish the exercise in five to seven minutes? Notice your beginning and end times.

1. What is the title of the chapter? Write the title in the form of a question. For example, the title of this chapter is "Improving Memory and Reading." A good question would be, "How can I improve my memory and reading?"

2. Briefly list one key idea mentioned in the introduction or first paragraph.

3. Write five questions you asked yourself while surveying this chapter. Read the bold section headings in the chapter and turn them into questions. For example, one heading in this chapter is "Myths about Reading." This heading might prompt you to ask, "What are some myths about reading? Do I believe in some of these myths?"

4. List three topics that interest you.

5. Briefly write one key idea from the last paragraph or chapter summary.

6. How long did it take you to do this exercise? Write your time here.

7. What did you think of this exercise on surveying and questioning a chapter?

CHAPTER 6

Taking Notes, Writing, and Speaking

Learning Objectives

Read to answer these key questions:

- Why is it important to take notes?

- What are some good listening techniques?

- What are some tips for taking good lecture notes?

- What are some note-taking systems?

- What is the best way to review my notes for the test?

- What is power writing?

- How can I make a good speech?

Knowing how to listen and take good notes can make your college life easier and may help you in your future career as well. Professionals in many occupations take notes as a way of recording key ideas for later use. Whether you become a journalist, attorney, architect, engineer, or other professional, listening and taking good notes can help you to get ahead in your career.

Good writing and speaking skills are important to your success in college and in your career. In college, you will be asked to write term papers and complete other writing assignments. The writing skills you learn in college will be used later in jobs involving high responsibility and good pay; on the job, you will write reports, memos, and proposals. In college, you will probably take a speech class and give oral reports in other classes; on the job, you will present your ideas orally to your colleagues and business associates.

Why Take Notes?

The most important reason for taking notes is to remember important material for tests or for future use in your career. If you just attend class without taking notes, you will forget most of the material by the next day.

How does taking notes enhance memory?

- In college, the lecture is a way of supplementing the written material in the textbook. Without good notes, an important part of the course is missing. Note taking provides material to rehearse or recite, so that it can be stored in long-term memory.
- When you take notes and impose your own organization on them, the notes become more personally meaningful. If they are meaningful, they are easier to remember.
- Taking notes helps you to make new connections. New material is remembered by connecting it to what you already know.
- For kinesthetic and tactile learners, the physical act of writing the material is helpful in learning and remembering it.
- For visual learners, notes provide a visual map of the material to be learned.
- For auditory learners, taking notes is a way to listen carefully and record information to be stored in the memory.
- Note taking helps students to concentrate, maintain focus, and stay awake.
- Attending the lectures and taking notes helps you to understand what the professor thinks is important and to know what to study for the exam.

© 2014, Monkey Business Images. Used under license with Shutterstock, Inc.

The College Lecture

You will experience many different types of lectures while in college. At larger universities, many of the beginning-level courses are taught in large lecture halls with 300 people or more. More advanced courses tend to have fewer students. In large lecture situations, it is not always possible or appropriate to ask questions. Under these circumstances, the large lecture is often supplemented by smaller discussion sessions where you can ask questions and review the lecture material. Although attendance may not be checked, it is important to attend both the lectures and the discussion sessions.

A formal college lecture is divided into four parts. Understanding these parts will help you to be a good listener and take good notes.

1. **Introduction.** The professor uses the introduction to set the stage and to introduce the topic of the lecture. Often an overview or outline of the lecture is presented. Use the introduction as a way to begin thinking about the organization of your notes and the key ideas you will need to write down.

2. **Thesis.** The thesis is the key idea in the lecture. In a one-hour lecture, there is usually one thesis statement. Listen carefully for the thesis statement and write it down in your notes. Review the thesis statement and related ideas for the exam.

3. **Body.** The body of the lecture usually consists of five or six main ideas with discussion and clarification of each idea. As a note taker, your job is to identify the main ideas, write them in your notes, and put in enough of the explanation or examples to understand the key ideas.

4. **Conclusion.** In the conclusion, the professor summarizes the key points of the lecture and sometimes asks for questions. Use the conclusion as an opportunity to check your understanding of the lecture and to ask questions to clarify the key points.

> "Education is not a problem. It is an opportunity."
> Lyndon B. Johnson

How to Be a Good Listener

Effective note taking begins with good listening. What is good listening? Sometimes students confuse listening with hearing. Hearing is done with the ears. Listening is a more active process done with the ears and the brain engaged. Good listening requires attention and concentration. Practice these ideas for good listening:

- **Be physically ready.** It is difficult to listen to a lecture if you are tired, hungry, or ill. Get enough sleep so that you can stay awake. Eat a balanced diet without too much caffeine or sugar. Take care of your health and participate in an exercise program so that you feel your best.

- **Prepare a mental framework.** Look at the course syllabus to become familiar with the topic of the lecture. Use your textbook to read, or at least survey, the material to be covered in the lecture. If you are familiar with the key concepts from the textbook, you will be able to understand the lecture and know what to write down in your notes. If the material is in your book, there is no need to write it down in your notes.

  The more complex the topic, the more important it is for you to read the text first. If you go to the lecture and have no idea what is being discussed, you may be overwhelmed and find it difficult to take notes on material that is totally new to you. Remember that it is easier to remember material if you can connect it to material you already know.

- **Find a good place to sit.** Arrive early to get a good seat. The best seats in the classroom are in the front and center of the room. If you were buying concert tickets, these would be the best and most expensive seats. Find a seat that will help you to hear and focus on the speaker. You may need to find a seat away from your friends to avoid distractions.

- **Have a positive mental attitude.** Convince yourself that the speaker has something important to say and be open to new ideas. This may require you to focus on your goals and to look past some distractions. Maybe the lecturer doesn't have the best speaking voice or you don't like his or her appearance. Focus on what you can learn from the professor rather than outward appearances.

- **Listen actively to identify the main points.** As you are listening to the lecture, ask yourself, "What is the main idea?" In your own words, write the main points down in your notes. Do not try to write down everything the professor says. This will be impossible and unnecessary. Imagine that your mind is a filter and you are actively sorting through the material to find the key ideas and write them down in your notes. Try to identify the key points that will be on the test and write them in your notes.

- **Stay awake and engaged in learning.** The best way to stay awake and focused is to listen actively and take notes. Have a mental debate with the professor. Listen for the main points and the logical connection between ideas. The physical act of writing the notes will help to keep you awake.

Tips for Good Note Taking

Here are some suggestions for taking good notes:

1. Attend all of the lectures. Because many professors do not take attendance, students are often tempted to miss class. If you do not attend the lectures, however, you will not know what the professor thinks is important and what to study for the test. There will be important points covered in the lectures that are not in the book.

2. Have the proper materials. A three-ring notebook and notebook paper are recommended. Organize notes chronologically and include any handouts given in class. You can have a small notebook for each class or a single large notebook with dividers for each class. Just take the notebook paper to class and later file it in your notebook at home. Use your laptop as an alternative to a paper notebook.

3. Begin your notes by writing the date of the lecture, so you can keep your notes in order.

4. Write notes on the front side only of each piece of paper. This will allow you to spread the pages out and see the big picture or pattern in the lectures when you are reviewing.

© 2014, Monkey Business Images. Used under license with Shutterstock, Inc.

5. Write notes neatly and legibly so you can read and review them easily.

6. Do not waste time recopying or typing your notes. Your time would be better spent reviewing your notes.

7. As a general rule, do not rely on a tape recorder for taking notes. With a tape recorder, you will have to listen to the lecture again on tape. For a semester course, this would be about 45 hours of tape! It is much faster to review carefully written notes.

8. Copy down everything written on the board and the main points from PowerPoint or other visual presentations. If it is important enough for the professor to write on the board, it is important enough to be on the test.

9. Use key words and phrases in your notes. Leave out unimportant words and don't worry about grammar.

10. Use abbreviations as long as you can read them. Entire sentences or paragraphs are not necessary and you may not have time to write them.

11. Don't loan your whole notebook to someone else because you may not get it back. If you want to share your notes, make copies.

12. If the professor talks too fast, listen carefully for the key ideas and write them down. Leave spaces in your notes to fill in later. You may be able to find the information in the text or get the information from another student.

13. Explore new uses of technology for note taking. Students are taking notes and sharing them on Facebook and GradeGuru, for example.

Journal Entry #1

Write one paragraph giving advice to a new student about taking notes in college. Use any of these questions to guide your thinking:

- Why is note taking necessary in college?
- How can you be a good listener?
- What are some tips for taking good notes?
- What are some ideas that don't work?

Note-Taking Systems

There are several systems for taking notes. How you take notes will depend on your learning style and the lecturer's speaking style. Experiment with these systems and use what works best for you.

Note-Taking Systems
- Cornell format
- Outline method
- Mind map

The Cornell Format

The Cornell format is an efficient method of taking notes and reviewing them. It appeals to students who are logical, orderly, and organized and have lectures that fit into this pattern. The Cornell format is especially helpful for thinking about key points as you review your notes.

Step 1: Prepare. To use the Cornell format, you will need a three-ring notebook with looseleaf paper. Draw or fold a vertical line 2½ inches from the left side of the paper. This is the recall column that can be used to write key ideas when reviewing. Use the

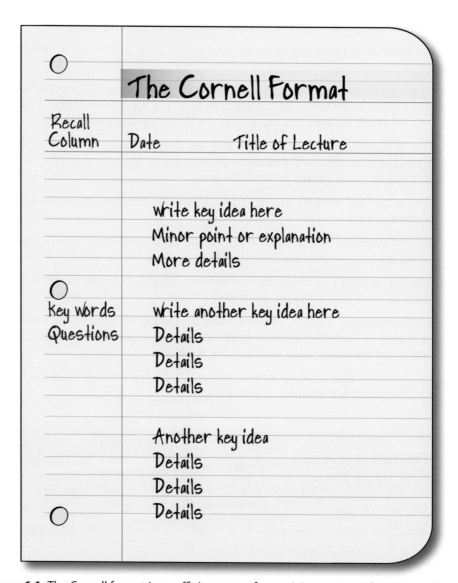

Figure 6.1 The Cornell format is an efficient way of organizing notes and reviewing them.

remaining section of the paper for your notes. Write the date and title of the lecture at the top of the page.

Step 2: Take notes. Use the large area to the right of the recall column to take notes. Listen for key ideas and write them just to the right of the recall column line, as in the diagram above. Indent your notes for minor points and illustrative details. Then skip a space and write the next key idea. Don't worry about using numbers or letters as in an outline format. Just use the indentations and spacing to highlight and separate key ideas. Use short phrases, key words, and abbreviations. Complete sentences are not necessary, but write legibly so you can read your notes later.

Step 3: Use the recall column for review. Read over your notes and write down key words or ideas from the lecture in the recall column. Ask yourself, "What is this about?" Cover up the notes on the right-hand side and recite the key ideas of the lecture. Another variation is to write questions in the margin. Find the key ideas and then write possible exam questions in the recall column. Cover your notes and see if you can answer the questions.

The Outline Method

If the lecture is well organized, some students just take notes in outline format. Sometimes lecturers will show their outline as they speak.

- Use Roman numerals to label main topics. Then use capital letters for main ideas and Arabic numerals for related details or examples.
- You can make a free-form outline using just indentation to separate main ideas and supporting details.
- Leave spaces to fill in material later.
- Use a highlighter to review your notes as soon as possible after the lecture.

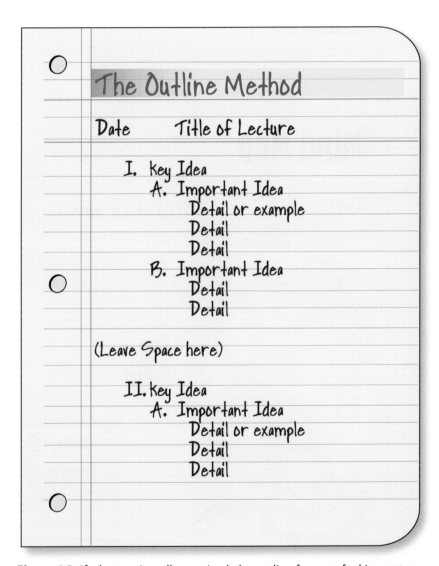

Figure 6.2 If a lecture is well organized, the outline format of taking notes works well.

The Mind Map

A mind map shows the relationship between ideas in a visual way. It is much easier to remember items that are organized and linked together in a personally meaningful way. As a result, recall and review is quicker and more effective. Mind maps have appeal to visual learners and those who do not want to be limited by a set structure, as in the outline formats. They can also be used for lectures that are not highly structured. Here are some suggestions for using the mind-mapping technique:

- Turn your paper sideways to give you more space. Use standard-size notebook paper or consider larger sheets if possible.
- Write the main idea in the center of the page and circle it.
- Arrange ideas so that more important ideas are closer to the center and less important ideas are farther out.

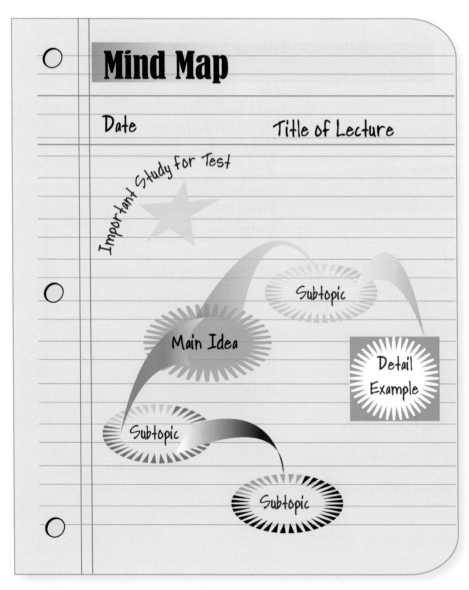

Figure 6.3 The mind map format of taking notes shows the relationship between ideas in a visual way.

- Show the relationship of the minor points to the main ideas using lines, circles, boxes, charts, and other visual devices. Here is where you can use your creativity and imagination to make a visual picture of the key ideas in the lecture.
- Use symbols and drawings.
- Use different colors to separate main ideas.
- When the lecturer moves to another main idea, start a new mind map.
- When you are done with the lecture, quickly review your mind maps. Add any written material that will be helpful in understanding the map later.
- A mind map can also be used as:
  - a review tool for remembering and relating the key ideas in the textbook;
  - a preparation tool for essay exams in which remembering main ideas and relationships is important; and
  - the first step in organizing ideas for a term paper.

Improving Note-Taking Efficiency

Improve note-taking efficiency by listening for key words that signal the main ideas and supporting details. Learn to write faster by using telegraphic sentences, abbreviations, and symbols.

Telegraphic Sentences

Telegraphic sentences are short, abbreviated sentences used in note taking. They are very similar to the text messages sent on a cell phone. There are four rules for telegraphic sentences:

1. Write key words only.
2. Omit unnecessary words (*a, an, the*).
3. Ignore rules of grammar.
4. Use abbreviations and symbols.

Here is an example of a small part of a lecture followed by a student's telegraphic notes:

Heavy drinking of alcoholic beverages causes students to miss class and to fall behind in schoolwork. College students who are considered binge drinkers are at risk for many alcohol-related problems. Binge drinking is simply drinking too much alcohol at one time. Binge drinking is defined by researchers as drinking five or more drinks in a row for men or four or more drinks in a row for women. Researchers estimate that two out of five college students (40 percent) are binge drinkers.

Binge drinking—too much alcohol at one time
    Men = 5 in row
    Women = 4
    2 out of 5 (40%) college students binge

Signal Words

Signal words are clues to understanding the structure and content of a lecture. Recognizing signal words can help you identify key ideas and organize them in your notes. The table on the following page lists some common signal words and their meaning.

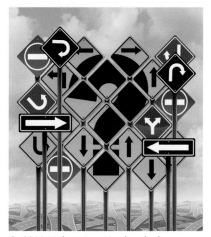

© 2014, Lightspring. Used under license with Shutterstock, Inc.

Signal Words

Type	Examples	Meaning
Main idea words	And most important A major development The basic concept is Remember that The main idea is We will focus on The key is	Introduce the key points that need to be written in your notes.
Example words	To illustrate For example For instance	Clarify and illustrate the main ideas in the lecture. Write these examples in your notes after the main idea. If multiple examples are given, write down the ones you have time for or the ones that you understand the best.
Addition words	In addition Also Furthermore	Add more important information. Write these points down in your notes.
Enumeration words	The five steps First, second, third Next	Signal a list. Write down the list in your notes and number the items.
Time words	Before, after Formerly Subsequently Prior Meanwhile	Signal the order of events. Write down the events in the correct order in your notes.
Cause and effect words	Therefore As a result If . . ., then	Signal important concepts that might be on the exam. When you hear these words, label them "cause" and "effect" in your notes and review these ideas for the exam.
Definition words	In other words It simply means That is In essence	Provide the meanings of words or simplify complex ideas. Write these definitions or clarifications in your notes.
Swivel words	However Nevertheless Yes, but Still	Provide exceptions, qualifications, or further clarification. Write down qualifying comments in your notes.
Compare and contrast words	Similarly Likewise In contrast	Present similarities or differences. Write these similarities and differences in your notes and label them.
Summary words	In conclusion To sum up In a nutshell	Restate the important ideas of the lecture. Write the summaries in your notes.
Test words	This is important. Remember this. You'll see this again. You might want to study this for the test.	Provide a clue that the material will be on the test. Write these down in your notes and mark them in a way that stands out. Put a star or asterisk next to these items or highlight them. Each professor has his or her own test clue words.

Abbreviations

If you have time, write out words in their entirety for ease of reading. If you are short on time, use any abbreviation as long as you can read it. Here are some ideas:

1. Use the first syllable of the word.

democracy	dem
education	ed
politics	pol
different	diff
moderate	mod
characteristic	char
develop	dev

2. Use just enough of the word so that you can recognize it.

republican	repub
prescription	prescrip
introduction	intro
intelligence	intell
association	assoc

3. Abbreviate or write out the word the first time, then use an acronym. For example, for the United States Department of Agriculture, abbreviate it as "US Dept of Ag" and then write it as USDA in subsequent references. Other examples:

short-term memory	STM
as soon as possible	ASAP

4. Omit vowels.

background	bkgrnd
problem	prblm
government	gvt

5. Use g in place of ing.

checking	ckg
decreasing	decrg

6. Write your notes in text message format.

Symbols

Use common symbols or invent your own to speed up the note-taking process.

Common Symbols Used in Note Taking

Symbol	Meaning	Symbol	Meaning
&	and	B4	before
w	with	BC	because
wo	without	esp	especially
wi	within	diff	difference
<	less than	min	minimum
>	more than	gov	government

(Continued)

Symbol	Meaning	Symbol	Meaning
@	at	ex	example
/	per	↑	increasing
2	to, two, too	↓	decreasing
∴	therefore	=	equal
vs	versus, against	≠	not equal

How to Review Your Notes

© 2014, Terence. Used under license with Shutterstock, Inc.

Immediate review. Review your notes as soon as possible after the lecture. The most effective review is done immediately or at least within 20 minutes. If you wait until the next day to review, you may already have forgotten much of the information. During the immediate review, fill in any missing or incomplete information. Say the important points to yourself. This begins the process of rehearsal for storing the information in long-term memory.

There are various methods for review depending on your note-taking system:

- For the Cornell format, use the recall column to write in key words or questions. Cover your notes and see if you can recall the main ideas. Place checkmarks by the items you have mastered. Don't worry about mastering all the key points from the beginning. With each review, it will be easier to remember the information.
- For the outline format, use a highlighter to mark the key ideas as you repeat them silently to yourself.
- For mind maps, look over the information and think about the key ideas and their relationships. Fill in additional information or clarification. Highlight important points or relationships with color.

Intermediate review. Set up some time each week for short reviews of your notes and the key points in your textbook from previous weeks. Quickly look over the notes and recite the key points in your mind. These intermediate reviews will help you to master the material and avoid test anxiety.

Test review. Complete a major review as part of your test preparation strategy. As you look through your notes, turn the key ideas into possible test questions and answer them.

Final review. The final review occurs after you have received the results of your test. Ask yourself these questions:

- What percentage of the test questions came from the lecture notes?
- Were you prepared for the exam? If so, congratulate yourself on a job well done. If not, how can you improve next time?
- Were your notes adequate? If not, what needs to be added or changed?

"You have to get your education. Then nobody can control your destiny."
Charles Barkley

Listening and Note Taking

Test what you have learned by selecting the correct answer to the following questions.

1. When taking notes on a college lecture, it is most important to

   a. write down everything you hear.
   b. write down the main ideas and enough explanation to understand them.
   c. write down names, dates, places, and numbers.

2. To be a good listener,

   a. read or skim over the material before you attend the lecture.
   b. attend the lecture first and then read the text.
   c. remember that listening is more important than note taking.

3. To stay awake during the lecture,

   a. drink lots of coffee.
   b. sit near your friends so you can make some comments on the lecture.
   c. listen actively by taking notes.

4. Since attendance is not always checked in college classes,

   a. it is not necessary to attend class if you read the textbook.
   b. it is acceptable to miss lectures as long as you show up for the exams.
   c. it is up to you to attend every class.

5. The best time to review your notes is

   a. as soon as possible after the lecture.
   b. within 24 hours.
   c. within one week.

How did you do on the quiz? Check your answers: 1. b, 2. a, 3. c, 4. c, 5. a

Journal Entry #2

Write five intention statements about improving your note-taking skills. Consider your note-taking system, how to take notes more efficiently, and the best way to review your notes. I intend to . . .

"The highest reward for a person's toil is not what they get for it, but what they become by it."
John Ruskin

Power Writing

Effective writing will help you in school, on the job, and in your personal life. Good writing will help you to create quality term papers. The writing skills that you learn in college will be used later in jobs involving high responsibility and good pay. You can become an excellent writer by learning about the steps in POWER writing: prepare, organize, write, edit, and revise.

Power Writing

- Prepare
- Organize
- Write
- Edit
- Revise

Prepare

Plan your time. The first step in writing is to plan your time so that the project can be completed by the due date. Picture this scene: It is the day that the term paper is due. A few students proudly hand in their term papers and are ready to celebrate their accomplishments. Many of the students in the class are absent, and some will never return to the class. Some of the students look as though they haven't slept the night before. They look stressed and weary. At the front of the class is a line of students wanting to talk with the instructor. The instructor has heard it all before:

- I had my paper all completed and my printer jammed.
- My hard drive crashed and I lost my paper.
- I was driving to school and my paper flew off my motorcycle.
- I had the flu.
- My children were sick.
- I had to take my dog to the vet.
- My dog ate my paper.
- My car broke down and I could not get to the library.
- My grandmother died and I had to go to the funeral.
- My roommate accidentally took my backpack to school.
- I spilled salad dressing on my paper, so I put it in the microwave to dry it out and the writing disappeared!

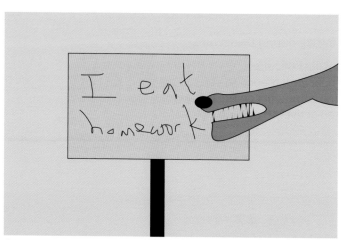

© 2014, Benjamin Howell. Used under license with Shutterstock, Inc.

To avoid being in this uncomfortable and stressful situation, plan ahead. Plan to complete your project at least one week ahead of time so that you can deal with life's emergencies. Life does not always go as planned. You or your children may get sick, or your dog may do strange things to your homework. Your computer may malfunction, leading you to believe it senses stress and malfunctions just to frustrate you even more.

To avoid stress and do your best work, start with the date that the project is due and then think about the steps needed to finish. Write these dates on your calendar or on your list of things to do. Consider all these components:

Prepare

- Plan your time
- Find space and time
- Choose general topic
- Gather information
- Write thesis statement

Project due date:

To do	By when?
1. Brainstorm ideas.	_____
2. Choose a topic.	_____
3. Gather information.	_____
4. Write a thesis statement.	_____
5. Write an outline.	_____
6. Write the introduction.	_____
7. Write the first draft.	_____
8. Prepare the bibliography.	_____
9. Edit.	_____
10. Revise.	_____
11. Print and assemble.	_____

Find a space and time. Find a space where you can work. Gather the materials that you will need to write. Generally, writing is best done in longer blocks of time. Determine when you will work on your paper and write the time on your schedule. Start right away to avoid panic later.

Choose a general topic. This task will be easy if your topic is already clearly defined by your instructor or your boss at work. Make sure that you have a clear idea of what is required, such as length, format, purpose, and method of citing references and topic. Many times the choice of a topic is left to you. Begin by doing some brainstorming. Think about topics that interest you. Write them down. You may want to focus your attention on brainstorming ideas for five or 10 minutes, and then put the project aside and come back to it later. Once you have started the process of thinking about the ideas, your mind will continue to work and you may have some creative inspiration. If inspiration does not come, repeat the brainstorming process.

Gather information. Go to your college library and use the Internet to gather your information. As you begin, you can see what is available, what is interesting to you, and what the current thinking is on your topic. Note the major topics of interest that might be useful to you. Once you have found some interesting material, you will feel motivated to continue your project. As you find information relevant to your topic, make sure to write down the sources of your information to use in your bibliography. The bibliography contains information about where you found your material. Write down the author, the title of the publication, the publisher, and the place and date of publication. For Internet resources, list the address of the website and the date accessed.

Write the thesis statement. The thesis statement is the key idea in your paper. It provides a direction for you to follow. It is the first step in organizing your work. To write a thesis statement, review the material you have gathered and then ask these questions:

- What is the most important idea?
- What question would I like to ask about it?
- What is my answer?

© 2014, Elena Elisseeva. Used under license with Shutterstock, Inc.

For example, if I decide to write a paper for my health class on the harmful effects of smoking, I would look at current references on the topic. I might become interested in how the tobacco companies misled the public on the dangers of smoking. I would think about my thesis statement and answer the questions stated above.

- **What is the most important idea?** Smoking is harmful to your health.
- **What question would I like to ask about it?** Did the tobacco companies mislead the public about the health hazards of smoking?
- **What is my answer?** The tobacco companies misled the public about the hazards of smoking in order to protect their business interests.
- **My thesis statement:** Tobacco companies knew that smoking was hazardous to health, but to protect their business interests, they deliberately misled the public.

The thesis statement helps to narrow the topic and provide direction for the paper. I can now focus on reference material related to my topic: research on health effects of smoking, congressional testimony relating to regulation of the tobacco industry, and how advertising influences people to smoke.

Organize

Organize
- List related topics
- Arrange in logical order
- Have an organizational structure

At this point you have many ideas about what to include in your paper, and you have a central focus, your thesis statement. Start to organize your paper by listing the topics that are related to your thesis statement. Here is a list of topics related to my thesis statement about smoking:

- Tobacco companies' awareness that nicotine is addictive
- Minimizing health hazards in tobacco advertisements
- How advertisements encourage people to smoke
- Money earned by the tobacco industry
- Health problems caused by smoking
- Statistics on numbers of people who have health problems or die from smoking
- Regulation of the tobacco industry
- Advertisements aimed at children

Think about the topics and arrange them in logical order. Use an outline, a mind map, a flowchart, or a drawing to think about how you will organize the important topics. Keep in mind that you will need an introduction, a body, and a conclusion. Having an organizational structure will make it easier for you to write because you will not need to wonder what comes next.

Write

Write the First Sentence

Begin with the main idea.

Write the Introduction

This is the road map for the rest of the paper. The introduction includes your thesis statement and establishes the foundation of the paper. It introduces topics that will be discussed in the body of the paper. The introduction should include some interesting points that provide a "hook" to motivate the audience to read your paper. For example, for a paper on the hazards of smoking, you might begin with statistics on how many people suffer from smoking-related illnesses and premature death. Note the large profits earned by the tobacco industry. Then introduce other topics: deception, advertisements, and regulation. The introduction provides a guide or outline of what will follow in the paper.

Write
- First sentence
- Introduction
- Body
- Conclusion
- References

Write the Body of the Paper

The body of the paper is divided into paragraphs that discuss the topics that you have introduced. As you write each paragraph, include the main idea and then explain it and give examples. Here are some good tips for writing:

1. Good writing reflects clear thinking. Think about what you want to say and write about it so the reader can understand your point of view.

2. Use clear and concise language. Avoid using too many words or scholarly-sounding words that might get in the way of understanding.

3. Don't assume that the audience knows what you are writing about. Provide complete information.

4. Provide examples, stories, and quotes to support your main points. Include your own ideas and experiences.

5. Beware of plagiarism. Plagiarism is copying the work of others without giving them credit. It is illegal and can cause you to receive a failing grade on your project or even get you into legal trouble. Faculty regularly uses software programs that identify plagiarized material in student papers. You can avoid plagiarism by using quotation marks around an author's words and providing a reference indicating where you found the material. Another way to avoid plagiarism is by carefully reading your source material while using critical thinking to evaluate it. Then look away from the source and write about the ideas in your own words, including your critical thinking about the subject. Don't forget to include a reference for the source material in your bibliography.

Write the Conclusion

The conclusion summarizes the topics in the paper and presents your point of view. It makes reference to the introduction and answers the question posed in your thesis statement. It often makes the reader think about the significance of your point and the implications for the future. Make your conclusion interesting and powerful.

Include References

No college paper is complete without references. References may be given in footnotes, endnotes, a list of works cited, or a bibliography. You can use your computer to insert these references. There are various styles for citing references depending on your subject area. There are computer programs that put your information into the correct style. Ask your instructor which style to use for your particular class or project. Three frequently used styles for citing references are APA, Chicago, and MLA.

1. The American Psychological Association (APA) style is used in psychology and other behavioral sciences. Consult the *Publication Manual of the American Psychological Association*, 6th ed. (Washington, DC: American Psychological Association, 2010). You can find this source online at www.apastyle.org.

2. Chicago style is used by many professional writers in a variety of fields. Consult the *Chicago Manual of Style*, 16th ed. (Chicago: University of Chicago Press, 2010). You can find this source online at www.chicagomanualofstyle.org/home.html.

3. The Modern Language Association (MLA) style is used in English, classical languages, and the humanities. Consult the *MLA Handbook for Writers of Research Papers*, 7th ed. (New York: Modern Language Association, 2009). This source is available online at www.mla.org/style.

Each of these styles uses a different format for listing sources, but all include the same information. Make sure you write down this information as you collect your reference material. If you forget this step, it is very time-consuming and difficult to find later.

- Author's name
- Title of the book or article
- Journal name
- Publisher
- City where book was published
- Publication date
- Page number (and volume and issue numbers, if available)

Here are some examples of citations in the APA style:

- **Book.** Include author, date of publication, title, city of publication, and publisher.
  Fralick, M. (2014). *College and career success* (6th ed.). Dubuque, IA: Kendall Hunt.
- **Journal article.** Include author, date, title, name of journal, volume and issue numbers, pages.
  Fralick, M. (1993). College success: A study of positive and negative attrition. *Community College Review, 20*(5), 29–36.
- **Website.** Include author, date listed or updated, document title or name of website, URL or website address, and date accessed. Include as many of the above items as possible. Methods of citing information from the Internet are still evolving.
  Fralick, M. (2014, October). *Note taking.* Retrieved October 2013 from College Success 1 at www.collegesuccess1.com/

Save Your Work

As soon as you have written the first paragraph, save it on your computer. If your computer is not backed up by a remote server such as iCloud or Carbonite, save another copy on a flash drive. When you are finished, print your work and save a paper copy. Then, if your hard drive crashes, you will still have your work at another location. If your file becomes corrupted, you will still have the paper copy. Following these procedures can save you a lot of headaches. Any writer can tell you stories of lost work because of computer problems, lightning storms, power outages, and other unpredictable events.

Put It Away for a While

The last step in writing the first draft is easy. Put it away for a while and come back to it later. In this way, you can relax and gain some perspective on your work. You will be able to take a more objective look at your work to begin the process of editing and revising.

Writer's Block

Many people who are anxious about writing experience "writer's block." You have writer's block if you find yourself staring at that blank piece of paper or computer screen not knowing how to begin or what to write. Here are some tips for avoiding writer's block.

- **Write freely.** Just write anything about your topic that comes to mind. Don't worry about organization or perfection at this point. Don't censure your ideas. You can always go back to organize and edit later. Free-writing helps you to overcome one of the main causes of writer's block: you think it has to be perfect from the beginning. This expectation of perfection causes anxiety. You freeze up and become unable to write. Perhaps you have past memories of writing where the teacher made many corrections on your paper. Maybe you lack confidence in your writing skills. The only way you will become a better writer is to keep writing and perfecting your writing skills, so to start the writing process, just write what comes to mind. Don't worry how great it is. You can fix it later. Just begin.

- **Use brainstorming if you get stuck.** For five minutes, focus your attention on the topic and write whatever comes to mind. You don't even need to write full sentences; just jot down ideas. If you are really stuck, try working on a different topic or take a break and come back to it later.

- **Realize that it is only the first draft.** It is not the finished product and it does not have to be perfect. Just write some ideas on paper; you can revise them later.

- **Read through your reference materials.** The ideas you find can get your mind working. Also, reading can make you a better writer.

- **Break the assignment up into small parts.** If you find writing difficult, write for five minutes at a time. Do this consistently and you can get used to writing and can complete your paper.

Tips to Overcome Writer's Block

1. Write freely
2. Use brainstorming
3. Realize it's a first draft
4. Read reference materials
5. Break up assignment
6. Find a good place to write
7. Beware of procrastination

© 2014, Creativa. Used under license with Shutterstock, Inc.

- **Find a good place for writing.** If you are an introvert, look for a quiet place for concentration. If you are an extrovert, go to a restaurant or coffee shop and start your writing.
- **Beware of procrastination.** The more you put off writing, the more anxious you will become and the more difficult the task will be. Make a schedule and stick to it.

Edit and Revise

The editing and revising stage allows you to take a critical look at what you have written. It takes some courage to do this step. Once people see their ideas in writing, they become attached to them. With careful editing and revising, you can turn in your best work and be proud of your accomplishments. Here are some tips for editing and revising:

1. **Read your paper as if you were the audience.** Pretend that you are the instructor or another person reading your paper. Does every sentence make sense? Did you say what you meant to say? Read what you have written, and the result will be a more effective paper.

2. **Read paragraph by paragraph.** Does each paragraph have a main idea and supporting details? Do the paragraphs fit logically together? Use the cut-and-paste feature on your computer to move sentences and paragraphs around if needed.

3. **Check your grammar and spelling.** Use the spell check and grammar check on your computer. These tools are helpful, but they are not thorough enough. The spell check will pick up only misspelled words. It will skip words that are spelled correctly but not the intended word—for example, if you use "of" instead of "on" or "their" instead of "there." To find such errors, you need to read your paper after doing a spell check.

4. **Check for language that is biased in terms of gender, disability, or ethnic group.** Use words that are gender neutral. If a book or paper uses only the pronoun "he" or "she," half of the population is left out. You can often avoid sexist language by using the plural forms of nouns:

   (singular)   The successful student knows *his* values and sets goals for the future.

   (plural)   Successful students know *their* values and set goals for the future.

   After all, we are trying to make the world a better place, with opportunity for all. Here are some examples of biased language and better alternatives.

Biased Language	*Better Alternatives*
policeman	police officer
chairman	chair
fireman	firefighter
postman	mail carrier
mankind	humanity
manmade	handcrafted
housewife	homemaker
crippled	persons with disabilities

5. **Have someone else read your paper.** Ask your reader to check for clarity and meaning. After you have read your paper many times, you do not really see it anymore. If you need assistance in writing, colleges offer tutoring or writing labs where you can get help with editing and revising.

6. **Review your introduction and conclusion.** They should be clear, interesting, and concise. The introduction and conclusion are the most powerful parts of your paper.

Tips for Editing
and Revising

1. Read your paper objectively
2. Read paragraph by paragraph
3. Check grammar and spelling
4. Check for biased language
5. Have someone else read your paper
6. Review the introduction and conclusion
7. Prepare final copy
8. Prepare title page

7. **Prepare the final copy.** Check your instructor's instructions on the format required. If there are no instructions, use the following format:

- Use double-spacing.

- Use 10- or 12-point font.

- Use one-inch margins on all sides.

- Use a three-inch top margin on the first page.

- Single-space footnotes and endnotes.

- Number your pages.

8. **Prepare the title page.** Center the title of your paper and place it one third of the page from the top. On the bottom third of the page, center your name, the professor's name, the name of the class, and the date.

Final Steps

Make sure you follow instructions about using a folder or cover for your paper. Generally professors dislike bulky folders or notebooks because they are difficult to carry. Imagine your professor trying to carry 50 notebooks to his or her office! Unless asked to do so, do not use plastic page protectors. Professors like to write comments on papers, and it is extremely difficult to write on papers with page protectors.

Turning your paper in on time is very important. Some professors do not accept late papers. Others subtract points if your paper is late. Put your paper in the car or someplace where you will have to see it before you go to class. **Then reward yourself for a job well done!**

Journal Entry #3

Write five intention statements about improving your writing. While thinking about your statements, consider the steps of POWER writing: prepare, organize, write, edit, and revise. Do you need to work on problems such as writer's block or getting your writing done on time? I intend to . . .

Effective Public Speaking

You may need to take a speech class in order to graduate from college, and many of your classes will require oral presentations. Being a good speaker can contribute to your success on the job as well. A study done at Stanford University showed that one of the top predictors of success in professional positions was the ability to be a good public speaker.[1] You will need to present information to your boss, your colleagues, and your customers or clients.

"Let us think of education as the means of developing our greatest abilities, because in each of us there is a private hope and dream which, fulfilled, can be translated into greater benefit for everyone and greater strength for our nation."

John F. Kennedy

Learn to Relax

Whenever I tell students that they will need to take a speech class or make an oral presentation, I see a look of panic on their faces. Good preparation can help you to feel confident about your oral presentation. Professional speaker Lilly Walters believes that you can deal with 75 percent of your anxiety by being well prepared.[2] You can deal with the remaining 25 percent by using some relaxation techniques.

- If you are anxious, admit to yourself that you are anxious. If it is appropriate, as in a beginning speech class, you can even admit to the audience that you are anxious. Once you have admitted that you are anxious, visualize yourself confidently making the speech.
- You do not have to be perfect; it is okay to make mistakes. Making mistakes just shows you are human like the rest of us.
- If you are anxious before your speech, take three to five deep breaths. Breathe in slowly and hold your breath for five seconds, and then breathe out slowly. Focus your mind on your breathing rather than your speech.
- Use positive self-talk to help you to relax. Instead of saying to yourself, "I will look like a fool up there giving the speech," tell yourself, "I can do this" or "It will be okay."
- Once you start speaking, anxiety will generally decline.
- With experience, you will gain confidence in your speaking ability and will be able to relax more easily.

Preparing and Delivering Your Speech

Write the Beginning of the Speech

The beginning includes a statement of your objective and what your speech will be about. It should prepare the audience for what comes next. You can begin your speech with a personal experience, a quote, a news article, or a joke. Jokes can be effective, but they are risky. Try out your joke with your friends to make sure that it is funny. Do not tell jokes that put down other people or groups.

Write the Main Body of the Speech

The main body of the speech consists of four or five main points. Just as in your term paper, state your main points and then provide details, examples, or stories that illustrate them. As you present the main points of your speech, consider your audience. Your speech will be different depending on whether it is made to a group of high school students, your college classmates, or a group of professionals. You can add interest to your speech by using props, pictures, charts, PowerPoint, music, or video clips. College students today are increasingly using PowerPoint software to make classroom presentations. If you are planning to enter a professional career, learning how to make PowerPoint presentations will be an asset.

Write the Conclusion

In your conclusion, summarize and review the key points of your speech. The conclusion is like the icing on a cake. It should be strong, persuasive, and interesting. Invest some time in your ending statement. It can be a call to action, a recommendation for the future, a quote, or a story.

Practice Your Speech

Practice your speech until you feel comfortable with it. Prepare a memory system or notes to help you deliver your speech. You will want to make eye contact with your audience, which is difficult if you are trying to read your speech. A memory system useful for delivering speeches is the loci system. Visualize a house, for example: the entryway is the introduction, and each room represents a main point in the speech. Visualize walking into each room and what you will say in each room. Each room can have items that remind you of what you are going to say. At the conclusion, you say good-bye at the door. Another technique is to prepare brief notes or outlines on index cards or sheets of paper. When you are practicing your speech, time it to see how long it is. Keep your speech within the time allowed. Most people tend to speak longer than necessary.

Review the Setup

If you are using props, make sure that you have them ready. If you are using equipment, make sure it is available and in working condition. Make arrangements in advance for the equipment you need and, if possible, check to see that it is running properly right before your presentation.

Deliver the Speech

Wear clothes that make you feel comfortable, but not out of place. Remember to smile and make eye contact with members of the audience. Take a few deep breaths if you are nervous. You will probably be less nervous once you begin. If you make a mistake, keep your sense of humor. I recall the famous chef Julia Child doing a live television production on how to cook a turkey. As she took the turkey out of the oven, it slipped and landed on the floor right in front of the television cameras. She calmly picked it up and said, "And remember that you are the only one that really knows what goes on in the kitchen." It was one of the shows that made her famous.

Writing and Speaking

Test what you have learned by selecting the correct answers to the following questions.

1. To make sure to get your paper done on time,

   a. have someone remind you of the deadline.
   b. write the due date on your calendar and the date for completion of each step.
   c. write your paper just before the due date to increase motivation.

2. The thesis statement is the

   a. most important sentence in each paragraph.
   b. key idea in the paper.
   c. summary of the paper.

3. If you have writer's block, it is helpful to

   a. delay writing your paper until you feel relaxed.
   b. make sure that your writing is perfect from the beginning.
   c. begin with brainstorming or free writing.

4. No college paper is complete without

   a. the references.
   b. a professional-looking cover.
   c. printing on quality paper.

5. You can deal with most of your anxiety about public speaking by

   a. striving for perfection.
   b. visualizing your anxiety.
   c. being well prepared.

How did you do on the quiz? Check your answers: 1. b, 2. b, 3. c, 4. a, 5. c

Journal Entry #4

Write one paragraph giving advice to a new college student on how to make a speech. Use any of these questions to guide your thinking:

- What are some ways to deal with anxiety about public speaking?
- How can you make your speech interesting?
- What are some steps in preparing a speech?
- What are some ideas that don't work?

KEYS TO SUCCESS

Be Selective

Psychologist and philosopher William James said, "The essence of genius is knowing what to overlook."[3] This saying has a variety of meanings. In reading, note taking, marking a college textbook, and writing, it is important to be able to pick out the main points first and then identify the supporting details. Imagine you are trying to put together a jigsaw puzzle. You bought the puzzle at a garage sale and all the pieces are there, but the lid to the box with the picture of the puzzle is missing. It will be very difficult, if not impossible, to put this puzzle together. Reading, note taking, marking, and writing are very much like putting a puzzle together. First you will need an understanding of the main ideas (the big picture) and then you can focus on the details.

How can you get the overall picture? When reading, you can get the overall picture by skimming the text. As you skim the text, you get a general outline of what the chapter contains and what you will learn. In note taking, actively listen for the main ideas and write them down in your notes. In marking your text, try to pick out about 20 percent of the most important material and underline or highlight it. In writing, think about what is most important, write your thesis statement, and then provide the supporting details.

To select what is most important, be courageous, think, and analyze.

Does this mean that you should forget about the details? No, you will need to know some details too. The supporting details help you to understand and assess the value of the main idea. They help you to understand the relationship between ideas. Being selective means getting the general idea first, and then the details will make sense to you and you will be able to remember them. The main ideas are like scaffolding or a net that holds the details in some kind of framework so you can remember them. If you focus on the details first, you will have no framework or point of reference for remembering them.

Experiment with the idea of being selective in your personal life. If your schedule is impossibly busy, be selective and choose to do the most important or most valuable activities. This takes some thinking and courage too. If your desk drawer is stuffed with odds and ends and you can never find what you are looking for, take everything out and only put back what you need. Recycle, give away, or throw away surplus items around the house. You can take steps toward being a genius by being selective and taking steps to simplify and organize your life and your work.

Journal Entry #5

How can being selective help you achieve success in college and in life? Use any of these questions to guide your thinking:

- How can being selective help you to be a better note taker, writer, or speaker?
- How can being selective help you to manage your time and your life?
- What is the meaning of this quote by William James: "The essence of genius is knowing what to overlook?"

JOURNAL ENTRIES

Taking Notes, Writing, and Speaking

Go to http://www.collegesuccess1.com/JournalEntries.htm for Word files of the Journal Entries

Success over the Internet

Visit the *College Success Website* at http://www.collegesuccess1.com/

The *College Success Website* is continually updated with new topics and links to the material presented in this chapter. Topics include:

- Note taking
- Mind maps
- Memory and note taking
- Telegraphic sentences
- Signal words
- Listening to lectures
- Grammar and style
- Quotes to use in speeches and papers
- The virtual public speaking assistant
- Researching, organizing, and delivering a speech
- Best speeches in history

Contact your instructor if you have any problems accessing the *College Success Website.*

Notes

1. T. Allesandra and P. Hunsaker, *Communicating at Work* (New York: Fireside, 1993), 169.

2. Lilly Walters, *Secrets of Successful Speakers: How You Can Motivate, Captivate, and Persuade* (New York: McGraw-Hill, 1993), 203.

3. Quoted in Rob Gilbert, ed., *Bits and Pieces,* August 12, 1999, 15.

Note-Taking Checklist

Name _____ Date _____

Place a checkmark next to the note-taking skills you have now.

_____ I attend every (or almost every) lecture in all my classes.

_____ I check the syllabus to find out what is being covered before I go to class.

_____ I read or at least skim through the reading assignment before attending the lecture.

_____ I attend lectures with a positive attitude about learning as much as possible.

_____ I am well rested so that I can focus on the lecture.

_____ I eat a light, nutritious meal before going to class.

_____ I sit in a location where I can see and hear easily.

_____ I have a laptop or a three-ring binder, looseleaf paper, and a pen for taking notes.

_____ I avoid external distractions (friends, sitting by the door).

_____ I am alert and able to concentrate on the lecture.

_____ I have a system for taking notes that works for me.

_____ I am able to determine the key ideas of the lecture and write them down in my notes.

_____ I can identify signal words that help to understand key points and organize my notes.

_____ I can write quickly using telegraphic sentences, abbreviations, and symbols.

_____ If I don't understand something in the lecture, I ask a question and get help.

_____ I write down everything written on the board or on visual materials used in the class.

_____ I review my notes immediately after class.

_____ I have intermediate review sessions to review previous notes.

_____ I use my notes to predict questions for the exam.

_____ I have clear and complete notes that help me to prepare adequately for exams.

Evaluate Your Note-Taking Skills

Name _____ Date _____

Use the note-taking checklist on the previous page to answer these questions.

1. Look at the items that you checked. What are your strengths in note taking?

2. What are some areas that you need to improve?

3. Write at least three intention statements about improving your listening and note-taking skills.

Assess Your College Writing Skills

Name _____ Date _____

Read the following statements and rate how true they are for you at the present time. Use the following scale:

5 Definitely true
4 Mostly true
3 Somewhat true
2 Seldom true
1 Never true

_____ I am generally confident in my writing skills.

_____ I have a system for reminding myself of due dates for writing projects.

_____ I start writing projects early so that I am not stressed by finishing them at the last minute.

_____ I have the proper materials and a space to write comfortably.

_____ I know how to use the library and the Internet to gather information for a term paper.

_____ I can write a thesis statement for a term paper.

_____ I know how to organize a term paper.

_____ I know how to write the introduction, body, and conclusion of a paper.

_____ I can cite references in the appropriate style for my subject.

_____ I know where to find information about citing material in APA, MLA, or Chicago style.

_____ I know what plagiarism is and know how to avoid it.

_____ I can deal with "writer's block" and get started on my writing project.

_____ I know how to edit and revise a paper.

_____ I know where I can get help with my writing.

_____ **Total**

60–70   You have excellent writing skills, but can always learn new ideas.
50–59   You have good writing skills, but there is room for improvement.
Below 50 You need to improve writing skills. The skills presented in this chapter will help. Consider taking a writing class early in your college studies.

Thinking about Writing

Name _____ Date _____

List 10 suggestions from this chapter that could help you improve your writing skills.

1.

2.

3.

4.

5.

6.

7.

8.

9.

10.

A Case Study

Name _____ Date _____

John is a new college student who needs help with college success skills. Using what you have learned in this chapter, give John some advice on how to take notes in class. This exercise can be done individually or as a group exercise in class.

> John is a new college student who has just graduated from high school. He is not sure what he wants to do with his life, but his parents want him to go to college. He misses the first class in Psychology 101 because he thinks nothing important happens on the first day. On the second day of class, John walks into class and finds some friends from high school. He takes a seat near them and starts a lively conversation. He has no books, paper, or pencil.
>
> The lecture is on the biological foundations of behavior. The topic is new for John and he is unfamiliar with the terms and concepts used in the lecture. He notices that the professor is wearing a tie that he must have purchased in 1970 and has an irritating habit of scratching his head. In addition, he is boring and speaks in a dull and monotonous way. John finds it difficult to concentrate. He becomes sleepy and starts to doze off during the lecture. At the end of the lecture, John realizes that he is going to have problems with psychology. For the next class, John brings a tape recorder and records the class. Again he finds it difficult to stay awake during the lecture. He works late at night and has scheduled this class for 8:00 in the morning.

What are the five most important suggestions you could make to help John take notes and be successful in this class?

1.

2.

3.

4.

5.

CHAPTER 7

Test Taking

Learning Objectives

Read to answer these key questions:

- What are some test preparation techniques?

- How should I review the material?

- How can I predict the test questions?

- What are some emergency test preparation techniques?

- How can I deal with test anxiety?

- How can I study math and deal with math anxiety?

- What are some tips for taking math tests?

- What are some tips for taking objective tests?

- How can I write a good essay?

An important skill for survival in college is the ability to take tests. Passing tests is also important in careers that require licenses, certificates, or continuing education. Knowing how to prepare for and take tests with confidence will help you to accomplish your educational and career goals while maintaining your good mental health. Once you have learned some basic test-taking and relaxation techniques, you can turn your test anxiety into motivation and good test results.

Preparing for Tests

Attend Every Class

The most significant factor in poor performance in college is lack of attendance. Students who attend the lectures and complete their assignments have the best chance for success in college. Attending the lectures helps you to be involved in learning and to know what to expect on the test. College professors know that students who miss three classes in a row are not likely to return, and some professors drop students after three absences. After three absences, students can fall behind in their schoolwork and become overwhelmed with makeup work.

© 2014, Robert Kneschke. Used under license with Shutterstock, Inc.

Distribute the Practice

The key to successful test preparation is to begin early and do a little at a time. Test preparation begins the first day of class. During the first class, the professor gives an overview of the course content, requirements, tests, and grading. These items are described in writing in the class calendar and syllabus. It is very important to attend the first class to obtain this essential information. If you have to miss the first class, make sure to ask the professor for the syllabus and calendar and read it carefully.

Early test preparation helps you to take advantage of the powerful memory technique called distributed practice. In distributed practice, the material learned is broken up into small parts and reviewed frequently. Using this method can enable you to learn a large quantity of material without becoming overwhelmed. Here are some examples of using distributed practice:

- If you have a test on 50 Spanish vocabulary words in two weeks, don't wait until the day before the test to try to learn all 50 words. Waiting until the day before the test will result in difficulty remembering the words, test anxiety, and a dislike of studying Spanish. If you have 50 Spanish vocabulary words to learn in two weeks, learn five words each day and quickly review the words you learned previously. For example, on Monday you would learn five words, and on Tuesday, you would learn five new words and review the ones learned on Monday. Give yourself the weekends off as a reward for planning ahead.

- If you have to read a history book with 400 pages, divide that number by the number of days in the semester or quarter. If there are 80 days in the semester, you will only have to read five pages per day or 10 pages every other day. This is a much easier and more efficient way to master a long assignment.

- Don't wait until the last minute to study for a midterm or final exam. Keep up with the class each week. As you read each chapter, quickly review a previous chapter. In this way you can comfortably master the material. Just before a major test, you can review the material that you already know and feel confident about your ability to get a good grade on the test.

Schedule a Time and a Place for Studying

To take advantage of distributed practice, you will need to develop a study schedule. Write down your work time and school time and other scheduled activities. Identify times that can be used for studying each day. Get in the habit of using these available times for studying each week. As a general rule, you need two hours of study time for each hour spent in a college classroom. If you cannot find enough time for studying, consider either reducing your course load or reducing work hours.

Use your study schedule or calendar to note the due dates of major projects and all test dates. Schedule enough time to complete projects and to finish major reviews for exams. Look at each due date and write in reminders to begin work or review well in advance of the due date. Give yourself plenty of time to meet the deadlines. It seems that around exam time, students are often ill or have problems that prevent them from being successful. Having some extra time scheduled will help you to cope with the many unexpected events that happen in everyday life.

Try to schedule your study sessions during your prime time, when you are awake and refreshed. For many people, one hour of study during the daylight hours is worth one and a half hours at night. Trying to study late at night may not be the best idea, because it is difficult to motivate yourself to study when you are tired. Save the time at the end of the day for relaxing or doing routine chores.

Find a place to study. This can be an area of your home where you have a desk, computer, and all the necessary supplies for studying. As a general rule, do not study at the kitchen table, in front of the television, or in your bed. These places provide powerful cues for eating, watching television, or sleeping instead of studying. If you cannot find an appropriate place at home, use the college library as a place to study. The library is usually quiet and others are studying, so there are not too many distractions.

© 2014, Alexander Raths. Used under license with Shutterstock, Inc.

Review Tools

- Flash cards
- Summary sheets
- Mind maps
- Study groups

Test Review Tools

There are a variety of tools you can use to review for tests. Choose the tools according to your learning style and what works for you. Learning styles include visual, auditory, kinesthetic, and tactile modes of learning. **Visual learners** find it easy to make mental pictures of the material to be learned. **Auditory learners** prefer listening and reciting material out loud. **Kinesthetic learners** benefit from moving around or acting out material to be learned. **Tactile learners** benefit from physical activities such as writing down items to be remembered.

- **Flash cards.** Flash cards are an effective way to learn facts and details for objective tests such as true-false, multiple-choice, matching, and fill-in-the-blank. For example, if you have 100 vocabulary words to learn in biology, put each word on one side of a card and the definition on the other side. First, look at each definition and see if you can recall the word. If you are a visual learner, look at the word and see if you can recall the definition. If you are an auditory learner, say the words and definitions. If you are a tactile or kinesthetic learner, carry the cards with you and briefly look at them as you are going about your daily activities. Make a game of studying by sorting the cards into stacks of information you know and information you still have to practice. Work with flash cards frequently and review them quickly. Don't worry about learning all the items at once. Each day that you practice, you will recall the items more easily. Check http://www.collegesuccess1.com/Links6Tests.htm for online tools for making flash cards.

- **Summary sheets.** Summary sheets are used to record the key ideas from your lecture notes or textbook. It is important to be selective; write only the most important ideas on the summary sheets. At the end of the semester, you might have approximately 10 pages of summary sheets from the text and 10 pages from your notes. If you are a kinesthetic learner, writing down the items you wish to remember will help you learn them. If you are a visual learner, the summary sheet becomes a picture of the ideas you need to remember. If you are an auditory learner, recite aloud the important ideas on the summary sheets.

- **Mind maps.** A mind map is a visual picture of the items you wish to remember. Start in the center of the page with a key idea and then surround it with related topics. You can use drawings, lines, circles, or colors to link and group the ideas. A mind map will help you to learn material in an organized way that will be useful when writing essay exams.

- **Study groups.** A study group is helpful in motivating yourself to learn through discussions of the material with other people. For the study group, select three to seven people who are motivated to be successful in class and can coordinate schedules. Study groups are often used in math and science classes. Groups of students work problems together and help each other understand the material. The study group is also useful in studying for exams. Give each member a part of the material to be studied. Have each person predict test questions and quiz the study group. Teaching the material to the study group can be the best way to learn it.

> "I can accept failure. Everyone fails at something. But I can't accept not trying."
> Michael Jordan

Reviewing Effectively

Begin your review early and break it into small parts. Remember that repetition is one of the effective ways to store information in long-term memory. Here are some types of review that help you to store information in long-term memory:

- **Immediate review.** This type of review is fast and powerful and helps to minimize forgetting. It is the first step in storing information in long-term memory. Begin the process by turning each bold-faced heading in the text into a question. Read each section to answer the question you have asked. Read your college texts with a highlighter in hand so that you can mark the key ideas for review. Some students use

© 2014, wavebreakmedia. Used under license with Shutterstock, Inc.

a variety of colors to distinguish main ideas, supporting points, and key examples, for instance. When you are finished using the highlighter, quickly review the items you have marked. As you complete each section, quickly review the main points. When you finish the chapter, immediately review the key points in the entire chapter again. As soon as you finish taking your lecture notes, take a few minutes to review them. To be most effective, immediate review needs to occur as soon as possible or at least within the first 20 minutes of learning something.

- **Intermediate review.** After you have finished reading and reviewing a new chapter in your textbook, spend a few minutes reviewing an earlier one. This step will help you to master the material and to recall it easily for the midterm or final exam. Another way to do intermediate review is to set up time periodically in your study schedule for reviewing previous chapters and classroom notes. Doing intermediate reviews helps to access the materials you have stored in long-term memory.

- **Final review.** Before a major exam, organize your notes, materials, and assignments. Estimate how long it will take you to review the material. Break the material into manageable chunks. For an essay exam, use mind maps or summary sheets to write down the main points that you need to remember and recite these ideas frequently. For objective tests, use flash cards or lists to remember details and concepts that you expect to be on the test. Here is a sample seven-day plan for reviewing 10 chapters for a final exam:

Day 1 Gather materials and study Chapters 1 and 2 by writing key points on summary sheets or mind maps. Make flash cards of details you need to remember. Review and highlight lecture notes and handouts on these chapters.

Day 2 Review Chapters 1 and 2. Study Chapters 3 and 4 and the corresponding lecture notes.

Day 3 Review Chapters 1 to 4. Study Chapters 5 and 6 and the corresponding lecture notes.

Day 4 Review Chapters 1 to 6. Study Chapters 7 and 8 along with the corresponding lecture notes.

Day 5 Review Chapters 1 to 8. Study Chapters 9 and 10 along with corresponding lecture notes.

Day 6 Review notes, summary sheets, mind maps, and flash cards for Chapters 1 to 10. Relax and get a good night's sleep. You are well prepared.

Day 7 Do one last quick review of Chapters 1 to 10 and walk into the test with the confidence that you will be successful on the exam.

Predicting Test Questions

There are many ways to predict the questions that will be on the test. Here are some ideas that might be helpful:

- Look for clues from the professor about what will be on the test. Many times professors put information about the tests on the course syllabus. During lectures, they often give hints about what will be important to know. If a professor repeats something more than once, make note of it as a possible test question. Anything written on the board is likely to be on the test. Sometimes the professor will even say, "This will be on the test." Write these important points in your notes and review them.

- College textbooks are usually written in short sections with bold headings. Turn each bold-faced heading into a question and read to answer the question. Understand and review the main idea in each section. The test questions will generally address the main ideas in the text.

- Don't forget to study and review the handouts that the professor distributes to the class. If the professor has taken the time and effort to provide extra material, it is probably important and may be on the test.

- Form a study group and divide up the material to be reviewed. Have each member of the group write some test questions based on the important points in each main section of the text. When the study group meets, take turns asking likely test questions and providing the answers.

- When the professor announces the test, make sure to ask what material is to be covered on the test and what kind of test it is. If necessary, ask the professor which concepts are most important. Know what kinds of test questions will be asked (essay, true-false, multiple-choice, matching, or short-answer). Some professors may provide sample exams or math problems.

- Use the first test to understand what is expected and how to study for future tests.

> "The will to win is not nearly as important as the will to prepare to win."
> Bobby Knight

Preparing for an Open-Book Test

In college, you may have some open-book tests. Open-book tests are often used in very technical subjects where specific material from the book is needed to answer questions. For example, in an engineering course, tables and formulas in the book may be needed to solve engineering problems on an exam. To study for an open-book test, focus on understanding the material and being able to locate key information for the exam. Consider making index tabs for your book so that you can locate needed information quickly. Be sure to bring your book, calculator, and other needed material to the exam.

Journal Entry # 1

Write one paragraph about the ideal way to prepare for a major exam such as a midterm or final. Consider these factors while thinking about your answer: attendance, distribute the practice, time management, review tools, predicting test questions and the most efficient way to review.

Emergency Procedures

If it is a day or two before the test and you have not followed the above procedures, it is time for the college practice known as "cramming." There are two main problems that result from this practice. First, you cannot take advantage of distributed practice, so it

© 2014, Mike Elliott. Used under license with Shutterstock, Inc.

will be difficult to remember large amounts of material. Second, it is not fun, and if done often will result in anxiety and a dislike of education. Because of these problems, some students who rely on cramming wrongly conclude that they are not capable of finishing their education.

If you must cram for a test, here are some emergency procedures that may be helpful in getting the best grade possible under difficult circumstances:

- When cramming, *it is most important to be selective*. Try to identify the main points and recite and review them.

- Focus on reviewing and reciting the lecture notes. In this way, you will cover the main ideas the professor thinks are important.

- If you have not read the text, skim and search each chapter looking for the main points. Highlight and review these main points. Read the chapter summaries. In a math textbook, practice sample problems.

- Make summary sheets containing the main ideas from the notes and the text. Recite and review the summary sheets.

- For objective tests, focus on learning new terms and vocabulary related to the subject. These terms are likely to be on the test. Flash cards are helpful.

- For essay tests, develop an outline of major topics and review the outline so you can write an essay.

- Get enough rest. Staying up all night to review for the test can result in confusion, reduced mental ability, and test anxiety.

- Hope for the best.

- Plan ahead next time so that you can get a better grade.

If you have very little time to review for a test, you will probably experience information overload. One strategy for dealing with this problem is based on the work of George Miller of Harvard University. He found that the optimum number of chunks of information we can remember is seven plus or minus two (or five to nine chunks of information).[1] This is also known as the Magical Number Seven Theory. For this last-minute review technique, start with five sheets of paper. Next, identify five key concepts that are likely to be on the test. Write one concept on the top of each sheet of paper. Then check your notes and text to write an explanation, definition, or answer for each of these topics. If you have more time, find two to four more concepts and research them, writing the information on additional sheets. You should have no more than nine sheets of paper. Arrange the sheets in order of importance. Review and recite the key ideas on these sheets. Get a regular night's sleep before the test and do some relaxation exercises right before the test.

© 2014, YanLev. Used under license with Shutterstock, Inc.

Ideas That Don't Work

Some students do poorly on tests for the following reasons.

- Attending a party or social event the evening before a major test rather than doing the final review will adversely affect your test score. Study in advance and reward yourself with the party after the test.
- Skipping the major review before the test may cause you to forget some important material.
- Taking drugs or drinking alcohol before a test may give you the impression that you are relaxed and doing well on the test, but the results are disastrous to your success on the exam and your good health.
- Not knowing the date of the test can cause you to get a low grade because you are not prepared.
- Not checking or knowing about the final exam schedule can cause you to miss the final.
- Missing the final exam can result in a lower grade or failing the class.
- Arriving late for the exam puts you at a disadvantage if you don't have time to finish or have to rush through the test.
- Deciding not to buy or read the textbook will cause low performance or failure.
- Having a fight, disagreement, or argument with parents, friends, or significant others before the test will make it difficult to focus on the exam.
- Sacrificing sleep, exercise, or food to prepare for the exam makes it difficult to do your best.
- Cheating on an exam can cause embarrassment, a lower grade, or failure. It can even lead to expulsion from college.
- Missing the exam because you are not prepared and asking the professor to let you make up the exam later is a tactic that many students try. Most professors will not permit you to take an exam late.
- Inventing a creative excuse for missing an exam is so common that some professors have a collection of these stories that they share with colleagues. Creative excuses don't work with most professors.
- Arriving at the exam without the proper materials such as a pencil, Scantron, paper, calculator, or book (for open-book exams) can cause you to miss the exam or start the exam late.

Test Preparation

Test what you have learned by selecting the correct answers to the following questions.

1. In test preparation, it is important to use this memory technique:

    a. Distribute the practice.
    b. Read every chapter just before the test.
    c. Do most of the review right before the test to minimize forgetting.

2. Schedule your study sessions

    a. late at night.
    b. during your prime time, which is generally earlier in the day.
    c. after all other activities are done.

3. Effective tools to learn facts and details are

    a. mind maps.
    b. summary sheets.
    c. flash cards.

4. The best way to review is

    a. to start early and break it into small parts.
    b. immediately before the test.
    c. in large blocks of time.

5. If you have to cram for an exam, it is most important to

    a. stay up all night studying for the exam
    b. focus on the lecture notes and forget about reading the text
    c. be selective and review and recite the main points

How did you do on the quiz? Check your answers: 1. a, 2. b, 3. c, 4. a, 5. c

Ten Rules for Success

Here are 10 rules for success on any test. Are there any new ideas you can put into practice?

1. **Make sure to set your alarm,** and consider having a backup in case your alarm doesn't go off. Set a second alarm or have someone call to make sure you are awake on time.

2. **Arrive a little early for your exam.** If you are taking a standardized test like the Scholastic Aptitude Test (SAT) or Graduate Record Exam (GRE), familiarize yourself with the location of the exam. If you arrive early, you can take a quick walk around the building to relax or spend a few minutes doing a review so that your brain will be tuned up and ready.

3. **Eat a light breakfast including some carbohydrates and protein.** Be careful about eating sugar and caffeine before a test, because this can contribute to greater anxiety and low blood sugar by the time you take the test. The worst breakfast would be something like a doughnut and coffee or a soda and candy bar. Examples of good breakfasts are eggs, toast, and juice or cereal with milk and fruit.

4. **Think positively about the exam.** Tell yourself that you are well prepared and the exam is an opportunity to show what you know.

5. **Make sure you have the proper materials:** Scantrons, paper, pencil or pen, calculator, books and notes (for open-book exams).

6. **Manage your time.** Know how long you have for the test and then scan the test to make a time management plan. For example, if you have one hour and there are 50 objective questions, you have about a minute for each question. Halfway through the time,

you should have completed 25 questions. If there are three essay questions in an hour, you have less than 20 minutes for each question. Save some time to look over the test and make corrections.

7. **Neatness is important.** If your paper looks neat, the professor is more likely to have a positive attitude about the paper before it is even read. If the paper is hard to read, the professor will start reading your paper with a negative attitude, possibly resulting in a lower grade.

8. **Read the test directions carefully.** On essay exams, it is common for the professor to give you a choice of questions to answer. If you do not read the directions, you may try to answer all of the questions and then run out of time or give incomplete answers to them.

9. **If you get stuck on a difficult question, don't worry about it.** Just mark it and find an easier question. You may find clues on the rest of the test that will aid your recall, or you may be more relaxed later on and think of the answer.

10. **Be careful not to give any impression that you might be cheating.** Keep your eyes on your own paper. If you have memory aids or outlines memorized, write them directly on the test paper rather than a separate sheet so that you are not suspected of using cheat notes.

Journal Entry #2

Write one paragraph about the most common mistakes students make while getting ready for an exam.

Dealing with Test Anxiety

Some anxiety is a good thing. It can provide motivation to study and prepare for exams. However, it is common for college students to suffer from test anxiety. Too much anxiety can lower your performance on tests. Some symptoms of test anxiety include:

- Fear of failing a test even though you are well prepared
- Physical symptoms such as perspiring, increased heart rate, shortness of breath, upset stomach, tense muscles, or headache
- Negative thoughts about the test and your grade
- Mental blocking of material you know and remembering it once you leave the exam

© 2014, Stuart Miles. Used under license with Shutterstock, Inc.

You can minimize your test anxiety by being well prepared and by applying the memory strategies described in earlier chapters. Prepare for your exams by attending every class, keeping up with your reading assignments, and reviewing during the semester. These steps will help increase your self-confidence and reduce anxiety. Apply the principles of memory improvement to your studying. As you are reading, find the important points and highlight them. Review these points so that they are stored in your long-term memory. Use distributed practice and spread out learning over time rather than trying to learn it all at once. Visualize and organize what you need to remember. Trust in your abilities and intend to remember what you have studied.

> "Luck is what happens when preparation meets opportunity."
> Darrell Royal

If you find that you are anxious, here are some ideas you can try to cope with the anxiety. Experiment with these techniques to see which ones work best for you.

- **Do some physical exercise.** Physical exercise helps to use up stress hormones. Make physical activity a part of your daily routine. Arrive for your test a little early and walk briskly around campus for about 20 minutes. This exercise will help you to feel relaxed and energized.

- **Get a good night's sleep before the test.** Lack of sleep can interfere with memory and cause irritability, anxiety, and confusion.

- **Take deep breaths.** Immediately before the test, take a few deep breaths; hold them for three to five seconds and let them out slowly. These deep breaths will help you to relax and keep a sufficient supply of oxygen in your blood. Oxygen is needed for proper brain function.

- **Visualize and rehearse your success.** Begin by getting as comfortable and relaxed as possible in your favorite chair or lying down in bed. Visualize yourself walking into the exam room. Try to imagine the room in as much detail as possible. If possible, visit the exam room before the test so that you can get a good picture of it. See yourself taking the exam calmly and confidently. You know most of the answers. If you find a question you do not know, see yourself circling it and coming back to it later. Imagine that you find a clue on the test that triggers your recall of the answers to the difficult questions. Picture yourself handing in the exam with a good feeling about doing well on the test. Then imagine you are getting the test back and you get a good grade on the test. You congratulate yourself for a job well done. If you suffer from test anxiety, you may need to rehearse this scene several times. When you enter the exam room, the visual picture that you have rehearsed will help you to relax.

- **Acknowledge your anxiety.** The first step in dealing with anxiety is to admit that you are anxious rather than trying to fight it or deny it. Say to yourself, "I am feeling anxious." Take a few deep breaths and then focus your attention on the test.

- **Do the easy questions first and mark the ones that may be difficult.** This will help you to relax. Once you are relaxed, the difficult questions become more manageable.

Tips to Minimize Anxiety

- Exercise
- Sleep
- Take deep breaths
- Visualize success
- Acknowledge anxiety
- Easy questions first
- Yell, "Stop!"
- Daydream
- Practice perspective
- Give yourself time
- Get help

- **Yell, "Stop!"** Negative and frightening thoughts can cause anxiety. Here are some examples of negative thoughts:

> I'm going to fail this test.
> I don't know the answer to number 10!
> I never do well on tests.
> Essays! I have a hard time with those.
> I'll never make it through college.
> I was never any good in math!

These types of thoughts don't help you do better on the test, so stop saying them. They cause you to become anxious and to freeze up during the test. If you find yourself with similar thoughts, yell, "Stop!" to yourself. This will cause you to interrupt your train of thought so that you can think about the task at hand rather than becoming more anxious. Replace negative thoughts with more positive ones such as these:

> I'm doing the best I can.
> I am well prepared and know most of the answers.
> I don't know the answer to number 10, so I'll just circle it and come back to it later.
> I'll make an outline in the margin for the essay question.
> College is difficult, but I'll make it!
> Math is a challenge, but I can do it!

- **Daydream.** Think about being in your favorite place. Take time to think about the details. Allow yourself to be there for a while until you feel more relaxed.
- **Practice perspective.** Remember, one poor grade is not the end of the world. It does not define who you are. If you do not do well, think about how you can improve your preparation and performance the next time.
- **Give yourself time.** Test anxiety develops over a period of time. It will take some time to get over it. Learn the best ways to prepare for the exam and practice saying positive thoughts to yourself.
- **Get help.** If these techniques do not work for you, seek help from your college health or counseling center.

Journal Entry #3

You have a friend who prepares for exams, but suffers from test anxiety. Review the section on test anxiety and write a one paragraph e-mail to your friend with some ideas on dealing with test anxiety. Consider both physical and mental preparation as well as some relaxation techniques that can be helpful.

I am taking a college success course and the book has some ideas on dealing with test anxiety. The book suggests . . .

Studying Math and Dealing with Math Anxiety

When I mention to students that they need to take math, I often see a look of fear on their faces. Everyone needs to take math. Most colleges require math classes and demonstrated math competency in order to graduate. Math is essential for many high-paying technical and professional occupations. Being afraid of math and avoiding it will limit your career possibilities.

© 2014, Creativa. Used under license with Shutterstock, Inc.

Begin your study of math with some positive thinking. You may have had difficulty with math in the past, but with a positive attitude and the proper study techniques, you can meet the challenge. The first step to success in math is to put in the effort required. Attend class, do your homework, and get help if needed. If you put in the effort and hard work, you will gain experience in math. If you gain experience with math, you will become more confident in your ability to do math. If you have confidence, you will gain satisfaction in doing math. You may even learn to like it! If you like the subject, you can gain competence. The process looks like this:

Hard work → Experience → Confidence → Satisfaction → Competence

Although you may have had difficulty with math in the past, you can become successful by following these steps. Your reward is self-satisfaction and increased opportunity in technical and professional careers.

- **Don't delay taking math.** You may need a sequence of math courses in order to graduate. If you delay taking math, you may delay your graduation from college.

- **Think positively about your ability to succeed in math.** You may have had difficulties in math classes before. Think about your educational history. Can you recall having difficulties in the past? These past difficulties cause a fear of math. You may have a picture of failure in your mind. You need to replace it with a picture of success. Acknowledge that you are afraid because of past experiences with math. Acknowledge that the future can be different, and spend the time and effort needed to be successful.

- **Start at the beginning.** Assess where your math skills are at the present time. If you have not taken math classes for some time, you may need to review. Take the college math assessment test, read the college catalog, and speak to a counselor about where you should start.

- **Ask questions in class.** Students are often afraid to ask questions in math classes because they are afraid other students will think they are not smart. It is more likely that other students are wishing that someone would ask a question because they don't understand either. Ask your questions early, as soon as you find something you don't understand.

- **Get help early.** If you are having difficulties, get tutoring right away. If you are confused, you will not understand the next step either.

- **Don't miss your math classes.** It is difficult to catch up if you miss class.

- **Do your math homework regularly.** Math skills depend on practice. Make sure you understand the examples given in the textbook. Practice as many questions as you can until you feel comfortable solving the problems. Assign yourself extra problems if necessary. It is difficult to cram for a math test.

- **Use a study group.** Work with groups of students to study math. Get the phone numbers of other students in the study group. If you do not understand, other students may be able to help.
- **Study for the math test.** Start early so that you will have time to go over each topic in the book and practice doing problems from each section. Check your work against the solutions given in the text.
- **Do the easiest problems first on a math test.** In this way, you can gain confidence and relax. Then focus on the problems that are worth the most points. Don't be distracted by problems that you do not know and that use up test time.
- **Solve problems systematically.** First make sure you understand the problem. Write out the given facts and equations you may need to use before working out the problem. Then make a plan for solving it. What have you learned in class that will help you to solve the problem? Carry out the plan. Then check your answer. Does the answer make sense? Check your calculator work over again at the end of the test.
- **Check for careless errors.** Go over your math test to see if you have made any careless errors. Forgetting a plus or minus sign or adding or subtracting incorrectly can have a big impact on your grade. Save at least five minutes to read over your test.
- **Get enough sleep before the math test.** If you are mentally sharp, the test will be easier.

Math Tests

Taking a math test involves some different strategies:

1. Some instructors will let you write down formulas on an index card or a small crib sheet. Prepare these notes carefully, writing down the key formulas you will need for the exam.

2. If you have to memorize formulas, review them right before the test and write them on the test immediately.

3. As a first step, quickly look over the test. Find a problem you can solve easily and do this problem first.

4. Manage your time. Find out how many problems you have to solve and how much time is available for each problem. Do the problems worth the most points first. Stay on track.

5. Try this four-step process:
   a. Understand the problem.
   b. Devise a plan to solve the problem. Write down the information that is given. Think about the skills and techniques you have learned in class that can help you to solve the problem.
   c. Carry out the plan.
   d. Look back to see if your answer is reasonable.

6. If you cannot work a problem, go on to the next question. Come back later when you are more relaxed. If you spend too much time on a problem you cannot work, you will not have time for the problems that you can work.

7. Even if you think an answer is wrong, turn it in. You may get partial credit.

8. Show all the steps in your work and label your answer. On long and complex problems, it is helpful to use short sentences to explain your steps in solving the problem.

9. Estimate your answer and see if it makes sense or is logical.

Tips for Avoiding Common Math Errors[2]

- Any quantity multiplied by zero is zero
- Any quantity raised to the zero power is one
- Any fraction multiplied by its reciprocal is one
- Only like algebraic terms may be combined
- Break down to the simplest form in algebra
- In algebra, multiply and divide before adding and subtracting
- If an algebraic expression has more than one set of parentheses, get rid of the inner parenthesis first and work outward
- Any operation performed on one side of the equation must be performed on the other side

10. Write your numbers as neatly as possible to avoid mistakes and to make them legible for the professor.

11. Leave space between your answers in case you need to add to them later.

12. If you have time left over at the end, recheck your answers.

Journal Entry #4

You are enrolled in a math course that is required for graduation and want to make sure that you are successful in this course. List and briefly explain five ideas that will help you to be successful in this math course.

© 2014, Ivelin Radkov. Used under license with Shutterstock, Inc.

Taking Tests

True-False Tests

Many professors use objective tests such as true-false and multiple-choice because they are easy to grade. The best way to prepare for these types of tests is to study the key points in the textbook, lecture notes, and class handouts. In the textbook, take each bold-faced topic and turn it into a question. If you can answer the questions, you will be successful on objective tests.

In addition to studying for the test, it is helpful to understand some basic test-taking techniques that will help you to determine the correct answer. Many of the techniques used to determine whether a statement is true or false can also be used to eliminate wrong answers on multiple-choice tests.

To develop strategies for success on true-false exams, it is important to understand how a teacher writes the questions. For a true-false question, the teacher identifies a key point in the book or lecture notes. Then he or she has two choices. For a true statement, the key idea is often written exactly as it appears in the text or notes. For a false statement, the key idea is changed in some way to make it false.

One way to make a statement false is to add a **qualifier** to the statement. Qualifiers that are **absolute** or extreme are generally, but not always, found in false statements. **General** qualifiers are often found in true statements.

Absolute Qualifiers (false)		General Qualifiers (true)	
all	none	usually	frequently
always	never	often	sometimes
only	nobody	some	seldom
invariably	no one	many	much
best	worst	most	generally
everybody	everyone	few	ordinarily
absolutely	absolutely not	probably	a majority
certainly	certainly not	might	a few
no	every	may	apt to

Seven Tips for Success on True-False Tests

1. **Identify the key ideas in the text and class notes and review them.**

2. **Accept the question at face value.** Don't overanalyze or create wild exceptions in your mind.

3. **If you don't know the answer, assume it is true.** There are generally more true statements because we all like the truth (especially teachers) and true questions are easier to write. However, some teachers like to test students by writing all false statements.

4. **If any part of a true-false statement is false, the whole statement is false.** Carefully read each statement to determine if any part of it is false. Students sometimes assume a statement is true if most of it is true. This is not correct.

   Example: Good relaxation techniques include deep breathing, exercise, and visualizing your failure on the exam.

   This statement is false because visualizing failure can lead to test anxiety and failure.

5. **Notice any absolute or general qualifiers.** Remember that absolute qualifiers often make a statement false. General qualifiers often make a statement true.

   Example: The student who crams **always** does poorly on the exam.

   This statement is false because **some** students are successful at cramming for an exam.

   Be careful with this rule. Sometimes the answer can be absolute.

   Example: The grade point average is always calculated by dividing the number of units attempted by the grade points. (true)

6. **Notice words such as *because, therefore, consequently,* and *as a result*.** They may connect two things that are true but result in a false statement.

   Example: Martha does not have test anxiety. (true)

   Martha makes good grades on tests. (true)
   Martha does not have test anxiety and therefore makes good grades on tests.

   This statement is false because she also has to prepare for the exam. Not having test anxiety could even cause her to lack motivation to study and do poorly on a test.

7. **Watch for double negatives.** Two nos equal a yes. If you see two negatives in a sentence, read them as a positive. Be careful with negative prefixes such as un-, im-, mis-, dis-, il-, and ir-. For example, the phrase "not uncommon" actually means "common." Notice that the word "not" and the prefix "un-" when used together form a double negative that equals a positive.

   Example: **Not** being **un**prepared for the test is the best way to earn good grades.

   The above sentence is confusing. To make it clearer, change both of the negatives into a positive:

   Being prepared for the test is the best way to earn good grades.

Practice True-False Test

Answer the following questions by applying the tips for success in the previous section. Place a T or an F in the blanks.

_____ 1. If a statement has an absolute qualifier, it is always false.

_____ 2. Statements with general qualifiers are frequently true.

_____ 3. If you don't know the answer, you should guess true.

_____ 4. Studying the key points for true-false tests is not unimportant.

_____ 5. Good test-taking strategies include eating a light breakfast that includes carbohydrates and protein and drinking plenty of coffee to stay alert.

_____ 6. Ryan attended every class this semester and therefore earned an A in the class.

How did you do on the test? Answers: 1. F, 2. T, 3. T, 4. T, 5. F, 6. F

Multiple-Choice Tests

College exams often include multiple-choice questions rather than true-false questions because it is more difficult to guess the correct answer. On a true-false question, the student has a 50 percent chance of guessing the correct answer, while on a multiple-choice question, the odds of guessing correctly are only 25 percent. You can think of a multiple-choice question as four true-false questions in a row. First, read the question and try to answer it without looking at the options. This will help you to focus on the question and determine the correct answer. Look at each option and determine if it is true or false. Then choose the **best** answer.

To choose the best option, it is helpful to understand how a teacher writes a multiple-choice question. Here are the steps a teacher uses to write a multiple-choice exam:

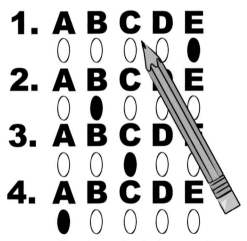

© 2014, WilleeCole. Used under license with Shutterstock, Inc.

1. Find an important point in the lecture notes, text, or handouts.

2. Write a **stem**. This is an incomplete statement or a question.

3. Write the correct answer as one of the options.

4. Write three or four plausible but incorrect options that might be chosen by students who are not prepared. These incorrect options are called **decoys**. Here is an example:

   Stem: If you are anxious about taking math tests, it is helpful to:

   a. Stay up the night before the test to review thoroughly. (**decoy**)

   b. Visualize yourself doing poorly on the test so you will be motivated to study. (**decoy**)

   c. Practice math problems regularly during the semester. (**correct answer**)

   d. Do the most difficult problem first. (**decoy**)

Learn to Recognize a Decoy
A Decoy is an Incorrect Answer

1. Decoys are all true or all false
2. Decoys contain absolute qualifiers
3. Decoys can be partly true
4. Decoys have conjunctions that make them false
5. Decoys have double negatives
6. Decoys can be foolish
7. Decoys are high or low numbers
8. Decoys can look like the correct answer
9. Decoys are often the shorter answer
10. Decoys may be grammatically incorrect
11. Decoys may be an opposite
12. Decoys may be the same as another answer

Being well prepared for the test is the most reliable way of recognizing the correct answer and the decoys. In addition, becoming familiar with the following rules for recognizing decoys can help you determine the correct answer or improve your chances of guessing the correct answer on an exam. If you can at least eliminate some of the wrong answers, you will improve your odds of selecting the correct answer.

Rules for recognizing a decoy or wrong answer:

1. **The decoys are all true or all false statements.** Read each option and determine which options are false and which statements are true. This will help you to find the correct answer.

   Example: To manage your time on a test, it is important to:

   a. Skip the directions and work as quickly as possible. (false)

   b. Skim through the test to see how much time you have for each section. (true)

   c. Do the most difficult sections first. (false)

   d. Just start writing as quickly as possible. (false)

   Read the stem carefully, because sometimes you will be asked to identify one false statement in a group of true statements.

2. **The decoy may contain an absolute qualifier.** The option with the absolute qualifier (e.g., always, only, every) is likely to be false because few things in life are absolute. There are generally exceptions to any rule.

3. **The decoy can be partly true.** However, if one part of the statement is false, the whole statement is false and an incorrect answer.

   Example: Memory techniques include visualization, organization, and telling yourself you won't remember.

   In this example, the first two techniques are true and the last part is false, which makes the whole statement false.

4. **The decoy may have a conjunction or other linking words that makes it false.** Watch for words and phrases such as *because, consequently, therefore,* and *as a result.*

5. **The decoy may have a double negative.** Having two negatives in a sentence makes it difficult to understand. Read the two negatives as a positive.

6. **The decoy may be a foolish option.** Writing multiple decoys is difficult, so test writers sometimes throw in foolish or humorous options.

   Example: In a multiple-choice test, a decoy is:

   a. a type of duck.

   b. an incorrect answer.

c. a type of missile used in air defense.

d. a type of fish.

The correct answer is b. Sometimes students are tempted by the foolish answers.

7. **The decoy is often a low or high number.** If you have a multiple-choice question with numbers, and you are not sure of the correct answer, choose the number in the middle range. It is often more likely to be correct.

   Example: George Miller of Harvard University theorized that the optimum number of chunks of material that we can remember is:

   a. 1–2 (This low number is a decoy.)

   b. 5–9 (This is the correct answer.)

   c. 10–12 (This is close to the correct answer.)

   d. 20–25 (This high number is a decoy.)

   There is an exception to this rule when the number is much higher or lower than the average person thinks is possible.

8. **The decoy may look like the correct answer.** When two options look alike, one is incorrect and the other may be the correct answer. Test writers often use words that look alike as decoys.

   Example: In false statements, the qualifier is often:

   a. absolute.

   b. resolute.

   c. general.

   d. exaggerated.

   The correct answer is a. Answer b is an incorrect look-alike option.

9. **Decoys are often shorter than the correct answer.** Longer answers are more likely to be correct because they are more complete. Avoid choosing the first answer that seems to be correct. There may be a better and more complete answer.

   Example: Good test preparation involves:

   a. doing the proper review for the test.

   b. good time management.

   c. a positive attitude.

   d. having good attendance, studying and reviewing regularly, being able to deal with test anxiety, and having a positive mental attitude.

   Option d is correct because it is the most complete and thus the best answer.

10. **Decoys may be grammatically incorrect.** The correct answer will fit the grammar of the stem. A stem ending with "a" will match an answer beginning with a consonant; stems ending with "an" will match a word beginning with a vowel. The answer will agree in gender, number, and person with the stem.

    Example: In test taking, a decoy is an:

    a. incorrect answer.

    b. correct answer.

    c. false answer.

    d. true answer.

    The correct answer is A. It is also the only answer that grammatically fits with the stem. Also note that decoys can be all true or all false. In standardized tests, the grammar is usually correct. On teacher-made tests, the grammar can be a clue to the correct answer.

11. **A decoy is sometimes an opposite.** When two options are opposites, one is incorrect and the other is sometimes, but not always, correct.

Example: A decoy is:

a. a right answer.

b. a wrong answer.

c. a general qualifier.

d. a true statement.

The two opposites are answers a and b. The correct answer is b.

12. **A decoy may be the same as another answer.** If two answers say the same thing in different ways, they are both decoys and incorrect.

Example: A true statement is likely to have this type of qualifier:

a. extreme

b. absolute

c. general

d. factual

Notice that answers a and b are the same and are incorrect. The correct answer is c.

Example: How much does a gallon of water weigh?

a. 8.34 pounds

b. 5.5 pounds

c. 5 pounds 8 ounces

d. 20 pounds

B and c are the same and are therefore incorrect answers. Answer d is a high number. The correct answer is a.

If you are unable to identify any decoys, these suggestions may be helpful:

- Mark the question and come back to it later. You may find the answer elsewhere on the test, or some words that help you remember the answer. After answering some easier questions, you may be able to relax and remember the answer.
- Trust your intuition and choose something that sounds familiar.
- Do not change your first answer unless you have misread the question or are sure that the answer is incorrect. Sometimes students overanalyze a question and then choose the wrong answer.
- The option "All of the above" is often correct because it is easier to write true statements rather than false ones. Options like A and B, B and D, or other combinations are also likely to be correct for the same reason.
- If you have no idea about the correct answer, guess option B or C. Most correct answers are in the middle.

Practice Multiple-Choice Test

Circle the letters of the correct answers. Then check your answers using the key at the end of this section.

1. The correct answer in a multiple-choice question is likely to be
   a. the shortest answer.
   b. the longest and most complete answer.
   c. the answer with an absolute qualifier.
   d. the answer that has some truth in it.

2. When guessing on a question involving numbers, it is generally best to
   a. choose the highest number.
   b. choose the lowest number.
   c. choose the mid-range number.
   d. always choose the first option.

3. If you have test anxiety, what questions should you answer first on the test?
   a. The most difficult questions
   b. The easiest questions
   c. The questions at the beginning
   d. The questions worth the least number of points

4. When taking a multiple-choice test, you should
   a. pick the first choice that is true.
   b. read all the choices and select the best one.
   c. pick the first choice that is false.
   d. choose the extreme answer.

5. A good method for guessing is to
   a. identify which choices are true and false.
   b. use the process of elimination.
   c. notice absolute qualifiers and conjunctions.
   d. all of the above.

6. The key to success when taking a multiple-choice test is
   a. cheating.
   b. good preparation.
   c. knowing how to guess.
   d. being able to recognize a qualifier.

(continued)

7. The following rule about decoys is correct:

   a. A decoy is always absolute.

   b. A decoy can be partly true.

   c. Every decoy has a qualifier.

   d. Decoys are invariably false statements.

8. An example of an absolute qualifier is

   a. generally.

   b. never.

   c. sometimes.

   d. frequently.

9. Statements with absolute qualifiers are generally

   a. true.

   b. false.

   c. irrelevant.

   d. confusing.

10. If two multiple-choice options are the same or very similar, they are most likely

   a. a decoy and a correct answer.

   b. a correct answer.

   c. a true answer.

   d. a mistake on the test.

11. It is generally not a good idea to change your answer unless

   a. you are very anxious about the test.

   b. you do not have good intuition.

   c. you notice that your intelligent friend has a different answer.

   d. you have misread the question and you are sure that the answer is incorrect.

How did you do on the quiz? Check your answers: 1. b, 2. c, 3. b, 4. b, 5. d, 6. b, 7. b (Notice the absolute qualifiers in the decoys), 8. b, 9. b (Notice the opposites), 10. a (Notice the grammar), 11. d

Matching Tests

A matching test involves two lists of facts or definitions that must be matched together. Here are some tips to help you successfully complete a matching exam:

1. Read through both lists to discover the pattern or relationship between the lists. The lists might give words and definitions, people and accomplishments, or other paired facts.

2. Count the items on the list of answers to see if there is only one match for each item or if there are some extra answer choices.

3. Start with one list and match the items that you know. In this way, you have a better chance of guessing on the items that you do not know.

4. If you have difficulty with some of the items, leave them blank and return later. You may find the answers or clues on the rest of the test.

Practice Matching Test

Match the items in the first column with the items in the second column. Write the letter of the matching item in the blank at the left.

_____ 1. Meaningful organization   **A.** Learn small amounts and review frequently.

_____ 2. Visualization   **B.** The more you know, the easier it is to remember.

_____ 3. Recitation   **C.** Tell yourself you will remember.

_____ 4. Develop an interest   **D.** Pretend you like it.

_____ 5. See the big picture   **E.** Make a mental picture.

_____ 6. Intend to remember   **F.** Rehearse and review.

_____ 7. Distribute the practice   **G.** Focus on the main points first.

_____ 8. Create a basic background   **H.** Personal organization.

Answers: 1. H,   2. E,   3. F,   4. D,   5. G,   6. C,   7. A,   8. B

Sentence-Completion or Fill-in-the-Blank Tests

Fill-in-the-blank and sentence-completion tests are more difficult than true-false or multiple-choice tests because they require the **recall** of specific information rather than the **recognition** of the correct answer. To prepare for this type of test, focus on facts such as definitions, names, dates, and places. Using flash cards to prepare can be helpful. For example, to memorize names, place each name on one side of a card and some identifying words on the other side. Practice looking at the names on one side of the card and then recalling the identifying words on the other side of the card. Then turn the cards over and look at the identifying words to recall the names.

Sometimes the test has clues that will help you to fill in the blank. Clues can include the length of the blanks and the number of blanks. Find an answer that makes sense in the sentence and matches the grammar of the sentence. If you cannot think of an answer, write a general description and you may get partial credit. Look for clues on the rest of the test that may trigger your recall.

Practice Fill-in-the-Blank Test

Complete each sentence with the appropriate word or words.

1. Fill-in-the-blank tests are more difficult because they depend on the _____ of specific information.

2. On a true-false test, a statement is likely to be false if it contains an _____ qualifier.

3. Test review tools include _____, _____, and _____.

4. When studying for tests, visualize your _____.

Answers: 1. recall, 2. absolute, 3. flash cards, summary sheets, and mind maps (also study groups and highlighters), 4. success

Essay Tests

Many professors choose essay questions because they are the best way to show what you have learned in the class. Essay questions can be challenging because you not only have to know the material, but must be able to organize it and use good writing techniques in your answer.

© 2014, Lucky Business. Used under license with Shutterstock, Inc.

Essay questions contain key words that will guide you in writing your answer. One of the keys to success in writing answers to essay questions is to note these key words and then structure your essay accordingly. As you read through an essay question, look for these words:

Analyze	Break into separate parts and discuss, examine, or interpret each part.
Argue	State an opinion and give reasons for the opinion.
Comment	Give your opinion.
Compare	Identify two or more ideas and identify similarities and differences.
Contrast	Show how the components are the same or different.
Criticize	Give your opinion and make judgments.
Defend	State reasons.
Define	Give the meaning of the word or concept as used within the course of study.
Describe	Give a detailed account or provide information.
Demonstrate	Provide evidence.
Diagram	Make a drawing, chart, graph, sketch, or plan.
Differentiate	Tell how the ideas are the same and how they are different.
Describe	Make a picture with words. List the characteristics, qualities, and parts.
Discuss	Describe the pros and cons of the issues. Compare and contrast.
Enumerate	Make a list of ideas, events, qualities, reasons, and so on.
Explain	Make an idea clear. Show how and why.
Evaluate	Describe it and give your opinion about something.
Illustrate	Give concrete examples and explain them. Draw a diagram.
Interpret	Say what something means. Describe and then evaluate.
Justify	Prove a point. Give the reasons why.
Outline	Describe the main ideas.
Prove	Support with facts. Give evidence or reasons.
Relate	Show the connections between ideas or events.
State	Explain precisely. Provide the main points.
Summarize	Give a brief, condensed account. Draw a conclusion.
Trace	Show the order of events.

Here are some tips on writing essays:

1. To prepare for an essay test, use a mind map or summary sheet to summarize the main ideas. Organize the material in the form of an outline or mental pictures that you can use in writing.

2. The first step in writing an essay is to quickly survey the test and read the directions carefully. Many times you are offered a choice of which and how many questions to answer.

3. Manage your time. Note how many questions need to be answered and how many points each question is worth. For example, if you have three questions to answer in one hour, you will have less than 20 minutes for each question. Save some time to check over your work.

   If the questions are worth different numbers of points, divide up your time proportionately. In the above example with three questions, if one question is worth 50 points and the other two are worth 25 points, spend half the time on the 50-point question (less than 30 minutes) and divide the remaining time between the 25-point questions (less than 15 minutes each).

4. If you are anxious about the test, start with an easy question in order to relax and build your confidence. If you are confident in your test-taking abilities, start with the question that is worth the most points.

5. Get organized. Write a brief outline in the margin of your test paper. Do not write your outline on a separate sheet of paper because you may be accused of using cheat notes.

6. In the first sentence of your essay, rephrase the question and provide a direct answer. Rephrasing the question keeps you on track and a direct answer becomes the thesis statement or main idea of the essay.

   Example: (Question:) Describe a system for reading a college textbook.
   (Answer:) A system for reading a college textbook is Survey, Question, Read, Review, Recite, and Reflect (SQ4R). (Then you would go on to expand on each part of the topic.)

7. Use the principles of good composition. Start with a thesis statement or main idea. Provide supporting ideas and examples to support your thesis. Provide a brief summary at the end.

8. Write your answer clearly and neatly so it is easy to grade. Grading an essay involves an element of subjectivity. If your paper looks neat and is easy to read, the professor is likely to read your essay with a positive attitude. If your paper is difficult to read, the professor will probably read your paper with a negative attitude.

9. Determine the length of your essay by the number of points it is worth. For example, a five-point essay might be a paragraph with five key points. A 25-point essay would probably be a five-paragraph essay with at least 25 key points.

10. Save some time at the end to read over your essays. Make corrections, make sure your answers make sense, and add any key information you may have forgotten to include.

What to Do When Your Test Is Returned

When your test is returned, use it as feedback for future test preparation in the course. Look at your errors and try to determine how to prevent these errors in the future.

- Did you study correctly?
- Did you study the proper materials?
- Did you use the proper test-taking techniques?
- Was the test more difficult than you expected?
- Did you run out of time to take the test?
- Was the test focused on details and facts or on general ideas and principles?
- Did you have problems with test anxiety?

Analyzing your test performance can help you to do better in the future.

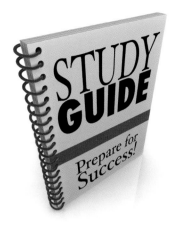

Journal Entry #5

Of course it is a good idea to be well prepared for exams, but there are times when you will have to figure out the answer or even make a guess on the correct answer. Review the section on "Taking Tests" and list five ideas for guessing that you can try in the future.

KEYS TO SUCCESS

Be Prepared

The key idea in this chapter is to be prepared. Good preparation is essential for success in test taking as well as in many other areas of life. Being successful begins with having a vision of the future and then taking steps to achieve your dream.

Sometimes people think of success in terms of good luck. Thomas Jefferson said, "I'm a great believer in luck, and I find the harder I work, the more I have of it." Don't depend on good luck. Work to create your success.

You can reach your dream of attaining a college education through preparation and hard work. Use the ideas in this chapter to ensure your success. Remember that preparation begins on the first day of class: it does not begin when the professor announces a test. On the first day of class, the professor provides an overview, or outline, of what you will learn. Attend every class. The main points covered in the class will be on the test. Read your assignments a little at a time starting from the first day. If you distribute your practice, you will find it easier to learn and to remember.

When it comes time to review for the test, you will already know what to expect on the test, and you will have learned the material by attending the lectures and reading your text. Reviewing for the test is just review; it is not original learning. It is a chance to strengthen what you have learned so that you can relax and do your best on the test. Review is one of the final steps in learning. With review, you will gain a sense of confidence and satisfaction in your studies.

If you are not prepared, you will need to cram for the test and you may not be as successful on the test as you could be. If you are not successful, you may get the mistaken idea that you cannot be successful in college. Cramming for the test produces stress, since you will need to learn a great deal of information in a short time. Stress can interfere with memory and cause you to freeze up on exams. It is also difficult to remember if you have to cram. The memory works best if you do a small amount of learning regularly over a period of time. Cramming is hard work and no fun. The worst problem with cramming is that it causes you to dislike education. It is difficult to continue to do something that you have learned to dislike.

Good preparation is the key to success in many areas of life. Whether you are taking a college course, playing a basketball game, going on vacation, planning a wedding, or building a house, good preparation will help to guarantee your success. Begin with your vision of the future and boldly take the first steps. The best preparation for the future is the good use of your time today.

> "The secret of getting ahead is getting started. The secret of getting started is breaking your complex, overwhelming tasks into small manageable tasks, and then starting on the first one."
> Mark Twain

> "The future starts today, not tomorrow."
> Pope John Paul II

Success over the Internet

Visit the *College Success Website* at http://www.collegesuccess1.com/

The *College Success Website* is continually updated with new topics and
links to the material presented in this chapter. Topics include:

- Tips for taking tests
- Dealing with math anxiety
- How to study for math tests
- How to take math tests
- How to guess on a test
- Test anxiety
- Multiple-choice exams
- Dealing with difficult questions

Contact your instructor if you have any problems accessing the *College
Success Website.*

Notes

1. G. A. Miller, "The Magical Number Seven, Plus or Minus Two: Some Limits on Our Capacity for Processing Information," *Psychological Review* 63 (March 1956): 81–97.

2. From Aguilar et al., *The Community College: A New Beginning*, 2nd ed. (Dubuque, IA: Kendall Hunt, 1998).

Test-Taking Checklist

Name _____   Date _____

Place checkmarks next to the test-taking skills you have now.

_____ Attend every class (or almost every class)

_____ Have a copy of the course syllabus with test dates

_____ Start test preparation early and study a little at a time

_____ Do not generally cram for exams

_____ Have a place to study (not the kitchen, TV room, or bedroom)

_____ Participate in a study group

_____ Review immediately after learning something

_____ Review previous notes and reading assignments on a regular basis

_____ Schedule a major review before the exam

_____ Know how to predict the test questions

_____ Get enough rest before a test

_____ Visualize my success on the exam

_____ Complete my math homework on a regular basis

_____ Eat a light but nutritious meal before the exam

_____ Maintain a regular exercise program

_____ Read all my textbook assignments before the exam

_____ Review my classroom notes before the exam

_____ Skim through the test and read all directions carefully before starting the test

_____ Answer the easy questions first and return later to answer the difficult questions

_____ Check over my test before handing it in

_____ Write an outline before beginning my essay answer

_____ Manage my study time to adequately prepare for the test

_____ Review my returned tests to improve future test preparation

_____ Write the test neatly and make sure my writing is legible

_____ Avoid test anxiety by being well prepared and practicing relaxation techniques

_____ Prepare adequately for tests

Name _____   Date _____

Use the test-taking checklist on the previous page to answer the following questions.

1. My strengths in test-taking skills are

2. Some areas I need to improve are

3. Write three intention statements about improving your test-taking skills.

Practice with Short Essays

Name _____ Date _____

Your professor may ask you to do this as a classroom exercise. Review the section in the text on how to write a short essay. Answer the following short essay question worth five points.

1. Explain how you can improve your chances of success when preparing for exams. Include the physical, mental, and emotional preparation necessary for success.

2. Rate your essay. Did you do the following?

   _____ I read the directions and the essay question thoroughly before I began.

   _____ I organized my thoughts or made a brief outline before starting.

   _____ The first sentence was a direct answer and rephrased the question.

   _____ My thesis statement or main idea was clear.

   _____ The remaining sentences in the essay supported my main idea.

   _____ Since this is a five-point essay, I made at least five key points in the essay.

   _____ My answer was written clearly and neatly. My handwriting was legible.

   _____ I spelled the words correctly and used good grammar.

   _____ I read over my essay to make sure it made sense.

3. For essay exams, I need to work on

How Well Do You Follow Directions?

Name _____ Date _____

1. Read all of the directions before you do anything.

2. Put your name at the top of this page.

3. In the bottom right-hand corner, write the name of this class.

4. In the bottom left-hand corner, write the name of your instructor.

5. Put a box around the class name.

6. Put a circle around your instructor's name.

7. Write the name of your college at the bottom of this page.

8. You have now completed the exercise, so let the class know you are finished by calling out "Done."

9. Return to the beginning and only do number one.

From Aguilar et al., *The Community College: A New Beginning*, 2nd ed. (Dubuque, IA: Kendall Hunt, 1998).

CHAPTER 8

Thinking Positively about the Future

Learning Objectives

Read to answer these key questions:

- How does positive thinking affect my future success?

- What are some beliefs of successful people?

- What is a dangerous opportunity?

- What are my values and how will they affect decisions about my future?

- What are some secrets to achieving happiness?

Thinking Positively about Your Life

Thinking positively about yourself and your life is one of the most important skills you can learn for your future success. Following are some ways to practice positive thinking.

© 2014, kentoh. Used under license with Shutterstock, Inc.

Optimism, Hope, and Future-Mindedness

You can increase your chances of success by using three powerful tools: optimism, hope, and future-mindedness. These character traits lead to achievement in athletics, academics, careers, and even politics. They also have positive mental and physical effects. They reduce anxiety and depression as well as contributing to physical well-being. In addition, they aid in problem solving and searching out resources to solve problems. A simple definition of optimism is expecting good events to happen in the future and working to make them happen. Optimism leads to continued efforts to accomplish goals, whereas pessimism leads to giving up on accomplishing goals. A person who sets no goals for the future cannot be optimistic or hopeful. Here are some ideas about optimism from Optimist International.[1]

Promise yourself:

- To talk health, happiness, and prosperity to every person you meet.
- To make all your friends feel that there is something important in them.
- To look at the sunny side of everything and make your optimism come true.
- To be just as enthusiastic about the success of others as you are about your own.
- To forget the mistakes of the past and press on to the greater achievements of the future.
- To give so much time to the improvement of yourself that you have no time to criticize others.
- To wear a cheerful countenance at all times and give every living creature you meet a smile.

Being hopeful is another way of thinking positively about the future. One research study showed for entering college freshmen, level of hope was a better predictor of college grades than standardized tests or high school grade point average.[2] Students who have a high level of hope set higher goals and work to attain these goals. If they are not successful, they change goals and move in a new direction with a renewed sense of hope for a positive future.

Future-mindedness is thinking about the future, expecting that desired events and outcomes will occur, and then acting in a way that makes the positive outcomes come true. It involves setting goals for the future and taking action to accomplish these goals as well as being confident in accomplishing them. Individuals with future-mindedness are conscientious and hardworking and can delay gratification. They make to-do lists and use schedules and day planners. Individuals who are future-minded would agree with these statements:[3]

- Despite challenges, I always remain hopeful about the future.
- I always look on the bright side.
- I believe that good will always triumph over evil.
- I expect the best.
- I have a clear picture in mind about what I want to happen in the future.
- I have a plan for what I want to be doing five years from now.
- If I get a bad grade or evaluation, I focus on the next opportunity and plan to do better.

Believe in Yourself

Anthony Robbins defines belief as "any guiding principle, dictum, faith, or passion that can provide meaning and direction in life . . . Beliefs are the compass and maps that guide us toward our goals and give us the surety to know we'll get there."[4] The beliefs that we have about ourselves determine how much of our potential we will use and how successful we will be in the future. If we have positive beliefs about ourselves, we will feel confident and accomplish our goals in life. Negative beliefs get in the way of our success. Robbins reminds us that we can change our beliefs and choose new ones if necessary.

> *"The birth of excellence begins with our awareness that our beliefs are a choice. We usually do not think of it that way, but belief can be a conscious choice. You can choose beliefs that limit you, or you can choose beliefs that support you. The trick is to choose the beliefs that are conducive to success and the results you want and to discard the ones that hold you back."[5]*

The Self-Fulfilling Prophecy

The first step in thinking positively is to examine your beliefs about yourself, your life, and the world around you. Personal beliefs are influenced by our environment, significant events that have happened in life, what we have learned in the past, and our picture of the future. Beliefs cause us to have certain expectations about the world and ourselves. These expectations are such a powerful influence on behavior that psychologists use the term "self-fulfilling prophecy" to describe what happens when our expectations come true.

For example, if I believe that I am not good in math (my expectation), I may not try to do the assignment or may avoid taking a math class (my behavior). As a result, I am not good in math. My expectations have been fulfilled. Expectations can also have a positive effect. If I believe that I am a good student, I will take steps to enroll in college and complete my assignments. I will then become a good student. The prophecy will again come true.

To think positively, it is necessary to recognize your negative beliefs and turn them into positive beliefs. Some negative beliefs commonly heard from college students include the following:

I don't have the money for college.
English was never my best subject.
I was never any good at math.

> "Attitude is the librarian of our past, the speaker of our present and the prophet of our future."
> John Maxwell

> "¡Sí, se puede!" (Yes, you can!)
> César Chavez

> "If I believe I cannot do something, it makes me incapable of doing it. But when I believe I can, then I acquire the ability to do it, even if I did not have the ability in the beginning."
> Mahatma Gandhi

When you hear yourself saying these negative thoughts, remember that these thoughts can become self-fulfilling prophecies. First of all, notice the thought. Then see if you can change the statement into a positive statement such as:

I can find the money for college.
English has been a challenge for me in the past, but I will do better this time.
I can learn to be good at math.

If you believe that you can find money for college, you can go to the financial aid office and the scholarship office to begin your search for money to attend school. You can look for a better job or improve your money management. If you believe that you will do better in English, you will keep up with your assignments and go to the tutoring center or ask the professor for help. If you believe that you can learn to be good at math, you will attend every math class and seek tutoring when you do not understand. Your positive thoughts will help you to be successful.

Positive Self-Talk and Affirmations

Self-talk refers to the silent inner voice in our heads. This voice is often negative, especially when we are frustrated or trying to learn something new. Have you ever had thoughts about yourself that are similar to these:

How could you be so stupid!
That was dumb!
You idiot!

ACTIVITY

What do you say to yourself when you are angry or frustrated? Write several examples of your negative self-talk.

Negative thoughts can actually be toxic to your body. They can cause biochemical changes that can lead to depression and negatively affect the immune system.[6] Negative self-talk causes anxiety and poor performance and is damaging to self-esteem. It can also lead to a negative self-fulfilling prophecy. Positive thoughts can help us build self-esteem, become confident in our abilities, and achieve our goals. These positive thoughts are called affirmations.

If we make the world with our thoughts, it is important to become aware of the thoughts about ourselves that are continuously running through our heads. Are your thoughts positive or negative? Negative thoughts lead to failure. What we hear over and over again shapes our beliefs. If you say over and over to yourself such things as, "I am stupid," "I am ugly," or "I am fat," you will start to believe these things and act in a way that supports your beliefs. Positive thoughts help to build success. If you say to yourself, "I'm a good person," "I'm doing my best," or "I'm doing fine," you will begin to believe these things about yourself and act in a way that supports these beliefs. Here are some guidelines for increasing your positive self-talk and making affirmations:

1. Monitor your thoughts about yourself and become aware of them. Are they positive or negative?

2. When you notice a negative thought about yourself, imagine rewinding a tape and recording a new positive message.

3. Start the positive message with "I" and use the present tense. Using an "I" statement shows you are in charge. Using the present tense shows you are ready for action now.

4. Focus on the positive. Think about what you want to achieve and what you can do rather than what you do not want to do. For example, instead of saying, "I will not eat junk food," say, "I will eat a healthy diet."

5. Make your affirmation stronger by adding an emotion to it.

6. Form a mental picture of what it is that you want to achieve. See yourself doing it successfully.

7. You may need to say the positive thoughts over and over again until you believe them and they become a habit. You can also write them down and put them in a place where you will see them often.

Here are some examples of negative self-talk and contrasting positive affirmations:

Negative: I'm always broke.

Affirmation: I feel really good when I manage my finances. See yourself taking steps to manage finances. For example, start a budget or savings plan.

Negative: I'm too fat. It just runs in the family.

Affirmation: I feel good about myself when I exercise and eat a healthy diet. See yourself exercising and eating a healthy diet.

Negative: I can't do this. I must be stupid.

Affirmation: I can do this. I am capable. I feel a sense of accomplishment when I accomplish something challenging. See yourself making your best attempt and taking the first step to accomplish the project.

"We are what we think.
All that we are arises
With our thoughts.
With our thoughts
we make the world."
Buddha

"Learn from yesterday, live for today, hope for tomorrow. The important thing is not to stop questioning."
Albert Einstein

Select one example of negative self-talk that you wrote earlier. Use the examples above to turn your negative message into a positive one and write it here.

Visualize Your Success

© 2014, Sergey Nivens. Used under license with Shutterstock, Inc.

Visualization is a powerful tool for using your brain to improve memory, deal with stress, and think positively. Coaches and athletes study sports psychology to learn how to use visualization along with physical practice to improve athletic performance. College students can use the same techniques to enhance college success.

If you are familiar with sports or are an athlete, you can probably think of times when your coach asked you to use visualization to improve your performance. In baseball, the coach reminds players to keep their eye on the ball and visualize hitting it. In swimming, the coach asks swimmers to visualize reaching their arms out to touch the edge of the pool at the end of the race. Pole-vaulters visualize clearing the pole and sometimes even go through the motions before making the jump. Using imagery lets you practice for future events and pre-experience achieving your goals. Athletes imagine winning the race or completing the perfect jump in figure skating. In this way they prepare mentally and physically and develop confidence in their abilities. It still takes practice to excel.

Just as the athlete visualizes and then performs, the college student can do the same. It is said that we create all things twice. First we make a mental picture, and then we create the physical reality by taking action. For example, if we are building a house, first we get the idea; then we begin to design the house we want. We start with a blueprint and then build the house. The blueprint determines what kind of house we construct. The same thing happens in any project we undertake. First we have a mental picture, and then we complete the project. Visualize what you would like to accomplish in your life as if you were creating a blueprint. Then take the steps to accomplish what you want.

As a college student, you might visualize yourself in your graduation robe walking across the stage to receive your diploma. You might visualize yourself in the exam room confidently taking the exam. You might see yourself on the job enjoying your future career. You can make a mental picture of what you would like your life to be and then work toward accomplishing your goal.

> "The future first exists in imagination, then planning, then reality."
> R.A. Wilson

Successful Beliefs

Stephen Covey's book *The 7 Habits of Highly Effective People* has been described as one of the most influential books of the 20th century.[7] In 2004, he released a new book called *The 8th Habit: From Effectiveness to Greatness.*[8] These habits are based on beliefs that lead to success.

1. **Be proactive.** Being proactive means accepting responsibility for your life. Covey uses the word "response-ability" for the ability to choose responses. The quality of your life is based on the decisions and responses that you make. Proactive people make things happen through responsibility and initiative. They do not blame circumstances or conditions for their behavior.

2. **Begin with the end in mind.** Know what is important and what you wish to accomplish in your life. To be able to do this, you will need to know your values and goals in life. You will need a clear vision of what you want your life to be and where you are headed.

3. **Put first things first.** Once you have established your goals and vision for the future, you will need to manage yourself to do what is important first. Set priorities so that you can accomplish the tasks that are important to you.

4. **Think win-win.** In human interactions, seek solutions that benefit everyone. Focus on cooperation rather than competition. If everyone feels good about the decision, there is cooperation and harmony. If one person wins and the other loses, the loser becomes angry and resentful and sabotages the outcome.

5. **First seek to understand, then to be understood.** Too often in our personal communications, we try to talk first and listen later. Often we don't really listen: we use this time to think of our reply. It is best to listen and understand before speaking. Effective communication is one of the most important skills in life.

6. **Synergize.** A simple definition of synergy is that the whole is greater than the sum of its parts. If people can cooperate and have good communication, they can work together as a team to accomplish more than each individual could do separately. Synergy is also part of the creative process.

7. **Sharpen the saw.** Covey shares the story of a man who was trying to cut down a tree with a dull saw. As he struggled to cut the tree, someone suggested that he stop and sharpen the saw. The man said that he did not have time to sharpen the saw, so he continued to struggle. Covey suggests that we need to take time to stop and sharpen the saw. We need to stop working and invest some time in ourselves by staying healthy physically, mentally, spiritually, and socially. We need to take time for self-renewal.

8. **Find your voice, and inspire others to find theirs.** Believe that you can make a positive difference in the world and inspire others to do the same. Covey says that leaders "deal with people in a way that will communicate to them their worth and potential so clearly that they will come to see it in themselves." Accomplishing this ideal begins with developing one's own voice or "unique personal significance."[9]

> **Successful Beliefs**
> - Be proactive
> - Begin with the end in mind
> - Put first things first
> - Think win-win
> - First seek to understand, then to be understood
> - Synergize
> - Sharpen the saw
> - Find your voice, and inspire others to find theirs

Words Are Powerful

The words that we choose have a powerful influence on thoughts and behavior. One of the least powerful words is the word "should." This word is heard frequently on college campuses:

I should do my homework.
I should go to class.
I should get started on my term paper.

The problem with "should" is that it usually does not lead to action and may cause people to feel guilty. If you say, "I should get started on my term paper," the chances are that you will not start on it.

If you say, "I might get started on my term paper," at least you are starting to think about possibilities. You might actually get started on your term paper. If you say, "I want to get started on my term paper," the chances are getting better that you will get started. You are making a choice. If you say, "I intend to start on my term paper," you have at least expressed good intentions. The best way to get started is to make a promise to yourself

Figure 8.1 The Ladder of Powerful Speaking.

"*I promise*" *or* "*I will*"

"*I intend to*"

"*I want to*"

"*I might*"

"*I should*"

that you will start. The words "should," "might," "want," "intend," and "promise" represent a ladder of powerful communication. As you move up the ladder, you are more likely to accomplish what you say you will do. This ladder moves from obligation to promise, or a personal choice to act.

Next time you hear yourself saying that you "should" do something, move one more step up the ladder. Move from obligation to making a personal decision to do what is important to you. For example, if a friend wants to borrow money from you, which response is the most powerful?

- I really should pay the money back.
- Well, I might pay the money back.
- I really want to pay the money back.
- I intend to pay the money back.
- I promise to pay the money back.

Promise yourself to get your studying done in order to accomplish your goal of a college education.

Life Is a Dangerous Opportunity

Even though we may do our best in planning our career and education, life does not always turn out as planned. Unexpected events happen, putting our life in crisis. The crisis might be loss of employment, divorce, illness or death of a loved one. How we deal with the crisis events in our lives can have a great impact on our current well-being and the future.

Journal Entry #1

Write five statements about your future. I will . . .

© 2014, Shutter_M. Used under license with Shutterstock, Inc.

The Chinese word for crisis has two characters: one character represents danger and the other represents opportunity. Every crisis has the danger of loss of something important and the resulting emotions of frustration, sorrow, and grief. But every crisis also has an opportunity. Sometimes it is difficult to see the opportunity because we are overwhelmed by the danger. A crisis, however, can provide an impetus for change and growth. A crisis forces us to look inside ourselves to find capabilities that have always been there but we just did not know it. If life goes too smoothly, there is no motivation to change. If we get too comfortable, we stop growing. There is no testing of our capabilities. We stay in the same patterns. As a practical application, consider the example of someone who has just lost a job.

John had worked as a construction worker for nearly ten years when he injured his back. His doctor told him that he would no longer be able to do physical labor. John was 30 years old, had two children and large house and truck payments. He was having difficulty finding a job that paid as well as his construction job. He was suffering from many negative emotions resulting from his loss of employment.

John decided that he would have to use his brain rather than his back. As soon as he was up and moving, he started taking some general education courses at the local college. He assessed his skills and identified his strengths. He was a good father and communicated well with his children. He had wanted to go to college but got married early and started to work in construction instead. John decided that he would really enjoy being a marriage and family counselor. It would mean getting a bachelor's and a master's degree, which would take five or more years.

John began to search for a way to accomplish this new goal. He first tackled the financial problems. He investigated vocational rehabilitation, veteran's benefits, financial aid, and scholarships. He sold his house and his truck. His wife took a part-time job. He worked out a careful budget. He began to work toward his new goal with a high degree of motivation and self-satisfaction. He had found a new opportunity.

To find the opportunity in a crisis, focus on what is possible in the situation. Expect things to work out well. Expect success. To deal with negative emotions, consider that feelings are not simply a result of what happens to us but of our interpretation of events. If we focus on the danger, we cannot see the possibilities. Every adversity has the seed of a greater benefit or possibility.

QUIZ

Positive Thinking

Test what you have learned by selecting the correct answers to the following questions.

1. The self-fulfilling prophecy refers to

   a. expectations about ourselves that become true.
   b. a prediction about the future.
   c. using the past to predict the future.

2. Positive self-talk results in

   a. lower self-esteem.
   b. overconfidence.
   c. higher self-esteem.

3. The statement "We create all things twice" refers to

   a. doing the task twice to make sure it is done right.
   b. creating and refining.
   c. first making a mental picture and then taking action.

4. A win-win solution means

   a. winning at any cost.
   b. seeking a solution that benefits everyone.
   c. focusing on competition.

5. The statement by Stephen Covey, "Sharpen the saw," refers to

   a. proper tool maintenance.
   b. studying hard to sharpen thinking skills.
   c. investing time to maintain physical and mental health.

6. To be successful in accomplishing your goal, use this phrase:

   a. I should
   b. I want
   c. I will

7. "Life is a dangerous opportunity" means that

   a. life is dangerous
   b. crisis can lead to growth and change
   c. danger is always to be avoided

How did you do on the quiz? Check your answers: 1. a, 2. c, 3. c, 4. b, 5. c, 6. c, 7. b

Journal Entry #2

Write five intention statements about thinking positively about your life. In thinking about your statements, consider these factors: optimism, hope, future-mindedness, belief in yourself, the self-fulfilling prophecy, positive self-talk, affirmations, visualizing your success, words are powerful, life is a dangerous opportunity, and successful beliefs.

Using Values to Make Important Life Decisions

Values are what are most important to you; they are your highest principles. They provide the road map to your success and happiness. You will face important turning points along life's journey. Should I go to college? What will be my major? What career will I have? Who should I marry? What job should I take? Where shall I live? You can find good answers to these questions by being aware of your values and using them to make decisions and guide your actions. If your decisions follow your values, you can get what you want out of life.

Values come from many sources, including your parents, friends, the media, religious background, culture, society and the historical time in which we live. Our values make us different and unique individuals. Knowing your values helps you to make good decisions about work and life. For example, consider a situation in which a person is offered a high-paying job that involves a high degree of responsibility and stress. If the person values challenge and excitement and views stress as a motivator, the chances are that it would be a good decision to take the job. If the person values peace of mind and has a difficult time coping with stress, it might be better to forgo the higher income and maintain quality of life. Making decisions consistent with your values is one of the keys to happiness and success.

The first step is knowing your values. You may need some time to think about your values and change them if they are not right for you. What values were you taught as a child? What values do you want to keep as an adult? Look around at people that you admire. What are their values? What values have you learned from your religion? Are these values important to you? Ask your friends about their values and share yours. Revise and rethink your values periodically. Make sure your values are your own and not necessarily values that someone has told you were important. When you begin to think about values, you can come up with many things that are important. The key is to find out which values are most important. In this way, when you are faced with a choice, you will not be confused. You will know what is most important to you.

Values Checklist

Assessing Your Personal Values

Use the following checklist to begin to think about what values are important to you.
Place a checkmark next to any value that is important to you. There are no right or wrong answers. If you
think of other values that are important to you, add them to the bottom of the list.

_____ Having financial security	_____ Having good family relationships
_____ Making a contribution to humankind	_____ Preserving the environment
_____ Being a good parent	_____ Having the respect of others
_____ Being honest	_____ Becoming famous
_____ Acquiring wealth	_____ Happiness
_____ Being a wise person	_____ Freedom and independence
_____ Becoming an educated person	_____ Common sense
_____ Believing in a higher power (God)	_____ Having pride in my culture
_____ Preserving civil rights	_____ Doing community service
_____ Never being bored	_____ Achieving my goals in life
_____ Enjoying life and having fun	_____ Having adventures
_____ Making something out of my life	_____ Having leisure time
_____ Being an ethical person	_____ Having good health
_____ Feeling safe and secure	_____ Being loyal
_____ Having a good marriage	_____ Having a sense of accomplishment
_____ Having good friends	_____ Participating in church activities
_____ Having social status	_____ Being physically fit
_____ Being patriotic	_____ Helping others
_____ Having power	_____ Being a good person
_____ Having good morals	_____ Having time to myself
_____ Being creative	_____ Loving and being loved
_____ Having control over my life	_____ Being physically attractive
_____ Growing and developing	_____ Achieving something important
_____ Feeling competent	_____ Accepting who I am
_____ Feeling relaxed	_____ Appreciating natural beauty
_____ Having prestige	_____ Using my artistic talents
_____ Improving society	_____ Feeling good about myself

_____ Having good mental health	_____ Making a difference
_____ Being a good athlete	_____ Other: _____
_____ Enjoying the present moment	_____ Other: _____
_____ Maintaining peace of mind	_____ Other: _____

Knowing about values is not enough. It is important to act consistently with your values and to follow them. For example, if people value health but continue to smoke, they are saying one thing but doing another. If they value family but spend all of their time at work, they are not acting consistently with their values. As a result, they might find that their family is gone and they have lost something that is really valuable.

Use your actions to question or reaffirm your values. Do you really value your health and family? If so, take action to preserve your good health and spend time with your family. It is necessary to periodically look at your patterns of behavior. Do you act out of habit or do you act according to what is important to you? Habits might need to be changed to get what you value most out of life.

In times of doubt and difficulty, your values can keep you going. If you truly value getting a college education, you can put in the effort to accomplish your goal. When you have doubts about whether you can be successful, examine your values again and remind yourself of why you are doing what you are doing. For example, if you value being an independent business entrepreneur, you will put in the effort to be successful. If you value being a good parent, you will find the patience and develop the skill to succeed. Reminding yourself of your values can help you to continue your commitment to accomplishing your goals.

By knowing your values and following them, you have a powerful tool for making decisions, taking action, and motivating yourself to be successful.

Secrets to Happiness

Many of you probably have happiness on your list of lifetime goals. It sounds easy, right? But what is happiness, anyway?

Psychologist Martin Seligman says that real happiness comes from identifying, cultivating, and using your personal strengths in work, love, play, and parenting.[10] You have identified these strengths by learning about your personality type, learning style, interests, and values.

Seligman contrasts authentic happiness with hedonism. He states that a hedonist "wants as many good moments and as few bad moments as possible in life."[11] Hedonism is a shortcut to happiness that leaves us feeling empty. For example, we often assume that more material possessions will make us happy. However, the more material possessions we have, the greater the expectations, and we no longer appreciate what we have.

"Suppose you could be hooked up to a hypothetical 'experience machine' that, for the rest of your life, would stimulate your brain and give you any positive feelings you desire. Most people to whom I offer this imaginary choice refuse the machine. It is not just positive feelings we want, we want to be entitled to our positive feelings. Yet we have invented myriad shortcuts to feeling good: drugs, chocolate, loveless sex, shopping, masturbation, and television are all examples. (I am not, however, suggesting that you should drop these shortcuts altogether.) The belief that we can rely on shortcuts to happiness, joy, rapture, comfort, and ecstasy, rather than be entitled to these feelings by the exercise of personal strengths and virtues, leads to the legions of people who in

"Most folks are about as happy as they make up their minds to be."
Abraham Lincoln

the middle of great wealth are starving spiritually. Positive emotion alienated from the exercise of character leads to emptiness, to inauthenticity, to depression, and as we age, to the gnawing realization that we are fidgeting until we die."[12]

Most people assume that happiness is increased by having more money to buy that new car or HDTV. However, a process called hedonistic adaptation occurs that makes this type of happiness short-lived. Once you have purchased the new car or TV, you get used to it quickly. Soon you will start to think about a better car and a bigger TV to continue to feel happy. Seligman provides a formula for happiness:[13]

$$Happiness = S + C + V$$

In the formula S stands for set range. Psychologists believe that 50 percent of happiness is determined by heredity. In other words, half of your level of happiness is determined by the genes inherited from your ancestors. In good times or bad times, people generally return to their set range of happiness. Six months after receiving a piece of good fortune such as a raise or promotion or winning the lottery, unhappy people are still unhappy. Six months after a tragedy, naturally happy people return to being happy.

The letter C in the equation stands for circumstances such as money, marriage, social life, health, education, climate, race, gender, and religion. These circumstances account for 8 to 15 percent of happiness. Here is what psychologists know about how these circumstances affect happiness:

- Once basic needs are met, greater wealth does not increase happiness.
- Having a good marriage is related to increased happiness.
- Happy people are more social.
- Moderate ill health does not bring unhappiness, but severe illness does.
- Educated people are slightly happier.
- Climate, race, and gender do not affect level of happiness.
- Religious people are somewhat happier than nonreligious people.

The letter V in the equation stands for factors under your voluntary control. These factors account for approximately 40 percent of happiness. Factors under voluntary control include positive emotions and optimism about the future. Positive emotions include hope, faith, trust, joy, ecstasy, calm, zest, ebullience, pleasure, flow, satisfaction, contentment, fulfillment, pride, and serenity. Seligman suggests the following ideas to increase your positive emotions:

- Realize that the past does not determine your future. The future is open to new possibilities.
- Be grateful for the good events of the past and place less emphasis on the bad events.
- Build positive emotions through forgiving and forgetting.
- Work on increasing optimism and hope for the future.
- Find out what activities make you happy and engage in them. Spread these activities out over time so that you will not get tired of them.
- Take the time to savor the happy times. Make mental photographs of happy times so that you can think of them later.
- Take time to enjoy the present moment.
- Build more flow into your life. Flow is the state of gratification we feel when totally absorbed in an activity that matches our strengths.

Are you interested in taking steps to increase your happiness? Here are some activities proposed by Sonya Lyubomirsky, a leading researcher on happiness and author of *The How of Happiness.*[14] Choose the ones that seem like a natural fit for you and vary them so that they do not become routine or boring. After putting in some effort to practice these activities, they can become a habit.

1. **Express gratitude.** Expressing gratitude is a way of thinking positively and appreciating good circumstances rather than focusing on the bad ones. It is about appreciating and thanking the people who have made positive contributions to your life. It is feeling grateful for the good things you have in life. Create a gratitude journal and at the end of each day write down things for which you are grateful or thankful. Regularly tell those around you how grateful you are to have them in your life. You can do this in person, by phone, in a letter, or by email. Being grateful helps us to savor positive life experiences.

2. **Cultivate optimism.** Make a habit of looking at the bright side of life. If you think positively about the future, you are more likely to take the effort to reach your goals in life. Spend some time thinking or writing about your best possible future. Make a mental picture of your future goals as a first step toward achieving them. Thinking positively boosts your mood and promotes high morale. Most importantly, thinking positively can become a self-fulfilling prophecy. If you see your positive goals as attainable, you are more likely to work toward accomplishing them and invest the energy needed to deal with obstacles and setbacks along the way.

3. **Avoid overthinking and social comparison.** Overthinking is focusing on yourself and your problems endlessly, needlessly, and excessively. Examples of overthinking include "Why am I so unhappy?" "Why is life so unfair?" and "Why did he/she say that?" Overthinking increases sadness, fosters biased thinking, decreases motivation, and makes it difficult to solve problems and take action to make life better.

Social comparison is a type of overthinking. In our daily lives, we encounter people who are more intelligent, beautiful, richer, healthier, or happier. The media fosters images of people with impossibly perfect lives. Making social comparisons can lead to feelings of inferiority and loss of self-esteem.

Notice when your are overthinking or making comparisons with others and stop doing it. Use the "Yell, 'Stop!'" technique to refocus your attention. This technique involves yelling, "Stop!" to yourself or out loud to change your thinking. Another way to stop over-thinking is to distract yourself with more positive thoughts or activities. Watch a funny movie, listen to music, or arrange a social activity with a friend. If these activities are not effective, try writing down your worries in a journal. Writing helps to organize thoughts and to make sense of them. Begin to take some small steps to resolve your worries and problems.

4. **Practice acts of kindness.** Doing something kind for others increases your own personal happiness and satisfies your basic need for human connection. Opportunities for helping others surround us each day. How about being courteous on the freeway, helping a child with homework, or helping your elderly neighbor with yard work? A simple act of kindness makes you feel good and often sets off a chain of events in which the person who receives the kindness does something kind for someone else.

5. **Increase flow activities.** Flow is defined as intense involvement in an activity so that you do not notice the passage of time. Musicians are in the flow when they are totally involved in their music. Athletes are in the flow when they are totally focused on their sport. Writers are in the flow when they are totally absorbed in writing down their ideas. The key to achieving flow is balancing skills and challenges. If your skills are not sufficient for the activity, you will become frustrated. If your skills are greater than what is demanded for the activity, you will become bored. Work often provides an opportunity to experience flow if you are in a situation in which your work activities are matched to your skills and talents.

As our skills increase, it becomes more difficult to maintain flow. We must be continu-ally testing ourselves in ever more challenging activities to maintain flow. You can take

> "Finish each day and be done with it. You have done what you could; some blunders and absurdities have crept in; forget them as soon as you can. Tomorrow is a new day; you shall begin it serenely and with too high a spirit to be encumbered with your old nonsense."
> Ralph Waldo Emerson

some action to increase the flow in your life by learning to fully focus your attention on the activity you are doing. It is important to be open to new and different experiences. To maintain the flow in your life, make a commitment to lifelong learning.

6. **Savor life's joys.** Savoring is the repetitive replaying of the positive experiences in life and is one of the most important ingredients of happiness. Savoring happens in the past, present, and future. Think often about the good things that have happened in the past. Savor the present by relishing the present moment. Savor the future by anticipating and visualizing positive events or outcomes in the future.

> "Happiness consists more in small conveniences or pleasures that occur every day, than in great pieces of good fortune that happen but seldom."
> Benjamin Franklin

There are many ways to savor life's joys. Replay in your mind happy days or events from the past. Create a photo album of your favorite people, places, and events and look at it often. This prolongs the happiness. Take a few minutes each day to appreciate ordinary activities such as taking a shower or walking to work. Engage the senses to notice your environment. Is it a sunny day? Take some time to look at the sky, the trees, and the plants. Landscape architects incorporate artwork, trees, and flowers along the freeways to help drivers to relax on the road. Notice art and objects of beauty. Be attentive to the present moment and be aware of your surroundings. Picture in your mind positive events you anticipate in the future. All of these activities will increase your "psychological bank account" of happy times and will help deal with times that are not so happy.

7. **Commit to accomplishing your goals.** Working toward a meaningful life goal is one of the most important things that you can do to have a happy life. Goals provide structure and meaning to our lives and improve self-esteem. Working on goals provides something to look forward to in the future.

> "An aim in life is the only fortune worth finding."
> Robert Louis Stevenson

The types of goals that you pursue have an impact on your happiness. The goals that have the most potential for long-term happiness involve changing your activities rather than changing your circumstances. Examples of goals that change your circumstances are moving to the beach or buying a new stereo. These goals make you happy for a short time. Then you get used to your new circumstances and no longer feel as happy as when you made the initial change. Examples of goals that change your activities are returning to school or taking up a new sport or hobby. These activities allow you to take on new challenges that keep life interesting for a longer period of time. Choose intrinsic goals that help you to develop your competence and autonomy. These goals should match your most important values and interests.

8. **Take care of your body.** Engaging in physical activity provides many opportunities for increasing happiness. Physical activity helps to:
   - Increase longevity and improve the quality of life.
   - Improve sleep and protect the body from disease.
   - Keep brains healthy and avoid cognitive impairments.
   - Increase self-esteem.
   - Increase the opportunity to engage in flow.
   - Provide a distraction from worries and overthinking.

© 2014, Efired. Used under license with Shutterstock, Inc.

Journal Entry #3

Psychologists Martin Seligman and Sonya Lyubomirsky write about the secrets to happiness. Write about four of their ideas with which you agree or disagree.

David Myers, a professor of psychology at Hope College in Michigan, is a leading researcher on happiness. He says that 90 percent of us are naturally happy. He adds that if most of us "were characteristically unhappy, the emotional pain would lose its ability to alert us to an unusual and possibly harmful condition."[15]

Just as you have made a decision to get a college degree, make a decision to be happy. Make a decision to be happy by altering your internal outlook and choosing to change your behavior. Here are some suggestions for consciously choosing happiness.

1. Find small things that make you happy and sprinkle your life with them. A glorious sunset, a pat on the back, a well-manicured yard, an unexpected gift, a round of tennis, a favorite sandwich, a fishing line cast on a quiet lake, the wagging tail of the family dog, or your child finally taking some responsibility—these are things that will help to create a continual climate of happiness.

2. Smile and stand up straight. Michael Mercer and Maryann Troiani, authors of *Spontaneous Optimism: Proven Strategies for Health, Prosperity and Happiness*, say that "unhappy people tend to slouch, happy people don't. . . . Happy people even take bigger steps when they walk."[16]

3. Learn to think like an optimist. "Pessimists tend to complain; optimists focus on solving their problems."[17] Never use the word "try"; this word is for pessimists. Assume you will succeed.

4. Replace negative thoughts with positive ones.

5. Fill your life with things you like to do.

6. Get enough rest. If you do not get enough sleep, you will feel tired and gloomy. Sleep deprivation can lead to depression.

7. Learn from your elders. Psychologist Daniel Mroczek says that "people in their sixties and seventies who are in good health are among the happiest people in our society. . . . They may be better able to regulate their emotions, they've developed perspective, they don't get so worried about little things, and they've often achieved their goals and aren't trying to prove themselves."[18]

8. Reduce stress.

9. Take charge of your time by doing first things first.

10. Close relationships are important. Myers and Mroczek report higher levels of happiness among married men and women.[19]

11. Keep things in perspective. Will it matter in six months to a year?

Journal Entry # 4

Write five intention statements about increasing your future happiness.
I intend to . . .

Learn to Laugh at Life

> "Have a laugh at life and look around you for happiness instead of sadness. Laughter has always brought me out of unhappy situations. Even in your darkest moment, you usually can find something to laugh about if you try hard enough."
> Red Skelton

All of us face difficult times in life; but if we can learn the gift of laughter and have a good sense of humor, it is easier to deal with the difficulties. Laughter has important physical as well as emotional benefits. Laughter relaxes the body, boosts the immune system, and even improves the function of blood vessels and increases blood flow, which can protect the heart. It adds joy and zest to life, reduces anxiety, relieves stress, improves mood, and enhances resilience. Being more relaxed can help you to shift perspective, solve problems, and be more creative.

Just putting a smile on your face can help. German psychologist Fritz Strack had his subjects watch a cartoon with a pencil in their mouths. Half of his subjects held the pencil between their teeth, which made them smile. The other half of his subjects held the pencil between their lips, which made them frown. The smiling group thought that the cartoon was funnier. It seems that there is a connection between our physical responses and our internal feelings. The physical act of smiling actually makes you feel happier.[20]

If you do not feel happy, smile and pretend to feel happy. Neurophysicist Richard Hamilton says that if you pretend to be happy, you actually feel better because positive thoughts and behavior impact the biochemistry of the brain. Positive thinking helps the brain produce serotonin, a neurotransmitter linked with feelings of happiness.[21]

Humor has several components. Humor involves looking at the incongruities of life and laughing at them. It is looking at adversity and finding the humor in the situation. It is a playful attitude and the ability to make other people smile. Most children are playful, but socialization reduces their playfulness. You can develop your sense of humor by taking yourself less seriously and being grateful for the good things in your life. Learn to laugh at yourself by sharing your embarrassing moments and laughing at them. Be careful not to use humor that puts down other people or groups. Surround yourself with people who enjoy humor and laughter. Look for the humor in difficult situations. Life is full of irony and absurdity, and laughing about it unites people during difficult times. By laughing at the situation, you will be in a better position to deal with it. Keep a positive perspective by focusing on the good things that are happening in your life rather than dwelling on the negatives.

The author Mark Twain was a good example of using humor in life. Mark Twain said that he had never worked a day in his life. He said, "What I have done I have done because it has been play. If it had been work, I shouldn't have done it." He used humor throughout his life despite facing many adversities. His father died when he was 11 years old and he started work at age 12 as a printer's apprentice. He was constantly in trouble and spent some time in jail. He served in the Civil War. His wife died at an early age, and three out of four of his children died before he did.

As a child, Twain enjoyed playing pranks on his mother, and she responded with a sense of humor. After he played a prank on his mother, she told him that he gave her more trouble than all the other children. He replied, "I suppose you were afraid I wouldn't live," and she responded, "No, afraid you would." When Mark Train almost drowned in the river, she pulled him out and said, "I guess there wasn't much danger. People born to be hanged are safe in water." Mark Twain's children described him as "a very good man, and a very funny one . . . He does tell perfectly delightful stories." He started every day by making jokes at the breakfast table, and his humor is reflected in his famous books, including *Huckleberry Finn* and *Tom Sawyer.* He wrote that "humor is a great thing . . . the saving thing after all. The minute it crops up, all our hardnesses yield, all our irritations, and resentments flit away, and a sunny spirit takes their place."[22]

The path to achieving your goals is much smoother if you choose to be happy. So relax, smile, and be happy. Then work on making positive changes in your life.

> "Laugh at yourself first, before anyone else can."
> Elsa Maxwell
>
> "If we couldn't laugh, we would all go insane."
> Jimmy Buffett

© 2014, Dirk Ercken. Used under license with Shutterstock, Inc.

You Are What You Think

"Whether you think you can, or think you can't . . . you're right." Henry Ford

© 2014, iQoncept. Used under license with Shutterstock, Inc.

Sometimes students enter college with the fear of failure. This belief leads to anxiety and behavior that leads to failure. If you have doubts about your ability to succeed in college, you might not go to class or attempt the challenging work required in college. It is difficult to make the effort if you cannot see positive results ahead. Unfortunately, failure in college can lead to a loss of confidence and lack of success in other areas of life as well.

Henry Ford said, "What we believe is true, comes true. What we believe is possible, becomes possible." If you believe that you will succeed, you will be more likely to take actions that lead to your success. Once you have experienced some small part of success, you will have confidence in your abilities and will continue on the road to success. Success leads to more success. It becomes a habit. You will be motivated to make the effort necessary to accomplish your goals. You might even become excited and energized along the way. You will use your gifts and talents to reach your potential and achieve happiness. It all begins with the thoughts you choose.

"Watch your thoughts; they become words.
Watch your words; they become actions.
Watch your actions; they become habits.
Watch your habits; they become character.
Watch your character; it becomes your
destiny."[23]

—*Frank Outlaw*

To help you choose positive beliefs, picture in your mind how you want your life to be. Imagine it is here now. See all the details and experience the feelings associated with this picture. Pretend it is true until you believe it. Then take action to make your dreams come true.

Journal Entry #5

Henry Ford said, "Whether you think you can, or think you can't . . . you're right." Based on this quote, how can your thoughts help you to be successful in college and in your career?

Thinking Positively about the Future

Go to http://www.collegesuccess1.com/JournalEntries.htm for Word files of the Journal Entries

Success over the Internet

Visit the *College Success Website* at http://www.collegesuccess1.com/

The *College Success Website* is continually updated with new topics and links to the material presented in this chapter. Topics include:

- Adult development
- Happiness
- Self-improvement
- Self-esteem
- Sports psychology
- How to be successful

Contact your instructor if you have any problems in accessing the *College Success Website*.

Notes

1. Christopher Peterson and Martin Seligman, *Character Strengths and Virtues: A Handbook and Classification* (Oxford: University Press, 2004), 583–584.

2. Daniel Goleman, "Hope Emerges a Key to Success in Life," *New York Times*, December 24, 1991.

3. Peterson and Seligman, *Character Strengths and Virtues*, 570. Goleman, "Hope Emerges a Key to Success in Life."

4. Anthony Robbins, *Unlimited Power* (New York: Fawcett Columbine, 1986), 54–55.

5. Ibid., 54-55.

6. Joan Smith, "Nineteen Habits of Happy Women," *Redbook Magazine*, August 1999, 68.

7. Stephen R. Covey, *The 7 Habits of Highly Effective People* (New York: Simon and Schuster, 1989).

8. Stephen R. Covey, *The 8th Habit: From Effectiveness to Greatness* (New York: Free Press, 2004).

9. Ibid.

10. Martin Seligman, *Authentic Happiness: Using the New Positive Psychology to Realize Your Potential for Lasting Fulfillment* (New York: Free Press), xiii.

11. Ibid., 6.

12. Ibid., 8.

13. Ibid., 45.

14. Sonya Lyubomirsky, *The How of Happiness* (New York: The Penguin Press, 2008).

15. Quoted in Joan Smith, "Nineteen Habits of Happy Women," *Redbook Magazine*, August 1999, 66.

16. Quoted in Smith, "Nineteen Habits of Happy Women."

17. Ibid.

18. Ibid.

19. Ibid.

20. Joan Smith, "Nineteen Habits of Happy Women," *Redbook Magazine*, August 1999, 68.

21. Ibid.

22. Christopher Peterson and Martin Seligman, *Character Strengths and Virtues: A Handbook and Classification* (Oxford: University Press, 2004), 583–584.

23. Rob Gilbert, ed., *Bits and Pieces* (Fairfield, NJ: The Economics Press), Vol. R, No. 40, p. 7, copyright 1998.

Measure Your Success

Name _____ Date _____

Now that you have finished the text, complete the following assessment to measure your improvement. Compare your results to the assessment taken at the beginning of class.

Read the following statements and rate how true they are for you at the present time.

5 Definitely true
4 Mostly true
3 Somewhat true
2 Seldom true
1 Never true

_____ I am motivated to be successful in college.

_____ I know the value of a college education.

_____ I know how to establish successful patterns of behavior.

_____ I understand how health affects my learning.

_____ I am attending college to accomplish my own personal goals.

_____ I believe to a great extent that my actions determine my future.

_____ I am persistent in achieving my goals.

_____ **Total points for Getting Started**

_____ I can describe my personality type.

_____ I can list careers that match my personality type.

_____ I can describe my personal strengths and talents based on my personality type.

_____ I understand how my personality type affects how I manage my time and money.

_____ I know what college majors are most in demand.

_____ I am confident that I have chosen the best major for myself.

_____ Courses related to my major are interesting and exciting to me.

_____ **Total points for Personality and Major**

_____ I can describe my learning style.

_____ I can list study techniques that match my learning style.

_____ I understand how my personality affects my learning style.

_____ I understand the concept of emotional intelligence and how it affects personal and career success.

_____ I understand the concept of multiple intelligences.

_____ I can list my multiple intelligences and matching careers.

_____ I create my own success.

_____ Total points for Learning Style and Intelligence

_____ I have a list or mental picture of my lifetime goals.

_____ I know what I would like to accomplish in the next four years.

_____ I spend my time on activities that help me accomplish my lifetime goals.

_____ I effectively use priorities in managing my time.

_____ I can balance study, work, and recreation time.

_____ I generally avoid procrastination on important tasks.

_____ I am good at managing my money.

_____ Total points for Managing Time and Money

_____ I know memory techniques and can apply them to my college studies.

_____ I can read a college textbook and remember the important points.

_____ I know how to effectively mark a college textbook.

_____ I can quickly survey a college text and select the main ideas.

_____ I generally have good reading comprehension.

_____ I can concentrate on the material I am reading.

_____ I am confident in my ability to read and remember college-level material.

_____ Total points for Memory and Reading

_____ I know how to listen for the main points in a college lecture.

_____ I am familiar with note-taking systems for college lectures.

_____ I know how to review my lecture notes.

_____ I feel comfortable with writing.

_____ I know the steps in writing a college term paper.

_____ I know how to prepare a speech.

_____ I am comfortable with public speaking.

_____ Total points for Taking Notes, Writing, and Speaking

_____ I know how to adequately prepare for a test.

_____ I can predict the questions that are likely to be on the test.

_____ I know how to deal with test anxiety.

_____ I am successful on math exams.

_____ I know how to make a reasonable guess if I am uncertain about the answer.

_____ I am confident of my ability to take objective tests.

_____ I can write a good essay answer.

_____ **Total points for Test Taking**

_____ I have self-confidence.

_____ I use positive self-talk and affirmations.

_____ I have a visual picture of my future success.

_____ I have a clear idea of what happiness means to me.

_____ I usually practice positive thinking.

_____ I am confident of my ability to succeed in college.

_____ I am confident of my ability to succeed in my career.

_____ **Total points for Future**

Total your points:

_____ Getting Started

_____ Personality and Major

_____ Learning Style and Intelligence

_____ Managing Time and Money

_____ Memory and Reading

_____ Taking Notes, Writing, and Speaking

_____ Test Taking

_____ Future

_____ **Grand total points**

If you scored

253–280	You are very confident of your skills for success in college and your career.
225–252	You have good skills for success in college. You can always improve.
197–224	You have average skills for success in college.
Below 196	You need some help to survive in college. Visit your college counselor for further assistance or re-read some of the chapters in this text.

Use these scores to complete the exercise "Chart Your Success" as in Chapter 1.

Success Wheel

Name _____ Date _____

Use your scores from "Measure Your Success" to complete the following success wheel. Use different colored markers to shade in each section of the wheel.

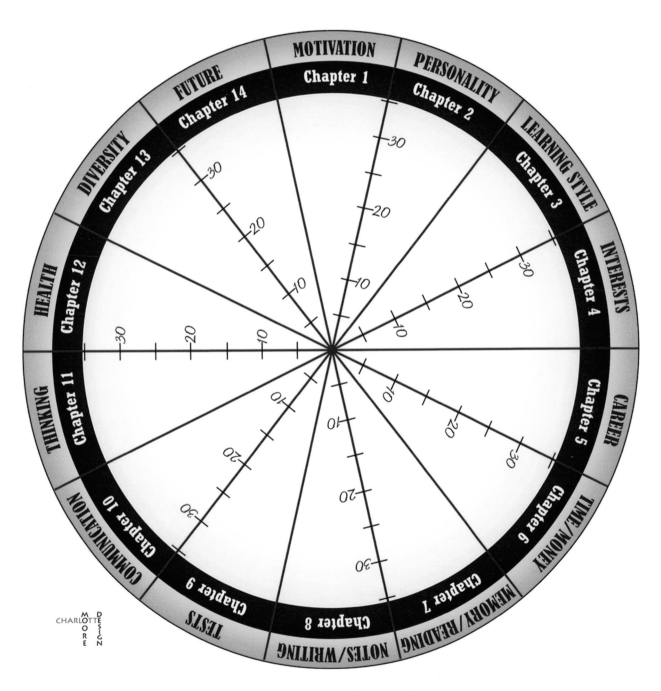

Compare your results to those on this same assessment in Chapter 1. How much did you improve?

Positive Thinking

Name _____ Date _____

Below are some negative thoughts. Transform each negative statement into a positive statement that could help a student to be successful. You may want to do this exercise as part of a group in your classroom.

Example: Negative thought: I have never been any good in math.
               Positive thought: I have had difficulty with math in the past, but I can do better this time.

1. I can't find a job.

   _____

2. I can never manage to save any money.

   _____

3. I hate physical education. Why do I have to take that class anyway?

   _____

4. I'm not very good at job interviews.

   _____

5. I'll never pass that test.

   _____

6. I'll never finish my college degree.

   _____

7. I was never good in school. I just want to play sports.

   _____

8. I'm not smart enough to do that.

   _____

9. Some people have all the luck.

   _____

Name _____ Date _____

To be successful, you will need a clear mental picture of what success means to you. Take a few minutes to create a mental picture of what success means to you. Include your education, career, family life, lifestyle, finances, and anything else that is important to you. Make your picture as specific and detailed as possible. Write about this picture or draw it in the space below. You may wish to use a mind map, list, outline, or sentences to describe your picture of success.

Summing Up Values

Name _____ Date _____

Look at the "Values Checklist" you completed on pages 282–283 of this chapter. Choose the 10 values most important to you and list them here.

_____   _____

_____   _____

_____   _____

_____   _____

_____   _____

Next, pick out the value that is most important and label it 1. Label your second most important value 2, and so on, until you have picked out your top five values.

1. My most important value is _____.
   Why?

2. My second most important value is _____.
   Why?

3. My third most important value is _____.
   Why?

4. My fourth most important value is _____.
   Why?

5. My fifth most important valus is _____
   Why?

Happiness Is . . .

Name _____ Date _____

Think of small things and big things that make you happy. List or draw them in the space below.

Intentions for the Future

Name _____ Date _____

Look over the table of contents of this book and think about what you have learned and how you will put it into practice. Write 10 intention statements about how you will use the material you have learned in this class to be successful in the future.

1.

2.

3.

4.

5.

6.

7.

8.

9.

10.

Course Evaluation

Name _____ Date _____

1. What did you think of this course?

   _____ **A.** This was one of the best courses I ever had.

   _____ **B.** This course was excellent.

   _____ **C.** This course was very good.

   _____ **D.** This course was satisfactory.

   _____ **E.** This course was not satisfactory.

2. How helpful was this course in choosing a major or career or confirming your choice of a major or career?

   _____ **A.** Extremely helpful

   _____ **B.** Very helpful

   _____ **C.** Helpful

   _____ **D.** Not helpful

   _____ **E.** Unknown

3. How helpful was this course in improving your chances for success in college?

   _____ **A.** Extremely helpful

   _____ **B.** Very helpful

   _____ **C.** Helpful

   _____ **D.** Not helpful

   _____ **E.** Unknown

4. How helpful was this course in improving your chances for success in your future career?

   _____ **A.** Extremely helpful

   _____ **B.** Very helpful

   _____ **C.** Helpful

   _____ **D.** Not helpful

   _____ **E.** Unknown

5. How helpful was this course in building your self-confidence?

_____ A. Extremely helpful

_____ B. Very helpful

_____ C. Helpful

_____ D. Not helpful

_____ E. Unknown

6. Please rate the textbook used for this class.

_____ A. Outstanding

_____ B. Excellent

_____ C. Satisfactory

_____ D. Needs Improvement

7. Please rate the instructor in this class.

_____ A. Outstanding

_____ B. Excellent

_____ C. Satisfactory

_____ D. Needs Improvement

8. Would you recommend this course to a friend?

_____ A. Yes

_____ B. No

9. Do you plan to continue your college studies next semester?

_____ A. Yes

_____ B. No

10. Please tell what you liked about this class and how it was useful to you.

11. Do you have any suggestions for improving the class or text?